BELMONT UNIVERSITY LIBRARY
BELMONT UNIVERSITY
1900 BELMONT BLVD.
NASHVILLE, TN 37212

Theological Essays

EBERHARD JÜNGEL

Theological Essays

Translated with an Introduction
by
J. B. Webster

T& T CLARK
EDINBURGH

T & T CLARK LTD
59 George Street
Edinburgh EH2 2LQ
Scotland

Copyright © T & T Clark Ltd, 1989

All rights reserved. No part of this publication may be reproduced, stored in a retrieval system, or transmitted, in any form or by any means, electronic, mechanical, photocopying, recording or otherwise, without the prior permission of T & T Clark Ltd.

First published 1989
Reprinted 1989

ISBN 0 567 09502 9 HB
ISBN 0 567 29502 8 PB

British Library Cataloguing in Publication Data

Jüngel, Eberhard
Theological essays
1. Theology. Theories of Jüngel, Eberhard
I. Title II. Webster, J.B. (John Bainbridge), 1955–
209'.2'4

195705
BELMONT UNIVERSITY LIBRARY

Typeset by C. R. Barber & Partners (Highlands) Ltd
Fort William, Scotland
Printed and bound in Great Britain

CONTENTS

Preface	vii
Abbreviations and Quotations	ix
Details of Publication	xi
Introduction	1

1 Metaphorical truth. Reflections on theological metaphor as a contribution to a hermeneutics of narrative theology — 16

2 Anthropomorphism: a fundamental problem in modern hermeneutics — 72

3 The world as possibility and actuality. The ontology of the doctrine of justification — 95

4 Humanity in correspondence to God. Remarks on the image of God as a basic concept in theological anthropology — 124

5 Invocation of God as the ethical ground of Christian action. Introductory remarks on the posthumous fragments of Karl Barth's ethics of the doctrine of reconciliation — 154

6 *Extra Christum nulla salus*—a principle of natural theology? Protestant reflections on the 'anonymity' of the Christian — 173

7 The church as sacrament? — 189

8 The effectiveness of Christ withdrawn. On the process of historical understanding as an introduction to Christology — 214

Bibliography — 232

Index — 233

TRANSLATOR'S PREFACE

The essays collected together here constitute only a small selection of Jüngel's shorter pieces from the last two decades. His writings in this form, which represent some of the best of his published work, are voluminous, but so far very little has been made available to readers without sufficient knowledge of German to tackle the originals. The essays have been selected both for their intrinsic interest and for the purpose of showing at least something of the range of Jüngel's intellectual contribution. They are a sample, but only a sample, from which to make further explorations.

'The task of translating a German theological work is never quite straightforward,' wrote Sir Edwyn Hoskyns in the preface to his memorable translation of Barth's *Epistle to the Romans*.[1] In the case of the present collection, there have been the inevitable difficulties of turning Jüngel's complex German into English—difficulties shared, I discovered with some relief, by others who have tried to translate his work. I have not attempted to reproduce every nuance or allusion, and in a few places I have trimmed the apparatus of scholarly references and footnotes. I have aimed at producing as clear and faithful a rendering as possible—though anyone closely familiar with the original is bound to be in some measure dissatisfied with this, as with any, translation.

The problems were compounded by a transatlantic move: the project was begun in England at St John's College, Durham, and finished in Canada at Wycliffe College, Toronto, much too far behind schedule. In addition to interrupting progress, moving to North America faced me with the necessity of producing a translation using inclusive language about human persons; this I have done, except in the case of quotations, where non-inclusive language has been left undisturbed.

I am grateful to the publishers for their initial enthusiasm for the project and for their patience in awaiting its completion. I am deeply indebted to Ulrike Lohmann, formerly of St John's, Durham and now of the University of Erlangen. In the midst of her own studies, she prepared careful draft translations of a substantial portion of the material. Though I am responsible for the final form in which the essays appear, her work made my own a great deal less onerous, and without her the project would have been difficult to finish. But most of all, I am indebted to Jane, Tommy and Joe, who allowed me to get on with it, and provided enough interruptions to keep me sane.

J. B. W.
Toronto, Pentecost 1988

[1] Oxford, 1933, p. xiii

ABBREVIATIONS AND QUOTATIONS

BC   T. G. Tappert, ed., *The Book of Concord. The Confessions of the Evangelical Lutheran Church* (Philadelphia, 1959)
CD   K. Barth, *Church Dogmatics* I/1–IV/4 (Edinburgh, 1956–75)
CT   *The Church Teaches. Documents of the Church in English Translation* (Rockford, Ill., 1973)
DS   H. Denzinger, A. Schönmetzer, *Enchiridion Symbolorum Definitionum et Declarationum de Rebus Fidei et Morum*, 36th edition (Freiburg, 1976)
DV   A. P. Flannery, ed., *Documents of Vatican II* (New York, 1975)
Freeman   K. Freeman, *Ancilla to the Presocratic Philosophers* (Oxford, 1962)
LW   *Luther's Works* (Philadelphia, 1955–86)
WA   D. *Martin Luthers Werke. Kritische Gesamtausgabe* (Weimar, 1883–)

Quotations from Aristotle are taken from J. Barnes, ed., *The Complete Works of Aristotle*, 2 vols (Princeton, 1984). Quotations from Plato are taken from E. Hamilton, H. Cairns, ed., *The Collected Dialogues of Plato* (Princeton, 1963). Biblical quotations are taken from the Revised Standard Version.

DETAILS OF PUBLICATION

The essays translated in this volume were published in German as follows:
1 'Metaphorical truth'—'Metaphorische Wahrheit. Erwägungen zur theologischen Relevanz der Metapher als Beitrag zur Hermeneutik einer narrativen Theologie' in P. Ricoeur, E. Jüngel, *Metapher. Zur Hermeneutik religiöser Sprache* (*Evangelische Theologie* Sonderheft 1974), pp. 71–122; reprinted in E. Jüngel, *Entsprechungen. Gott—Wahrheit—Mensch. Theologische Erörterungen* (Chr Kaiser Verlag, Munich, 1980), pp. 103–57
2 'Anthropomorphism: a fundamental problem in modern hermeneutics'—'Anthropomorphismus als Grundproblem neuzeitlicher Hermeneutik' in E. Jüngel, J. Wallmann, W. Werbeck, ed., *Verifikationen. Festschrift für Gerhard Ebeling zum 70. Geburtstag* (J. C. B. Mohr (Paul Siebeck) Tübingen, 1982), pp. 499–521
3 'The world as possibility and actuality'—'Die Welt als Möglichkeit und Wirklichkeit. Zum ontologischen Ansatz der Rechtfertigungslehre', *Evangelische Theologie* 29 (1969), pp. 417–442; reprinted in E. Jüngel, *Unterwegs zur Sache. Theologische Bemerkungen* (Chr Kaiser Verlag, Munich, 1972), pp. 206–233
4 'Humanity in correspondence to God'—'Der Gott entsprechende Mensch. Bemerkungen zur Gottebenbildlichkeit des Menschen als Grundfigur theologischer Anthropologie' in H.-G. Gadamer, P. Vogler, ed., *Neue Anthropologie* VI/1 (G. Thieme Verlag, Stuttgart, 1975), pp. 342–371; reprinted in *Entsprechungen*, pp. 290–317
5 'Invocation of God as the ethical ground of Christian action'— 'Anrufung Gottes als Grundethos christlichen Handelns. Einführende Bemerkungen zu den nachgelassenen Fragmenten der Ethik der Versöhnungslehre Karl Barths' in H. Weber, D. Mieth, ed., *Anspruch der Wirklichkeit und christlicher Glaube. Probleme und Wege theologischer Ethik heute* (Patmos, Düsseldorf, 1980), pp 208–224; reprinted in *Barth-Studien* (Mohn, Gütersloh, 1982), pp. 315–331.

6 '*Extra Christum nulla salus*—a principle of natural theology?'—
'Extra Christum nulla salus—als Grundsatz natürlicher Theologie? Evangelische Erwägungen zur "Anonymität" des Christenmenschen', *Zeitschrift für Theologie und Kirche* 72 (1975), pp. 337–352; reprinted in *Entsprechungen*, pp. 178–92.

7 'The Church as sacrament?'—'Die Kirche als Sakrament?' *Zeitschrift für Theologie und Kirche* 80 (1983), pp. 432–457.

8 'The effectiveness of Christ withdrawn'—'Die Wirksamkeit des Entzogenen. Zum Vorgang geschichtlichen Verstehens als Einführung in die Christologie' in B. Aland, ed., *Gnosis. Festschrift für Hans Jonas* (Vandenhoeck und Ruprecht, Göttingen, 1978), pp. 15–32.

The translator and publishers are grateful to the various copyright holders for permission to translate the material in this volume.

INTRODUCTION

The essays collected here form a series of attempts to restate the priority of grace in the way in which we think about ourselves, our history and our language. They all flow from a central conviction that the human world is 'to be understood in the context of (faith's) language about God' (p. 18). Their primary images for the relation of human and the divine—gift, interruption, being addressed, being created anew—all present a vision of God as a reality freely presenting itself, sheerly gratuitous, unconstrained and unexpected. And at the same time, they suggest a picture of human history as lying open to an active divine presence which does not so much enforce dependence as issue a summons to responsibility within the limits set to us. Like the rest of Jüngel's writings, these essays treat of ourselves and our history because and only because they are essays about God.

Clearly, to undertake this kind of theology is to go against the grain of many of the assumptions of the Western intellectual tradition since the seventeenth century. To put the matter rather too simply: philosophical developments in the seventeenth and eighteenth centuries led to the widespread breakup of a set of convictions about the interrelationship of God and creation, chiefly by shifting the centre of gravity away from mind-independent realities (God and a world ordered through creation and providence) towards the human self as the consciousness through which and around which reality is organized. 'One hallmark of the modern period in Western cultural history has been the rise of a distinctive set of root convictions about personhood ... To be a person is to be a centre or "subject" of consciousness who is at once a knower of "objects", a knower of the moral law, and a possible enactor of moral duties. Both as knower and as doer, a subject is autonomous, historical, and self-constituting.'[1] The effect of these developments was to make language about the reality and action of God increasingly difficult to support, whether in the natural or the moral

[1] D. H. Kelsey, 'Human Being' in P. Hodgson, R. King, eds., *Christian Theology. An Introduction to its Traditions and Tasks* (Philadelphia, 1982), p. 152. For some further analysis of the issues here, see, for example, C. Gunton, *Enlightenment and Alienation* (Basingstoke, 1985) and the account—still a classic—offered by J. M. Creed in *The Divinity of Jesus Christ* (Cambridge, 1938).

order. In English theology, these problems have often recurred in discussions of creation, providence and divine intervention, for example, and made problematical any language about incarnation or the activity of God in the history of the Church. The particular legacy of the Lutheran Reformation in German Protestantism has meant that problems about revelation, justification and ethics arose with rather more sharpness there than they did in English divinity.

Jüngel's work parallels that of a number of other recent theologians and philosophers who represent a significant criticism of and departure from the model of intellectual activity which has largely held sway in the West since the Enlightenment. Richard Bernstein, himself a major contributor to the revision process, has remarked that 'there are many signs that we are in the process of exorcising the Cartesian Anxiety'—the anxious search, that is, for an indubitable foundation for true knowledge in the self and its consciousness.[2] In his major work *God as the Mystery of the World*, Jüngel himself has undertaken a lengthy analysis of the epistemological issues here by tracing the dismal fate of thought and speech about God in the Western metaphysical tradition from Descartes onwards.[3] Readers with some familiarity with 'post-critical' styles of philosophy will probably find the agenda of the essays, along with their intellectual manner and their conversation partners, fairly easy to assimilate, even if Jüngel's rather fierce realism sets him apart from these thinkers in other respects.[4]

For Jüngel, however, reinstating the priority of grace has involved a great deal more than chasing the Cartesian *cogito* from

[2] R. J. Bernstein, *Philosophical Profiles. Essays in a Pragmatic Mode* (Cambridge, 1986), p. 11. Besides the work of Bernstein himself, in, for example, *Beyond Objectivism and Relativism* (Philadelphia, 1983), see R. Rorty, *Philosophy and the Mirror of Nature* (Princeton, 1979) or A. MacIntyre, *After Virtue* (Notre Dame, 1981). For a treatment of the issues from a theological perspective, see F. Kerr, *Theology after Wittgenstein* (Oxford, 1986).

[3] E. Jüngel, *God as the Mystery of the World* (Edinburgh 1983), pp. 111–26. F. Kerr is correct to observe that the 'perspective within which Jüngel pursues his theological reflections is . . . resolutely anti-Cartesian' (op. cit., p. 8).

[4] Bernstein, again, speaks of 'the cracks and crevices that are beginning to appear in the solid walls that have divided Anglo-American and Continental philosophy', and of 'the breakup of the hegemony of analytic philosophy—a breakup that allows for other voices to be heard' (op. cit., pp. 11, 8f.).

the field. It has also led him to undertake detailed explorations in anthropology, ethics, ontology and, most strikingly, the theory of language. Before looking in a little more detail at how the essays address these areas, it will be worthwhile to identify some of the intellectual resources which Jüngel brings to the task.

From his work in the early 1960s, Jüngel's chief master has been Barth, upon whom he has written extensively and with great sensitivity and penetration.[5] At one level, Barth has furnished Jüngel with a dogmatic framework of trinitarian and christological theory—most of all, of course, in the affirmation of the centrality of the history of Jesus Christ as the root and ground of all Christian speech about the human and the divine and their interrelation. 'Judgments about God and humanity can only be made on the basis of one and the same event. For Christian faith, this event is God's identity with the life and death of the one man Jesus, revealed in the resurrection of Jesus Christ from the dead' (p. 132). Because Barth characterises divine grace in this way, Jüngel finds in him a basis for anthropology and ethics avoiding both abstract heteronomy and abstract autonomy, since God and the human world exist in reciprocal relation and harmonious correspondence.

But beyond this, Barth has also offered a massive example of fluent discourse about God and the world in relation to God, discourse which is free from apology, hesitation or anxiety about its own possibility or justification. What Jüngel has taken from Barth, then, is not only dogmatic positions but also a confidence about the enterprise of doing theology after the apparent erosion of many of its certainties. Something of the same could be said about the influence of Luther on Jüngel. Luther provides a major counter-example to the prejudice in favour of the self-constituting subject which has been so potent in the intellectual currents of the last three centuries. Earlier in his career, Jüngel looked to Luther's theology of the cross as an instance of thorough revision of the metaphysical concept of God by reference to Calvary. More recently, it is the anthropological dimensions of Luther's theology, especially of his doctrine of justification, which have attracted

---

[5] Perhaps Jüngel's best work is his paraphrase of Barth's doctrine of God, *The Doctrine of the Trinity* (Edinburgh 1976). Most of his essays on Barth are collected as *Barth-Studien* (Gütersloh, 1982), of which a small selection has been translated as *Karl Barth. A Theological Legacy* (Philadelphia, 1986).

attention.⁶ Here Luther has helped Jüngel approach certain issues about passivity and receptivity which have been a source of difficulty in Christian theology at least since Kant—and, it ought to be noted, presented Jüngel with a way of handling these issues which is significantly different from Barth's treatment of them.⁷

Jüngel's other major contemporary mentor has been the New Testament theologian and hermeneutical theorist Ernst Fuchs, under whom he wrote his doctorate, and from whom he took a fascination for language. In earlier years, Jüngel made a great deal in his published works of the somewhat abstract categories of 'Word' and 'speech-event'—the latter a catch-phrase amongst those associated with the 'New Hermeneutic', intend to express the notion that language is not so much an instrument or sign for expressing extra-linguistic realities as the real presence of that which is. More recently, his work on language has focussed on analysis of metaphor, analogy and anthropomorphism, and especially upon the implications such forms of language have both for ontology in general and for the way in which the Christian faith understands the distinction between the divine and the wordly. Increasingly, Jüngel has come to argue that the tropic modes of speech offer significant clues in understanding the historical nature of human existence—in seeing human life as a process of becoming, of receptivity towards augmentation through the gift of new possibilities in speech, thought and action.

Besides these and other theological authorities, Jüngel brings to all his writing a close familiarity with some of the major philosophical texts of the Western tradition—the Presocratics, Plato and Aristotle, Spinoza and Kant, Hegel and Heidegger all recur in the essays which follow. Not only does this make his work more philosophically acute than that of many of Barth's heirs; it also gives it a substance and weight which has secured it against fashion or enslavement to the occasion.

The context, then, of Jüngel's work is a long-standing set of

⁶ Cf., for example, his tract *Zur Freiheit eines Christenmenschen. Eine Erinnerung an Luthers Schrift* (Munich, 1978).

⁷ The two essays 'Invocation of God' and 'Humanity in correspondence to God' show how the legacies of (respectively) Barth and Luther tend to pull in different directions. Jüngel attempts to identify the issues which are at play in this disparity in his essay 'Gospel and Law' in *Karl Barth, A Theological Legacy*, pp. 105–26.

theological, metaphysical and moral problems in relating the divine to the human; his resources in setting to work on these problems are drawn largely from a wide number of major thinkers in the classical and contemporary traditions of Western theology and speculative philosophy. We now turn to review the specific contents of the collection.

The first two essays treat issues about religious language. The longest of these, 'Metaphorical truth', gives a highly important statement of some of Jüngel's main concerns and illustrates many aspects of his characteristic procedure. The essay's main proposal is that metaphor is the primary form of Christian religious speech. The heart of the argument is its fifth section, out of which the other parts of the essays can be seen to flow. Here Jüngel lays down what has become his foundational dogmatic affirmation, namely the premiss that 'for Christian faith we only speak of God if at the time we speak of a fundamental difference between God and the world' (p. 58). This difference, however, is not simple opposition; it is Christologically defined in the fact that God is 'the one who *came* to the world in Jesus Christ and as such does not cease to *come* to the world' (p. 59). The notion of God's 'coming' is important in Jüngel's work. Through it, he seeks to state the distinction between God and the world without either abstract transcendence or total immanence: the relation of God to his creation is grounded in the history of the divine advent, in an event which cannot be reduced to a principle or static truth.

How may such a reality as the coming of God to the world become a matter for human speech? 'Our language is wordly language' (p. 59). It is this worldliness which makes metaphor a theological necessity. For language about God 'must be transferred from other states of affairs. The difference between God and the world, and, indeed, God himself, can only come to speech metaphorically' (p. 60). Metaphor transfers language from one context to another, bringing together two horizons of meaning; religious metaphor as it were bridges the reality of God and the reality of the world. Jüngel's point is not simply that language about God, because of its transcendent referent, is wordly language stretched to fit a new object. Indeed, he argues explicitly that metaphorical language about God differs from analogical language on the model of the way of eminence in which wordly terms are applied in a superlative manner to the divine. The process of metaphorical prediction articulates the emergence of a radically new possibility rather than the extension of present actuality: 'the language of faith proclaims the existence of a *new creation*' (p. 67). Of this new creation, the paradigm is the identification of the risen one with the crucified—the bringing together, that is, of the old actuality of the condemned world and the creative activity of God. Here in language about the resurrection of the crucified, we have what is in effect the fundamental Christian metaphor.

To come to terms with the argument of the essay, we need to bear in mind four of its underlying principles.

First, metaphor has ontological value—it refers to that which is. Of course, metaphor does not simply purport to describe actuality in the way that propositional statements do. Rather it 'brings to speech' states of affairs which are *more than actual*. 'Actuality is not the sum total of being' (p. 32). Metaphor refers, it has its object; but its object is not the world as it is but the world as it is coming to be, and God as he is coming to the world. And so metaphor, far from being a rhetorical ornament, pedagogically useful but inappropriate for description or definition, is language which testifies to the pushing back of the ontological horizon. Metaphors 'expand the horizon of being' (p. 68).

Second, because of this, 'metaphors are the articulation of discoveries' (p. 68), and contain 'the possibility of innovation' (p. 52 n. 87). Jüngel often uses imagery of renewal as a way of talking about the relation of God to the world ('God cannot be spoken of as if everything remained as it was' (p. 65)). His point here is that God is not to be spoken of as simply the foundation and guarantor of actuality and its continuity. Rather, God is the ground of the world's *becoming*, of a process in which the creation constantly goes beyond itself. As a mode of expression for the new possibilities which emerge as God comes to the world, metaphor is eminently suitable since it brings together the old and the new in a way which expresses 'the event of a gain to being' (p. 41).

Third, metaphor is in this way '*the event of truth*' (p. 53). Much of 'Metaphorical truth' is given over to disputing those traditions of Western philosophy which define truth in terms of correspondence between mind and actuality. The weakness of such a definition on Jüngel's reading is its orientation to actuality and its unsuitability in accounting for the truth-value of that which exceeds the actual.

'Metaphor does say more than is actual, and yet precisely in so doing it is true' (p. 57).

Fourth, Jüngel's account of metaphor cannot be separated from the notion of revelation in its broadest sense as the activity of external reality upon the human subject. The new world beyond the actual is a gift, originating from a source external to the world. And so the renewal of actuality is not born of some intrinsic capacity for enhancement; it occurs as an interruption, the emergence of the unexpected and uncaused. It is, indeed, for this very reason that metaphor is a linguistic process in which we see the horizons of being pushed back: the 'surprise of linguistic novelty' (p. 40) which a metaphor brings about is paralleled by surprise at the world's becoming other than it is or can be on its own resources. Metaphor is movement generated from without.

All this may seem very far removed from Aristotle's careful description of the rhetorical requirements for successful metaphorical predication, through which Jüngel guides us with such skill. But 'Metaphorical truth' offers not simply observations on linguistic usage but prescriptions for proper Christian speech. The language of faith is language in process of conversion, bearing in itself the marks of transformation by the new realities which it struggles to express and which do not, in one sense, *exist* apart from the converted language which the evoke. Moreover, the essay also provides significant pointers in the area of ontology. The next essay but one, 'The world as possibility and actuality', will take up these ontological issues at greater length; for the present, we see how the *historicality* of language is further elaborated in the essay on 'Anthropomorphism'.

This essay orients its account of anthropomorphism through a critique of Spinoza's account of religious language. Jüngel's chief objection to Spinoza is that he presupposes a notion of God which excludes in advance the validity of anthropomorphic language about God. Spinoza's entire method is underpinned by assumption of 'the unhistoricality of God' (p. 86); consequently anthropomorphic language can only be seen as accommodation to the human speaker, in no way expressive of the divine being. Jüngel counters Spinoza by arguing, as he has already done in 'Metaphorical truth', that the history of God's coming to the world in Jesus Christ determines the kind of speech which is appropriate for the Christian faith: 'If in the biblical texts there comes to speech the fact that God comes to the world, and if the history of God's coming to the world reaches its end in the man Jesus and in his history in the world, then the anthropomorphic character of human talk of God cannot be factually false. The formal character of the biblical texts as anthropomorphic language about God has to be seen as an expression of their material content' (pp. 89). Such anthropomorphism, Jüngel insists, is 'deliberate' (p. 89), in the sense that it is demanded by the object itself. Like metaphor, anthropomorphism is the result of transformation rather than accommodation, for 'words which bring God to speech are used in a way which changes their meaning' (p. 89). Behind Jüngel's account of anthropomorphism, then, we can discern the same understanding of religious language which found expression in his theory of metaphor: language which is appropriate to God, whilst it remains wordly language, is nevertheless language undergoing renewal as it 'brings to speech' that which lies beyond its own actuality. Hence 'anthropomorphic talk of God is only appropriate and responsible Christian language if it expresses the *freedom* of the God who *comes* to the world' (p. 94).

Anthropomorphism, like metaphor, is a speech-*event*, history taking place as language is changed and becomes new. It is also an expression of the historical nature of the human speaker. Anthropomorphism talks of God in terms drawn from the world of the speaker; such language is 'the most intense expression of the fact that in all that it says language also implicitly expresses the human person' (p. 91). Jüngel suggests, however, that this state of affairs is not to be understood 'in such a way that in language we relate everything to ourselves in a thoroughly egocentric way, *making* ourselves into the measures of all things (p. 92). The human speaker is not a fixed point to which all other realities are accommodated. Rather, the speaker is a subject of movement, a process of self-transcendence, not 'fixed and set in . . . *actuality* but . . . aligned to the *possibility* of a world' (p. 92).

These two terms, 'actuality' and 'possibility', have assumed great importance for Jüngel's theology, in both its ontological and its anthropological dimensions. The essay 'The world as possibility and actuality', written somewhat earlier than the other pieces, explores the ontological issues in some depth. In it, Jüngel calls into question an ontological presupposition deeply embedded in Western philosophy since Aristotle, namely the ontological prevalence of actuality over possibility. In the post-aristotelian tradition, 'possibility was pushed out of place by actuality' (p. 97) in such a way that 'being cannot properly be attributed to the possible. Only that which is actual can properly be said to be' (p. 99). Possibility 'stands in a teleological relation to actuality' and 'exists for the sake of actuality' (p. 100). Because of this, human agency assumes great importance in this ontological scheme, since it is through our acts that the possible is made actual, and so comes to be. 'According to Aristotle, our understanding of the structure of the world and of the divine which rules the world, is oriented to this complex of act and actuality. The ontological primacy of actuality leads . . . to the primacy of the act' (p. 100).

Jüngel attempts to dismantle this tradition with the aid of Luther's account of justification as gift rather than human work. Luther's ontology of the human person clearly de-emphasises human acts of self-realization and lays weight on the divine Word which creates the person *exnihilo*. 'The absolutising of actuality and the distinction between the actual and the non-actual as the measure of the world is subject to fundamental critique from the event of justification, a critique which understands the world . . . as creation out of nothing' (p. 110). In effect, this means that what has ontological priority is not the actuality which the world makes of itself but rather the possibility which God gives to the world, a possibility 'which unconditionally concerns actuality as a future which results from outside and from nothing—from no tendency in the actual' (p. 117). Such possibility occurs in the event of the Word, in language in which the regularity and continuity of the world's history is at the same time broken apart and set free for new possibilities.

The first three essays, then, examine aspects of language and ontology from the vantage point of 'becoming', attempting to show that the Christian faith and its speech are oriented to the history of the emergence of the new. Christian language testifies to a *possible* world, a world which both takes up into itself and transcends the actuality of the present, and which is realised by the action of God in Jesus Christ. Paul Ricoeur has suggested that one of the primary accomplishments of fiction and poetry is to 'intend being, not under the modality of being-given, but under the modality of power-to-be', in such a way that 'everyday reality . . . is metamorphosed'.[8] For Jüngel, Christian religious language operates

[8] P. Ricoeur, 'The hermeneutical function of distanciation' in *Hermeneutics and the human sciences* (Cambridge, 1981), p. 142.

in something of the same way. Undergirding his account, however, is an assertion that the metamorphosis of actuality is generated from without, by an external agency upon which the world is contingent. The next two essays look at the anthropological aspects of this contingency.

In theological anthropology, 'the hard questions come when one considers persons not as patients but as finite agents—active concrete powers in a shared and public world—and when one tries to reconcile the autonomy of finite agency with dependency on God'.[9] For one like Jüngel schooled in anthropology by Luther and Barth, answering these hard questions is a matter of considerable importance and difficulty. The essay 'Humanity in correspondence to God' shows both the acuteness of the difficulty and at least the rudiments of a possible solution.

The essay's starting-point is that Christian anthropology 'is concerned in a very special way with the *new humanity*', so that 'the Christian faith stands in critical relation to every actuality of human existence, in that it understands humanity *eschatologically*' (p. 124). In the same way that his theory of language and his ontology focus upon the emergence of the new, so Jüngel's anthropology is concerned with 'new being' (p. 124). This initial delimitation of concern leads to two important moves in the argument.

The first is methodological. Jüngel proposes that Christian anthropology 'transcends . . . that which we may ascertain about ourselves through analysis of our existence' (p. 125), concentrating upon a Word with which we are addressed rather than upon what we may be able to say of ourselves. Humanity is accordingly 'defined *a priori* from outside itself' (p. 127).It is this which makes Jüngel's anthropology so very different from that of his rough contemporary Pannenberg: whereas the latter seeks to interweave theological affirmations and the findings of the social, human and historical sciences, Jüngel insists that theology is anthropological soley because it is theological, and that theological anthropology of necessity has its own distinct grounds and procedures.[10] This distinctiveness is a function of the fact that 'for the Christian faith the meanings of "God" and "humanity" are defined by reference

[9] D. H. Kelsey, op. cit., p. 165.
[10] Cf. W. Pannenberg, *Anthropology in Theological Perspective* (Edinburgh, 1985), pp. 11–23.

to the person of Jesus Christ' (p. 132). In its understanding of itself as an intellectual discipline, then, theological anthropology is referred beyond the horizon of human history.

Second, the eschatological character of humanity means in substantive terms that we are most appropriately defined *nos extra nos*: 'if we wish to experience ourselves as whole persons, we must experience more than ourselves' (p. 127). We are, that is, self-transcending beings, brought about and augmented by that which is beyond us. This kind of strategy is, of course, very familiar in much contemporary Christian writing on human nature. Jüngel's particular way of handling the issues here is to use justification by faith as an anthropological motif, stressing the passivity of the human subject as formed from without. As God acts upon us in the event of justification we are brought into correspondence to him: 'Prior to our relationship to ourselves is the relation which another bears to us. We could not relate to ourselves at all if we did not already exist out of the relation borne to us by another' (p. 133). 'Ontologically, we are in no way grounded in ourselves' (p. 133). Hence to *become* human, to have a human *history*, is to be involved in 'an event which is to our benefit but which does not arise out of ourselves' (p. 134).

The difficulty which much of this argument raises is whether it will enable a consistent affirmation of human agency. Jüngel's sharp distinction between the person as 'hearer' and the person as 'worker' aggravates the difficulty here. One of the ways in which he has sought to address the problem is through reflection on Barth's last writings, in which Barth gives his fullest account of the self as agent. The essay on 'Invocation of God', which is a commentary upon the posthumous volume of the *Church Dogmatics* entitled *The Christian Life* (which Jüngel co-edited for the collected edition of Barth's writings), offers a useful sample of Jüngel's writings here.

One of the central themes of Jüngel's writings on Barth has been the latter's use of analogy: his earliest published piece on Barth was an analysis of the function of analogy in Barth's theological anthropology.[11] Thus in 'Invocation of God' he suggests that for Barth 'the love of God which wills and accomplishes salvation

[11] See the 1962 essay 'Die Möglichkeit theologischer Anthropologie auf dem Grunde der Analogie', reprinted in *Barth-Studien* pp. 210–32, and the later (and more subtle) study 'Von der Dialektik zur Analogie' in ibid., pp. 127–79.

demands a human action which is analogous to itself' (p. 158). The force of the term 'analogous' is that human moral action is neither a usurpation of the action of God nor overwhelmed and rendered superfluous by it. Within this lies a characterization of divine grace as an invitation and enabling to act. From this perspective, the stark alternatives of heteronomy and autonomy (Jüngel unearths them in the work of Wilhelm Herrmann) can be exposed as false: 'Analogy guards the difference between God and humanity, in that it emphasises as strongly as possible their partnership' (p. 159). Abstract heteronomy is ruled out on a Christological basis: because the command of God is actual in and as the history of Jesus Christ, then 'the condition for moral behaviour is virtually the opposite of submission to an almighty will' (p. 168). And here the significance of Barth's choice of the rubric of invocation emerges: 'This ... is the fundamental ethical analogy: that in our invocation of God commanded of us by the God whose "being is in act", we are exalted to a life in act which corresponds to God, so that in our very relation to God we "may and should be truly active". In the same way that God is no *deus otiosus* (redundant God), so also the human person is no *homo otiosus* (redundant human person) ... The notion of a *co-operatio* (co-operation) between God and the human person in their mutual dealings with one another has here found a genuine Protestant, "evangelical" formulation' (p. 161). If Luther presses Jüngel towards an anthropology of human passivity, Barth (at least in his later writings) has encouraged him to give greater attention to the world of moral action.

One of the major effects of the changed intellectual conditions in which Christian theology found itself in the seventeenth and eighteenth centuries was to force theology into an increasingly apologetic mode, in the attempt to demonstrate that reflection upon the structure of the created order could yield knowledge of God.[12] As the Enlightenment seriously damaged notions of the interrelation of self, knowledge, nature and God, however, the project of demonstration became largely futile. It is sometimes argued, especially by English writers with an interest in the residues of natural theology, that Barth's decisive 'No!' to Brunner in the 1930s put an end to the matter once and for all amongst German

[12] In a rather different context, F. Schüssler Fiorenza has offered some acute characterizations of the effects of this period on Christian theology in *Foundational Theology: Jesus and the Church* (New York, 1985).

Protestants of the school of Barth. With others like Wolf Krötke and Christian Link, Jüngel has sought to argue otherwise, and some of his most interesting recent writing has been devoted to addressing issues in natural theology. The essay 'Extra Christum nulla salus' is in part a response to Rahner's notion of 'anonymous Christianity', but its most important suggestions are in the area of natural theology.

The core of the problem of 'traditional' natural theology (Jüngel's target here is not too clear: he quotes a formulation from Vatican I) lies in its attempt to discern God in the actualities of the natural order. The effect of this attempt is to envisage revelation taking place in and as actuality, rather than allowing that revelation is that which calls actuality into question and effects its renewal. 'Revelation is not simply a highly particular repetition of that which is the case in general; rather, it is a unique event which must establish itself historically in the horizon of the world and which must often, though not always, do this over against the prevailing *sensus communis*, and over against that which is . . . held to be self-evident' (p. 182f.). A divine reality available within 'untransformed' actuality would no longer be able to function as what Jüngel calls a '*critical comparative*, which brings that which is hitherto self-evident into a new light' (p. 183). On the other hand, as that which transcends actuality, revelation is the root of the 'historicality of the self-evident' (p. 183), bringing about an 'experience with experience', a new apprehension of the familiar world. On this basis, natural theology is not so much concerned with the universal demonstrability of the Christian claim as with the universal validity of the specific event of God's revelation in Jesus Christ, and with the capacity of that event to effect the renewal and furtherance of human history, making us 'ever more human' (p. 184).

The final two essays in the collection represent somewhat different interests from the other pieces, though readers will detect common themes and methods of approach.

The first of these, 'The church as sacrament?' was chosen partly to provide a sample of Jüngel's writing on sacramental theology, a topic on which he has published on several occasions.[13] It is also an interesting essay in that it represents a style of ecumenical theology

---

[13] See, for example, E. Jüngel/K. Rahner, *Was ist ein Sakrament?* (Freiburg, 1971), and *Barth-Studien*, pp. 246–314.

which is significantly at variance with most contemporary writing in the area. It is more sensitive and detailed in its handling of classical Reformation texts, less conciliatory in tone, ill at ease with some of the ecclesiological and sacramental orthodoxies of ecumenism. Focusing its attention on the sacramental nature of the church as it has been espoused in much recent Roman Catholic writing, the essay devotes a good deal of space to discussing the nature of the church's agency in the sacraments. Jüngel assumes from Luther a set of convictions in sacramental theology—that God's agency in the sacraments of necessity excludes human agency, that the proper human disposition vis-à-vis the sacraments is receptivity and faith, and that any emphasis on human mediation of grace runs the risk of a ruinous transformation of what is properly a 'matter of faith' into a 'matter of works'. To talk of the church as sacrament seems to run counter to such convictions. This is because, first, such language appears to be inevitably associated with a notion of the church 'representing' Christ—a notion which for Jüngel threatens to usurp Christ's priestly office (cf. p. 193). But, second, Jüngel also has serious doubts about the propriety of thinking of the church as *agent* in its representation of Christ, since, he suggests, this can easily become a matter of an 'identity of action' between the 'primary acting subject' Jesus Christ and the church or priest as 'secondary acting subject' (p. 200).

Already the argument betrays Jüngel's major theological preoccupation—'how can God's work and human work be distinguished?' (p. 199). The essay makes a number of recommendations about how this distinction may be safeguarded. One is a more consistent emphasis on liturgical and sacramental action as *reception*: '*To let God perform his work*—this and this alone is the function of the church's action' (p. 203). Liturgy is testimony to Christ's own act through the Spirit in distributing the merits of his finished work. Another recommendation is that worship is not so much an ecclesial work as a word-event. Understanding the liturgy in this way serves to ensure that 'in the liturgical action of the church God himself is experienced as the real acting subject, with whom neither the priest nor the congregation can be brought into union' (pp. 203). The word-event proclaims 'a divine work which has already been accomplished' (p. 204) and with which its testimony cannot be equated. 'Representation of Christ' is thus not accomplished in action, but 'occurs in a fundamental way in the form of the hearing church and in the form of the gathering of believers who receive the grace of Christ' (p. 206). In this way, the church is not the fundamental sacrament so much as 'the great *sacramental sign* which represents Jesus Christ' (p. 206). The final brief piece, 'The effectiveness of Christ withdrawn', is interesting on two levels. First, it is one of the few pieces which Jüngel has published directly on Christology, even those his entire theology shares Barth's Christological method of construction. Second, it picks up and develops a concern from Jüngel's very early work which has already surfaced in most of the essays in this volume: the temporal nature of human existence. The essay reflects on the interweaving of the past and the present, and elaborates upon the notion of the possibilities belonging to an historical state of affairs, which do not necessarily pass away as the present recedes into the unreachable past. Whilst the theological dimensions of this are only hinted at towards the end of the essay, there is much here which could be developed in the theology of the person and of the atonement—areas where Christian theology finds itself inescapably and often problematically wedded to a contingent fragment of the past.

'God,' remarked Barth, 'is the essence of the possible'.[14] In their various ways, all the essays collected here are an expansion of that suggestion. To read them through with care ought to be a rich intellectual experience. British and North American readers will more likely than not experience a number of barriers, of course. A major hurdle is stylistic: the essays adopt a tone of high seriousness and rhetorical formality, features which tend to be heightened in the passage from German to English. A further difficulty may be that of reference to unfamiliar traditions, especially those of German idealism or classical philosophy. Reading these essays, then will prove hard work for most, but work in which the diligent will hopefully find themselves well rewarded.

[14] K. Barth, *Dogmatics in Outline* (London, 1949), p. 48.

METAPHORICAL TRUTH

Reflections on the theological relevance of metaphor as a contribution to the hermeneutics of narrative theology

For Martin Heidegger on his 85th birthday with respect and gratitude

I

1. Religious language necessarily accords to actuality more than an actual state of affairs can show for itself at any particular time, more, indeed, than it is capable of showing for itself at any particular time. For all its uniqueness, the language of the Christian faith shares this characteristic of religious language: religious language can only be true religious language when it goes beyond actuality without talking around it. Precisely in going beyond actuality, it gets to grips with it. 'Today is born to you a Saviour' or 'This man was the Son of God' are judgments of faith of this kind which augment the being of actuality and in that very way do justice to it.

If such a claim is to make sense, it implies the presupposition that actuality is not of itself sufficient. Actuality desires that which is more than actual. Intrinsic to our notion of actuality, it seems, is the fact that the actual accepts itself as only a limited measure of that which is. Actuality is not the sum total of being; it represents being only in time. More is possible. Of course, actuality is itself possible. But the possibility of an actual state of affairs is something other than its actuality. In the dimension of possibility, the being of an actual state of affairs encounters possibilities which, although they are not themselves actualised, still belong to the being of that actual state of affairs. Part of the process of understanding actuality is discovering what would and what would not count as such possibilities. Religious language, then, accords certain possibilities to actuality as intrinsic to its being. Christianity is quite specific in that it understands such possibilities as a *donum* (something given) to which actuality is not of itself entitled, i.e. as a *potentia aliena* (outside power) which, however, still belongs to the being of actuality. Possibility is a gift. And in the judgment of faith, actuality lives by such gifts of possibility, however much this escapes our attention as our minds fasten onto actuality. The language of faith presupposes revelation.

So not the least demonstration of the truth of what faith has to say is the fact that the language of faith does not simply accord with actuality. Because Christian faith has to talk about God if it wishes to speak the truth, it has to say more than the actuality of the world is able to say. This means, however, that faith is inevitably involved in a dispute about truth, for in the Western intellectual tradition, truth is conceived as the correspondence of the judgments of the mind (*intellectus*) with actuality (*res*), as *adaequatio intellectus et rei* (correspondence of mind and thing) in the sense of *adaequatio intellectus* [*humani*] *ad rem* (correspondence of the human mind to the thing). Seen from the standpoint of this understanding of truth, religious language seems to be the exact opposite of true language; it seems to be a kind of error, if not a lie. If, in order to be true according to the criteria of religion and faith, a text has to say more than what is actual, it does not correspond to actuality. In order to be able to make the claim to be religiously true, its statements seem to be untrue when judged by the actuality of the *res*. That which claims to be religiously true does not really seem to be true at all.

Since, however, the Christian faith by no means wishes to evade talking of actuality, and can only go beyond actuality by attending to it, the untruth of the language of faith seems very little different from a lie. Since faith does not want simply to do without any *adaequatio intellectus et rei*, but rather claims to make judgments about actuality, it seems that the *adaequatio intellectus ad rem* is infiltrated by an *adaequatio rei ad intellectum* (correspondence of the thing to the mind). But such a correspondence can only count as truth if the *res* (and not simply a concept of the *res*) is *in actuality* brought into correspondence with the mind, for this would otherwise be simply a correspondence of *intellectus* and *intellectus* with reference to the *res*. The human mind is, however, only capable of this if it *actually changes* the world of the *res*. Once this has been done, it would again be possible to view truth as *adaequatio intellectus ad rem* [*mutatam*], correspondence of the mind to a changed thing; the *adaequatio rei ad intellectum* would then appear to have been nothing but a cognitive anticipation of the goal of a *res mutanda* (changing thing). Between actuality and the judgment which expresses actuality there would stand nothing but the will to change and the corresponding act.

This model of truth cannot, however, satisfactorily explain the phenomenon of religious language. Religious language is not, of course, wholly uninterested in altering actuality: in certain respects one of its vital interests is that of altering the world. But for the language of faith, change initiated by the human will and enacted in corresponding acts is to be understood in the context of its language about God. Its concern is to change actuality so that it may be brought into correspondence with faith's judgment about actuality. But the judgments of faith talk about actuality only insofar as they at the same time talk—whether explicitly or implicitly—about a divine being and the acts of a divine being. Because of this, judgments of faith disturb actuality in a way quite different from a will which effects change without regard for God. Leaving aside the possibility of eventually effecting an *adaequatio rei et intellectum*, they disturb the correspondence of mind and thing by talking of a further event which concerns actuality, and so do not refrain from claiming to be true judgments about actuality. And so judgments of faith are necessarily exposed to the suspicion of being false—for the sake of truth. Can then truth be a lie?

We best understand the peculiarity of religious language when we take as our starting-point a process which is fundamental to the phenomenon of all human language. To state something about an actual state of affairs which is in actuality not predicable of it would not be a lie if it were a *metaphor*. 'Achilles is a lion'; 'Jesus is the Son of God'—though they are quite incomparable, both statements have something in common from a hermeneutical viewpoint. Each in its own way contradicts actuality and is nevertheless, again in its own way, true. According to the rules of rhetoric, the sentence 'Achilles is a lion' is an example of figurative speech; 'lion' is used as a predicate of the subject 'Achilles' metaphorically, or, we might say, *only* metaphorically. Is the statement 'Jesus is the Son of God' to be understood on the same linguistic model?

Giving an affirmative answer to that last question would involve us in a dispute about the antithesis made between literal and figurative modes of speech. A hermeneutical reflection on the

METAPHORICAL TRUTH

function of metaphor may be useful in this regard, not only, first, because metaphor is a fundamental characteristic of religious language, but also, second, because it is regarded as an example of permissible figurative language. But what literally is a literal use of language?

2. One of the peculiarities of language is that we readily call things by a variety of names. For many things we have more than one name. On the other hand, a good many words have more than one meaning, so that the same expression can signify both this and that. At first sight these states of affairs do not appear to be connected. The first testifies to the superfluity of language, the second, taken on its own, indicates its poverty. Both, however, suggest that language lacks any final univocity. If we were to insist on univocity, we would still have the escape route of rendering everyday language univocal by formalization. However, formalized everyday language would no longer be everyday language. A convention of signifying a thing with one sign and one only, and the construction of an artificial language in which each sign has one meaning and only one, would certainly ensure univocal statements. Within certain limits it has become a matter of absolute necessity to work with such formalized languages: in scientific work they are in some cases indispensable. But for day-to-day communication they are less appropriate. However much we may wish to use them to crack the code of life, they appear remote from life. Evidently everyday language really does express in human communication the living manifoldness of being, despite its lack of univocity.

In truth, however, everyday language is not burdened with the charge of a basic incapacity to function univocally. It is univocal by creating univocity. Univocity is established in the process of dealing with the world in language, through the use of words which have by no means always been univocal. In this way, univocity could be an event, although the use of language which led up to the event could well be regarded as 'figurative'. This is the case when a statement which leads to the event of univocity is metaphorical, as in the sentence 'Achilles is a lion'. This sentence is to be regarded as figurative since by the measure of the actual, Achilles is by no means a lion. The sentence, that is, does not satisfy the criterion of *adaequatio intellectus ad rem*. That criterion is only not contradicted on the condition that in this case, truth is stated metaphorically.

The condition is to be noted. In order to come to a decision about its legitimacy, we need to reflect on the nature of metaphor. And so: what is metaphorical language? How does μεταφορά (metaphor) relate to ἀλήθεια (truth)?

3. Traditional theory of language regards metaphor as a figurative mode of speech, since it is understood as *brevior similitudo*. As an 'abbreviated parable' it falls under the definition of all parables as figurative modes of speech.[1] The older theory of parables understood the parable proper as the 'figurative part' in which the 'factual part' had to be recognised; similarly, the older theory of metaphor[2] defined μεταφορά as a semantically meaningful substitute for the anticipated *verbum proprium* (the usual word), i.e. as *immutatio verborum*, exchange of words; this substitute is permitted to deviate from the purity and perspecuity which is usually required of eloquent speech. In this process, the word which replaces the usual word adds a new meaning to its own proper meaning, so that it can no longer be regarded as a *verbum univocum* (univocal word). Aristotle[3] defines the univocal use of a word as a use of language in which a word signifies a number of objects which have in common not only their name (τὸ ὄνομα) but also the concept of their nature which belongs to the name (the λόγος τῆς οὐσιάς). If I call Achilles a lion, I replace the expression 'brave warrior' by a word which

[1] The definition of metaphor as a short form of comparison can claim the authority of Aristotle, Rhet. 1406b 20. At the same time, for Aristotle the opposite seems to be the case: in their specific character as comparisons, parables are expanded metaphors (cf Rhet. 1407a 11–18). According to him the peculiar attractiveness of metaphor is lost in this process because the parable is more verbose, and because it *explicitly* identifies the two compared facts, thereby withholding from the reader the excitement of intellectual discovery (Rhet. 1410b 18f). The *immediate* identification in a metaphorical statement is more exciting and more demanding. G. Söhngen has dealt with the problem of metaphor from a theological and philosophical point of view on several occasions, most recently in his book *Analogie und Metapher. Kleine Philosophie und Theologie der Sprache* (Munich, 1962).
[2] For what follows, see H. Lausberg, *Handbuch der literarischen Rhetorik. Eine Grundlegung der Literaturwissenschaft* (Munich, 1960), §§ 558–564; idem., *Elemente der Literaturwissenschaft* (Munich, 1967), §§ 228–231.
[3] Cat. 1a 6f: 'When things have the name in common and the definition of being which corresponds to the name is the same thing, they are called synonymous'.

expresses the meaning of the sentence 'Achilles is a brave warrior', but I thereby change the meaning of that word. The word 'lion' cannot signify both the animal in the wilderness and the brave warrior Achilles in a univocal way. It functions as a *verbum proprium* only with reference to the animal in the wilderness, whilst it is transferred to Achilles, ostensibly to render the speech more interesting and agreeable.

In this sense, traditional theory of language regarded metaphor as primarily a rhetorical ornament (*ornatus*), and so as a rhetorical trope. In the rhetorical tradition, metaphor is the basic form of tropic language: Aristotle still understands μεταφορά as a generic term for what would later be called the tropes. Later, metaphor was contrariwise understood as a specific instance of τρόπος, i.e. of that process in language which there occurs a τρέπεσθαι, a '"turn" ... of the semantic arrow of signification which belongs to the substance of the word, away from the original content of the word to a different content'.[4] This 'turn' was understood as 'the artistic alteration of a word or phrase from its proper meaning to another.[5]

The rhetorical tradition allowed such figurative speech as a decoration or elucidation of language, provided that a relation of similarity obtains between the literal meaning of the word to be replaced and the literal meaning of the word which replaces it, or rather, between the latter and the nature of the object, represented by the logical subject of the statement, of which the metaphor is to be predicated. Because of this similarity the logical subject has to allow that it is spoken of with the aid of a word used metaphorically, however much the logic of language may fight against this. The logical subject opens up a hermeneutical horizon of expectation, which the metaphor as predicate can certainly distance but which it cannot completely miss, because of this similitude. An analysis in terms of the logic of language of that which a metaphorical statement seeks to express would, by contrast, demand some kind of translation of what was expressed in metaphorical and supposedly improper terms into what is regarded as the proper way of speaking.

[4] H. Lausberg, *Elemente*, §174.
[5] H. Lausberg, *Handbuch*, §552, from Quintilian, *Inst. or.* 8.6.1.

4. Modern theory of language has raised weighty objections to the understanding of metaphor as non-literal speech. The very definition of a metaphor as an abbreviated parable is problematic. The Aristotelian view that a parable is an expanded metaphor is once again being considered.[6] And apart from this controversy, modern theological research on the parables has cast doubt upon the old theory which understood the parables as non-literal speech. Taken together, the works of Ernst Lohmeyer, Ernst Fuchs, Eugen Biser, Georg Eichholz, Erhardt Güttgemans, D. O. Via, Walter Magass and others show that the parable is a highly distinctive kind of literal speech. There is substantial common ground between recent parable research and a variety of recent attempts in the theory of language to attain a better understanding of metaphor. If it is inadequate to characterise parable as figurative speech, it is similarly inadequate to characterise metaphor in the same way.

In this sense, a number of linguists and philosophers have made contributions to a new theory of metaphor which are of considerable theological relevance. In the light of the works of Karl Bühler, Bruno Snell, Karl Löwith, Beda Allemann, Hans Blumenberg, Paul Ricoeur and others, a revision of the conventional understanding of metaphor is necessary.[7] Such a revision would no longer view metaphor as a peripheral linguistic

[6] On this, see H. Weinrich, 'Die Metapher' *Poetica* 2 (1968), pp. 100–130. Weinrich's discussion should be referred to for what follows.

[7] There are, of course, precedents here also. Obviously it became unavoidable in certain significant contexts to assert the fundamental hermeneutical and anthropological significance of the creation of metaphors and their anything but figurative linguistic function. Thus, to cite but a few examples, it was Luther, the translator and interpreter of the Bible who had a highly particular understanding of language, who, in setting out the exegetical grounds of his doctrine of the Lord's Supper fought very vigorously against Zwingli's understanding of metaphor as a non-literal mode of speech. Giambattista Vico, in his repudiation of the Cartesian ideal of the intellect as judging only *clare et distincte* (clearly and distinctly) in such a way as to 'de-essentialise history', 'declared metaphorical language to be as "literal" as language that is commonly thought to be "literal".' (H. Blumenberg, 'Paradigmen zu einer Metaphorologie' *Archiv für Begriffgeschichte* 6 (1960), pp. 7–142; see pp. 8 and 10). For Vico's own thinking here, see the second chapter of the second book of the *Scienza Nuova* which deals with the logic of poetry: 'From all this it follows that all the tropes . . ., which have hitherto been considered ingenious inventions of writers, were necessary modes of expression of all the first poetic nations,

phenomenon but rather as a process fundamental to language. Indeed, the observation that even those words regarded as *verba propria* are often something like metaphors which have become independent, already contradicts a 'merely rhetorical' understanding of metaphor. Some philosophical concepts could serve as examples here, however much philosophy is concerned for literal speech.

Furthermore, a theological theory of language has to accord to metaphorical speech a dogmatically fundamental and therefore hermeneutically decisive function which is not congruous with an understanding of metaphor as merely a rhetorical figure. This is because linguistic expressions often have to assume a new meaning in order to signify theological states of affairs. For Luther it was both necessary and certain that 'all names receive a new meaning in Christ'.[8] This theological principle expresses the general hermeneutical experience that words take their meaning from the context in which they are used. For theology, however, a special problem arises. For *in Christo* (in Christ) there is given an eschatologically new context, which stands over against *all* other contexts in which words have hitherto been used; words used in *this* context necessarily acquire a new meaning. This context, which

and had originally their full native propriety. But these expressions of the first nations became figurative when, with the further development of the human mind, words were invented which signified abstract forms or genera comprising species or relating parts to their wholes. And here begins the overthrow of two common errors of the grammarians: that prose speech is proper speech and poetic speech improper speech, and that prose speech came first, and afterwards speech in verse' (G. Vico, *The New Science* (Ithaca, 1948), p. 118. In the same way, Jean Paul, who was highly sensitive to language, proposes that 'in that metaphor signifies relations rather than objects, (it) is the most primitive language, which gradually paled into literal speech' (*Vorschule der Aesthetik*, §50, in *Werke* V (Munich, 1973), p. 184). Standing in the same tradition, Nietzsche, himself a master of metaphor, calls the 'drive toward the formation of metaphors ... the fundamental human drive, which one cannot for a single instant dispense with in thought, for one would thereby dispense with man himself' (*On Truth and Lies in a Nonmoral Sense* in D. Breazeale, ed., *Philosophy and Truth. Selections from Nietzsche's Notebooks of the Early 1870s* (Atlantic Highlands, 1979), pp. 88f). Consideration of the 'wide spread of metaphorical phrases and techniques in representational language', which takes up this tradition from the perspective of the theory of language, has been given by K. Bühler in *Sprachtheorie* (Jena, 1965), §23.

[8] M. Luther, *Disputatio de divinitate et humanitate Christi*, WA 39/11, 94.17f.

is announced by the name of Jesus Christ, is nevertheless dependent upon words of other contexts, since it brings with it no words of its own to signify its own states of affairs. In this eschatologically new context, set over against all worldly contexts, words have to function as metaphors. The language of faith is constituted by μεταφορά. The dogmatic tradition treats this problem as the question of the analogy of signification and the analogy of being. Naming by analogy was, as we have yet to show, fundamentally understood as metaphorical speech. The complex problem of analogy was, however, to a large extent shaped by the attempt to move beyond the figurativeness of metaphorical speech to a more literal way of speaking which would, nevertheless, use words in an extended way. The theological problem of analogy can therefore only profit from the dismantling of the idea that metaphor is a merely figurative mode of speech.

5. The judgment that metaphor is a non-literal mode of speech is connected at a very deep level with the understanding of truth as *adaequatio intellectus et rei*. Figurative speech seems to fall short of the actuality of the *res*; by saying more than what is actual, it seems in truth to say too little. 'Achilles is a lion' predicates more of Achilles than he actually is. And so by the standard of truth, defined as *adaequatio intellectus ad rem*, the sentence says too little. In truth Achilles is not a lion.

Achilles was not actually a lion. In actuality he was a brave warrior. But in truth? Was he actually in truth only what he was in actuality? Is it only words which describe the actual Achilles that tell the truth to the hearer of this predication which is accomplished in these words, whereas the word which normally signifies a wild animal tells that hearer an untruth, when taken in its literal sense? If we include the relation of a statement to its hearer in our consideration of metaphor, then the value accorded to metaphorical speech is obviously altered. And so our reservation about a 'merely rhetorical' understanding of metaphor has critically to question the notion that the relation of the statement to its hearer is of only secondary importance when compared to the value of the statement 'as such'. The fact that metaphor is treated in a rhetorical context makes all the more obvious the decisive importance of the relation between what is expressed metaphorically and the one to whom it is addressed. All that is usually established by that is that metaphor has neither logical nor ontological relevance.

METAPHORICAL TRUTH

The fact that metaphor is treated in the context of rhetoric (as a discipline concerned with the effect of a statement) can be understood in terms of a philosophical theory characteristic of the ancient world which asserted the correspondence of being and concept. One should not, of course, forget remarks such as that of Plato in his seventh letter. But one could well say that 'for the ancient world, *logos* in principle matched up to the whole of being; *cosmos* and *logos* were correlates'. Accordingly, metaphor has nothing to add in asking after the 'what' of things: 'it is only a means of increasing the *effect* of a statement, of its attacking or striking home at its political or juridical opponents ... The rhetorician or the poet essentially cannot say anything specific about the "what" but only about the "how".'[9] The question of truth is the question of the 'what'. The question of the 'how' is only concerned with the problem of how that which has already been accepted can be accepted by others. Certainly it would be hard to overestimate the relevance of this problem for the ancient world, characterised as it was by the public nature of life. Today we are prone to devalue something as 'merely rhetorical', whereas in the ancient world rhetoric was intrinsic to the proper discharge of truth.[10] In this sense, metaphor deviates from actuality only insofar as it remains within the bounds of truth. Or, to put the point from the perspective of the understanding of truth as *adaequatio intellectus ad rem*: metaphor deviates from truth by remaining within the bounds of truth. In terms of the rhetorical tradition, this is done for the sake of the one addressed. The relation to the hearer, that is, serves to permit a deviation from literal speech, whereas for literal speech the one addressed is in no way a constitutive factor. Here, however, we reach the intractable problem of treating metaphor in a rhetorical context. If we deal with metaphor in this way, we have

[9] H. Blumenberg, op. cit., p. 8.
[10] 'The possibility and power of persuasion was an elementary experience of life in the ancient *polis* ... The significance of rhetoric, which it is hard for us to value highly enough today, shows how important it was for philosophy to set forth both persuasive power as a quality of truth itself, and rhetoric and its methods as simply an appropriate putting into effect and strengthening of this quality. Wrestling with the functional coordination of rhetoric and disputing the sophist claim for the autonomy of the technique of persuasion, were fundamental to the history of classical philosophy, whose ramifications in our entire history of ideas have by no means been shown clearly enough' (ibid., pp. 8f).

already decided that the function of addressing the hearer is only of secondary importance in language (understood as literal speech). It is just this which must be contested. We must dispute the hermeneutical concession which allows words used metaphorically to deviate from truth whilst remaining within the bounds of truth – as if poets and theologians, for whom metaphor is necessary, even indispensable, were permitted to be 'liars in the service of truth', as if their task were to deceive the truth.[11]

In objecting to the placing of metaphor within rhetoric and to the corresponding idea that metaphor is only able to state the truth figuratively, we can draw upon the insight that the desire for metaphor is, as Nietzsche put it, 'the fundamental human drive'— that it is intrinsic to the human condition. If it is correct to claim that 'one cannot for a single instant dispense with (this drive) in thought—for one would thereby dispense with man himself',[12] then metaphor deserves a different hermeneutical value than traditional theory of language was prepared to accord to it. Here the dependence of the language of faith upon metaphorical speech would encounter a basic anthropological process whose importance for our understanding of human language can hardly be overestimated. This being the case, we cannot escape the question of the relation between language and truth. The understanding of metaphor as non-literal speech always regarded propositional language as a presupposition of truth. As a statement, the proposition was interesting because and insofar as it expressed a mental judgment. Truth was propositional truth, located in the mind making the judgment, and so was defined as *adaequatio intellectus et rei*.[13] 'Falsity and truth,' says Aristotle, 'are not in things

[11] In his instructive article 'Die Metapher und das metaphorische Wesen der Sprache', *Weltgespräch* 4 (1968), pp. 29–43, B. Allemann makes (p. 31) positive use of this paradox, seeking to understand the poet as a 'liar in the service of truth'. But this leads to a rather unhelpful use of the word 'liar' which is not only metaphorical but especially equivocal. A liar certainly goes beyond actuality, but in doing this the liar abuses the fact that actuality wishes to be surpassed. The possibility of such abuse rests on the fact that the emergence of truth in the surpassing of actuality is the condition under which lying is possible. It is only because actuality wishes to be surpassed that it can also be surpassed in a way in which it neither wishes to be nor should be surpassed.
[12] Nietzsche, op. cit. pp. 88f.
[13] Cf. M. Heidegger, 'On the Essence of Truth' in *Existence and Being* (Chicago, 1970), p. 298: if we 'limit the concept of truth to propositional

but in thought'.[14] Over against this, a hermeneutic which kept in mind the fundamental anthropological function of metaphor would have to set about the task of 'drawing near to the substructure of thinking' and of disclosing 'with what "courage" the mind is ahead of itself in its pictures, and how its history is conceived in this courage to speculate'.[15] Could it be the mark of truth always to follow the mind which is always ahead of itself, always to lag behind, and to exist only in this way? Or could we conceive of truth as accompanying the discovery of what would later be called 'true'? And so: how can truth be brought to speech?

The discussion which follows sets out some reflections on these themes. We start from Nietzsche's thesis—which he intended to be destructive—that truth is nothing but μεταφορά; from there we move to look in greater detail at Aristotle's rhetorical theory of metaphor.

II

If truth is located in the judging mind, this is because the mind combines things by affirmation and separates them by negation, in accord with the state of affairs about which the judgment is exercised. Aristotle explains: 'that which *is* in the sense of being true, or *is not* in the sense of being false, depends on combination and separation, and truth and falsity together are concerned with the apportionment of a contradiction (for truth has the affirmation in the case of what is compounded and the negation in the case of what is divided, while falsity has the contradictory of this apportionment)'. And he continues: 'it is another question, how it happens that we think things together or apart'.[16] But it is precisely this last question which is of interest to us in inquiring into the truth-value of metaphor. Is not metaphor a proportion between

truth, then we are at once brought face to face with an old ... tradition of thought, according to which truth is the *likeness* or *agreement* of a statement to or with a given thing'.

[14] Meta. 1027 b 25–7. In *Being and Time* (Oxford, 1978), p. 268, however, Martin Heidegger explicitly denies that Aristotle claims that a statement of judgment is the location of truth.

[15] Blumenberg, op. cit., p. 8.

[16] Meta. 1027b 18–24. Similarly, De anima 432a 11f: 'what is true or false involves a synthesis of thoughts'. The Aristotelian understanding of truth is handled with masterly brevity by F. Brentano in *On the Several*

combining and separating? And could not this be the way in which truth occurs? Friedrich Nietzsche explicitly affirmed the metaphorical structure of truth. In our present context his remarks deserve particular consideration.[17] Nietzsche, of course, was not so much concerned with preserving the honour of metaphor as with discrediting truth. Nevertheless, his definition of the relationship between ἀλήθεια (truth) and μεταφορά (metaphor) is instructive for the quite contrary hermeneutical attempt to come to think of metaphor as an event of truth.

Nietzsche's remarks on 'Truth and Lies in a Nonmoral Sense' (1873) expound the nature of truth by looking at the nature of dissimulation. For him, dissimulation is a basic activity of the individual, an activity which serves the goal of self-preservation through the use of the intellect. The love of hiding which Heraclitus ascribed to nature ('nature likes to hide'[18]) is, according to Nietzsche, perfected into dissimulation as the intellectual means of self-preservation on the part of the animal individual. 'As a means for the preserving of the individual, the intellect unfolds its principal

Senses of Being in Aristotle (Berkeley, 1975). Brentano shows that divergences in Aristotle's use of language which seem to attribute 'true' or 'false' to instances other than mental judgments can be explained as analogical use of lanuage. Hence 'What Aristotle emphasises several times' is true, namely that 'truth and falsity can be found only in affirmative or negative judgments ... There is indeed another kind of mental cognizing which is not judging, and through which we grasp the undivided, the simple, and conceptually represent to ourselves the nature of things ... But neither truth nor falsity belong to it ... (and) they can also not be found outside the mind. And so it happens that in the *De interpretatione* 4, where he wants to give a definition of judgment, he defines it through the characteristic that it has truth and falsity. "It is not the case," he says, "that every utterance is an affirmation, only that of which it holds that it says something true or false"' (ibid., pp. 15f). Cf. De int. 17a 1–6: 'Every sentence is significant ... but not every sentence is a statement-making sentence, but only those in which there is truth or falsity. There is not truth of falsity in all sentences: a prayer is a sentence but it is neither true nor false. The present investigation deals with the statement-making sentence; the others we can dismiss, since consideration of them belongs rather to the study of rhetoric or poetry'.
[17] The significance of Nietzsche's remarks for a metaphorical conception of language has been pointed out above all by B. Allemann in the article already mentioned.
[18] Freeman, p. 33 fr. 123.

powers in dissimulation . . . This art of dissimulation reaches its peak in man. Deception, flattering, lying, deluding, talking behind the back, putting up a false front, living in borrowed splendour, wearing a mask, hiding behind convention, playing a role for others and for oneself—in short, a continuous fluttering around the *solitary flame of vanity*—is so much the rule and law among men that there is almost nothing which is less comprehensible than how an honest and pure drive for truth could have arisen among them.'[19] The expression 'an honest and pure drive for truth' is probably an ironical quotation drawn from the bourgeois world. For whilst Nietzsche's following remarks do treat of the formation of a 'drive for truth', it is anything but honest and pure.

According to Nietzsche, something like truth occurs because the impulse to dissimulation has necessarily to limit itself. This necessity is given with the desire for social existence which sometimes accords and sometimes conflicts with the will to self-assertion. 'Insofar as the individual wants to maintain himself against other individuals, he will under natural circumstances employ the intellect mainly for dissimulation. But at the same time, from boredom and necessity, man wishes to exist socially and with the herd; therefore, he needs to make peace and strives accordingly to banish from his world at least the most flagrant *bellum omni contra omnes*.'[20] This conclusion of peace is truth's hour of birth: 'that which shall count as "truth" from now on is established'. This establishing happens, according to Nietzsche, as 'a uniformly valid and binding designation of things is invented for things, and this legislation of language likewise establishes the first laws of truth'.[21] Nietzsche understands these 'laws of truth' out of the opposition of truth and falsity, in exactly the same way that he understood the birth of truth out of the necessary self-limitation of dissimulation as a means of self-preservation. '(T)he contrast between truth and lie arises here for the first time. The liar is a person who uses the valid designations, the words, in order to make something which is unreal appear to be real . . . He misuses fixed conventions by means of arbitrary substitutions or even reversals of names.'[22] And the reason why the liar who behaves in this way is mistrusted by society is not love of

[19] F. Nietzsche, op. cit., p. 80.
[20] Ibid., p. 81.
[21] Ibid.
[22] Ibid.

truth so much as fear of the harmful consequences of falsity. 'What men avoid by excluding the liar is not so much being defrauded as it is being harmed by means of fraud . . . It is in a similarly restricted sense that man wants nothing but the truth.'[23] So we are concerned with truth and lies only with respect to their social consequences, whether beneficial or harmful. Truth is as little worth valuing for itself as a lie is worth hating for itself. '(Man) desires the pleasant, life-preserving consequences of truth. He is indifferent towards pure knowledge which has no consequences; towards those truths which are possibly harmful or destructive he is even hostilely inclined.'[24] Truth is thus a linguistic regulation, and a utilitarian one at that.

Deducing truth from the regulation of language, from the regulation of useful dealings with actuality, Nietzsche wants to make the human 'drive for truth' seem untruthful. In actuality, we are beyond truth and falsity; and despite the rather disparaging examples which Nietzsche adduces, dissimulation is by no means falsity.

Nietzsche's dismantling of the notion of 'pure truth' is underpinned by a second train of thought, which calls into question the claim that 'linguistic conventions' are apt representations of things. 'And besides, what about these linguistic conventions themselves?' he asks. 'Are they perhaps products of knowledge, that is, of the sense of truth? Are designations congruent with things? Is language the adequate expression of all realities?'[25] To ask the questions means to answer: no.

In offering his reasons, Nietzsche sets over against one another 'truth in the form of tautology' and 'illusions' which are regarded as truths. Truth which exists in the form of tautology can only satisfy one who is content 'with empty husks'.[26] The conventions of language go beyond the tautological form of truth, by which Nietzsche is thinking of mathematics and formal logic. Language, however, does not say the same thing; it says and means something different. But does it articulate and signify actuality as it actually is? Does it speak the truth? For Nietzsche, who takes over the understanding of truth as *adaequatio intellectus et rei*, language is quite incapable of speaking the truth so defined. The non-

[23] Ibid.
[24] Ibid.
[25] Ibid.
[26] Ibid.

METAPHORICAL TRUTH 31

tautological nature of language is not an indication of a difference of adequacy, but rather of the discrepancy between the speaker and the being of things, which the speaker believes has been integrated into the consciousness through the words of his or her language, but which has not in fact been so integrated. That which language and its words express is not actuality. Words belong to the immanent world of the subjectivity of the ego. 'What is a word? It is the copy in sound of a nerve stimulus. But the further inference from the nerve stimulus to a cause outside of us is already the result of a false and unjustifiable application of the principle of sufficient reason ... The "thing-in-itself" (which is precisely what the pure truth, apart from any of its consequences, would be) is likewise something quite incomprehensible to the creator of language and something not in the least worth striving for. This creator only designates the relations of things to men, and for expressing these relations he lays hold of the boldest metaphors.'[27]

In the context of our present discussion, Nietzsche's use of the notion of metaphor seems itself to be metaphorical when compared with normal usage. Nietzsche first understands the process of μεταφορά as a physiological transference: 'To begin with, a nerve stimulus is transferred into an image: first metaphor. The image, in turn, is imitated in a sound: second metaphor. And each time there is a complete overleaping of one sphere, right into the middle of an entirely new and different one.'[28] Μεταφορά is not a (rhetorical) process within language, but rather an anthropological process of orientation – conceived of by analogy to the former – used by the human subject to master the world which impinges upon that subject's nerves. The world makes an impression upon us. The concrete physiological form of this is the nerve-stimulus. This nerve-stimulus pushes the subject to assimilate the impression received; impressions have to be assimilated. But this cannot be done unless the subject in his or her turn expresses the impression received. As receivers, we are already active: we lay hold of the world's impression upon us in order to make something of it. Mastering this impression of the world entails the expression of impressions. In the first step of this process, the subject assimilates the sensations received through affected nerves by using the power of imagination. In this

[27] Ibid., pp. 81f.
[28] Ibid., p. 82.

anthropological process of orientation, a physiological quantity is made into a mental quality. We form a picture to represent what affects us. The ego makes a picture of the world, the ego's picture. This process engenders the appearance that the thing which affects has somehow been assimilated by the affected subject, so that, in a mode appropriate to its actuality, it is in the subject. But the appearance is deceptive. The ego remains within itself. The thing remains the 'thing in itself'. All that the subject has achieved is the transference of one of its own subjective states to another such state, however much this may not have been self-caused. The transference has thereby leapt out of one sphere 'right into the middle of an entirely new and different one'. And thus metaphor occurs as μετάβασις, transition.

A further transference into an entirely different, new sphere occurs when the subject attempts to express the impression of the world which was transferred into a picture. Μεταφορά now occurs as μετάβασις into the dimension of a sensuous sound, the mental quality of the picture so engendered being preserved as the semiotic quality of the sound. The human person is a maker of sounds, and freights this sound with the semantic content of his or her picture of the world of things or of a thing in the world. What is expressed in these utterances is the subject's assimilated impression of the world, but not, however, the world of things which impressed the subject. '(W)e believe that we know something about the things themselves when we speak of trees, colours, snow, and flowers; and yet we possess nothing but metaphors for things – metaphors which correspond in no way to the original entities.'[29]

At first sight, the expression 'metaphor' in that last sentence appears to be used in the traditional way: metaphor as a rhetorical, figurative expression to signify a state of affairs. But in actuality Nietzsche is going beyond the traditional understanding of metaphor as non-literal mode of signification which belongs to the art of rhetoric. For according to Nietzsche *all* the words of our language are metaphors of things. This could never be admitted by the traditional understanding of metaphor, for, as a rhetorical figure, metaphor is defined by being set over against the *verbum proprium* which in certain cases it replaces. Every sign, every word is for Nietzsche a metaphor, whilst on the old view, the existence

[29] Ibid., pp. 82f.

METAPHORICAL TRUTH   33

of metaphor is dependent upon the fact that there are non-metaphorical words.

At this point it would be useful to elucidate the problem by looking at Aristotle's views of μεταφορά. In doing so, we will keep one eye on the question of whether Aristotle's observations on the metaphorical use of language, which as yet are by no means brought into a scholastic system, can offer lessons for a hermeneutic oriented in a quite different direction. Aristotle is an incomparable observer who still amply rewards each of his critics.

III

Aristotle's most decisive statements about metaphor are found in the *Poetics* and the *Rhetoric*. Besides these, there are important references in occasional remarks in other writings.

l. Aristotle mentions metaphor when discussing the classification of nouns. Metaphor is a name (ὄνομα). We are not, however, to think of the restricted use of the term 'name' in modern logic. The expression 'must be used not in the restricted sense of the proper or common names but must be taken as any sign whatsoever'.[30] More precisely: 'A noun is a spoken sound significant by convention, without time, none of whose parts is significant in separation'.[31] It signifies or names something. The noun is a word which names. Over against the noun so defined, Aristotle conceives of the verb (ῥῆμα) as a word which 'additionally signifies time, no part of it being significant separately' and which is 'a sign of things said of something else'.[32] Spoken alone – that is, without being connected to a noun – a verb becomes a noun: it 'signifies something ... but it does not yet signify whether it is or not'.[33] That nouns have their meaning by convention means that a sound is not a noun by nature; it only comes to be a noun when it becomes a symbol. This distinguishes nouns from animal sounds which, even if they indicate or reveal something, do so only as sounds, because of what they are by nature.[34]

[30] P. Henle, 'Metaphor' in P. Henle, ed., *Language, Thought and Culture* (Ann Arbor, 1958), p. 173.
[31] De int. 16a 19f.
[32] De int. 16b 6f.
[33] De int. 16b 19–22.
[34] Cf. De int. 16a 27–9: 'I say "by convention" because no name is a

Accordingly, speech (λόγος) is an utterance which signifies by convention; following the definitions of nouns and verbs, its parts also signify something, without, however, saying anything about the being or non-being of that which is signified.[35] A part of speech speaks; it speaks for itself; insofar as it says something it signifies something. But beyond that it does not affirm anything (as κατάφασις) or deny anything (as ἀπόφασις) about that of which it speaks. Nouns and verbs are simply concerned with saying something; they are not a form of speech which would make it possible for us to assert (ἀποφαίνεσθαι).[36] An utterance becomes an assertion (ἀπόφανσις, λόγος ἀποφαντικός) by asserting something true or false[37]; a statement is thus distinguished from its constitutive nouns and verbs insofar as they only have meaning as a whole whereas in an utterance the parts have meaning in isolation from one another. And so truth and falsity occur if the speech affirms or denies something of something.[38] Primarily by affirmation, but also by negation – by, in other words, stating something by affirmation or denial – an utterance comes together to become a unified language event which allows the being of things to appear (ἀποφαίνεσθαι); the utterance becomes a λόγος ἀποφαντικός.[39] The unity of a statement which lets that which is appear is a judgment which alone states the truth. For Aristotle, method demands that all other forms of utterance be excluded from this context; they are

name naturally but only when it has become a symbol. Even inarticulate noises (of beasts, for instance) do indeed reveal something, yet none of them is a name'.

[35] 'Every sentence is significant, not as a tool but, as we said, by convention' (De int. 17a 1f); cf. De int. 16b 26–8: 'A *sentence* is a significant spoken sound some part of which is significant in separation—as an expression, not as an affirmation'.

[36] 'Let us call a name or a verb simply an expression, since by saying it one cannot reveal anything by one's utterance in such a way as to be making a statement' (De int. 17a 17–19).

[37] 'Not every sentence is a statement-making sentence, but only those in which there is truth or falsity' (De int. 17a 2f).

[38] 'The simple statement is a significant spoken sound about whether something does or does not hold (in one of the divisions of time). An *affirmation* is a statement affirming something of something; a *negation* is a statement denying something of something' (De int. 17a 22–6).

[39] 'The first single statement-making sentence is the affirmation, next is the negation. The others are single in virtue of a connective' (De int. 17a 8f).

METAPHORICAL TRUTH

the concern of rhetoric or poetics, whose intellectual subject-matter is not the truth of a statement, but rather language which lives from and pleads for this truth. Rhetoric is of course necessary, since truth must assert itself. For although by nature truth is stronger than its opposite, human beings endowed with language have the capacity to assist in the victory of falsehood. And so the art of rhetoric has a special responsibility for truth.[40] Part of this rhetorical responsibility for truth is using speech in a way which is appropriate to the truth. Speech partly consists of nouns, and to them metaphor belongs.

2. Along with other kinds of nouns which in some way deviate from general linguistic usage, Aristotle sets metaphor over against the proper representative of nouns as a class, the ordinary word (ὄνομα κύριον).[41] By contrast to the ordinary word, μεταφορά is ὀνόματος ἀλλοτρίου ἐπιφορά.[42] The strange word really belongs to a different state of affairs, which it signifies in common linguistic usage. It is strange in respect of the new state of affairs which it is now used to signify by transference; and so over against common linguistic usage it is a strange word. Metaphor therefore presupposes that it is possible to signify (indicate) and express the world of things without metaphors. The Aristotelian conception of metaphor rests on the assumption that things are normally signified by the ordinary word in common usage, so that in respect of the state of affairs which it signifies the ὄνομα κύριον can also be regarded as τὸ οἰκεῖον ὄνομα, as the proper expression.[43] An ordinary word is defined by the fact that it is used by all.[44] It is ordinary in that all make use of it. This understanding of the ordinary word accords with the theory that

[40] 'Therefore rhetoric is useful because things that are true and things that are just have a natural tendency to prevail over their opposites, so that if the decisions of judges are not what they ought to be, the defeat must be due to the speeches themselves, and they must be blamed accordingly' (Rhet. 1355 a 22–4).
[41] 'Whatever its structure, a noun must be always either the ordinary word for the thing, or a strange word, or a metaphor, or an ornamental word, or a coined word, or a word lengthened out, or curtailed, or altered in form' (Poet. 1457b 1–3).
[42] 'Metaphor consists in giving the thing a name that belongs to something else' (Poet. 1457b 7–9).
[43] Cf. Rhet. 1404b 32.
[44] 'By the ordinary word I mean that in general use in a country' (Poet. 1457b 3f).

names, and speech which makes use of them, receive their semantic function by convention (κατὰ συνθήκην). Conventions which give meaning are the result of linguistic usage.

Over against this, metaphor deviates from common linguistic usage, at least in its first occurrence. It is, however, different from γλῶττα, a foreign word, which belongs to the class of nouns and is equally different from the ὄνομα κύριον, and which is used by foreigners (who, of course, regard it as the ordinary word).[45] It is different because it is accepted by everyone in ordinary linguistic usage.[46] And so metaphor gets itself adopted, either by being accepted by its hearers or by being repeated in speech. Thus a strange word's strangeness is appropriated. The strangeness is not abolished; rather in its very strangeness it becomes a means of heightening the familiarity of that which is familiar by highlighting a particular feature or by opening up the possibility of discovering something already known in such a way that a new familiarity arises. The strangeness of a strange word, which is intrinsic to metaphor, is altogether different from the strangeness of a foreign word, a γλῶττα. The strange word is manifest in its very strangeness. How can this be?

The peculiarity which we have observed can only be explained if the ἐπιφορά is not a matter of chance but rather occurs in accordance with a specific order. Aristotle himself sets out such an order. The transference from ... to ... is only hermeneutically permissible in certain cases: 'metaphor consists in giving the thing a name that belongs to something else; the transference being either from genus to species, or from species to genus, or from species to species, or on the grounds of analogy'.[47] We have an example of transference from species to genus when we talk of a ship standing in the water, for lying at anchor is a form of standing, so that 'standing' is the genus here.[48] There is a transference from genus to species when, for example, Homer talks of the 'ten thousand' rather than the 'many' noble deeds of Ulysses; 'many' here is the genus of the more particular term 'ten thousand'.[49] Or again, a

[45] Cf. Poet. 1457b 3–6.
[46] Cf. Rhet. 1404 b 26–35.
[47] Poet. 1457b 6–9.
[48] Cf. Poet. 1457b 9–11.
[49] Cf. Poet. 1457b 11–13.

transference 'from species to species' is examplified 'in "drawing the life with the bronze"', and in "severing with the enduring bronze", where the poet uses "draw" in the sense of "sever" and "sever" in the sense of "draw", both words meaning to "take away" something'.[50] Finally we have a transference by analogy in all cases in which the second term relates to the first term in the same way that the fourth term relates to the third, so that the fourth term is used instead of the second and vice-versa. Thus old age is to life as evening is to day, so that we can speak of the 'evening of life' or of a day growing old.[51] In the later rhetorical tradition, the term 'metaphor' was reserved exclusively for transference by analogy. It is, indeed, hermeneutically the most interesting of all the possibilities mentioned by Aristotle, though this does not explain why the 'later tradition . . . restricted the term "metaphor" to cases where analogy was the ground of the shift in sense' whilst using the general term 'trope' to cover all the other transferences and shifts of meaning which have been mentioned.[52]

Beyond its rhetorical functions, metaphor formed by analogy is especially valuable in that in certain cases it is indispensable for the signification of states of affairs. As we saw, the definition of metaphor as the transference of a strange word from . . . to . . . presupposes that the state of affairs signified metaphorically has its ὄνομα κύριον (or even more than one such) by which it is properly signified; the metaphor replaces this ὄνομα κύριον as it were out of extravagance. In some way or other, then, metaphor is, indeed, an indication of the richness of language, not simply in view of the quantity of available words, but much more so in view of the specific linguistic accomplishment which metaphor represents. This is shown by the exceptions to the rule just mentioned. For there are cases in which common usage lacks a proper signification for a well-known state of affairs. In such cases, a metaphor formed by analogy would be the only way in which we could speak at all.[53] In such cases, if we do not speak metaphorically, we do not speak at all. This being

[50] Poet. 1457b 13–16.
[51] Poet. 1457b 16–25.
[52] P. Henle, op. cit., p. 175. Henle concedes that 'the most recent tendency is to use "metaphor" in Aristotle's poetic sense' (ibid.), but does not himself follow this tendency. On 'tropes', see H. Lausberg, *Handbuch* §§ 552–98; *Elemente* §§ 174–236.
[53] As an example, Aristotle points out that 'to cast forth seed-corn is

said, it is still worth mentioning here that, in another context, of all four forms of metaphor, Aristotle praises that formed according to analogy as being 'the most taking'.[54]

Apart from the linguistic necessity we have just mentioned, language could in fact manage without metaphors. Such a language would, however, be extraordinarily dull. For Aristotle, the best language is spoken by those who know how to combine most appropriately the clarity of the normal, literal terms and the attractiveness of metaphors.[55] Such language would be neither too ordinary nor unduly elevated, but appropriate.[56] Language consisting only of common significations would be ordinary, although (because!) it would doubtless be the most clear.

An ordinary or low mode of expression becomes elevated if unusual, strange expressions (ξενικά) are added to the commonly used ordinary words (ὀνόματα κύρια); the most important of these expressions is metaphor.[57] It is highly important, however, that we should not be conscious of the strangeness. The speaker must introduce the element of strangeness without it being noticed, so that what is said does not appear to be artificially constructed but natural: 'naturalness is persuasive, artificiality is the contrary; for our hearers become prejudiced and think that we have some design against them, as if we were mixing their wines for them'.[58] One

---

called "sowing", but to cast forth its flame, as said of the sun, has no special name. This nameless act, however, stands in just the same relation to its object, sunlight, as sowing to the seed-corn. Hence the expression in the poet "sowing around a god-creating flame"' (Poet. 1457b 25–30).

[54] Rhet. 1411a 1f.

[55] Poet. 1458a 18–23: 'The excellence of diction is for it to be at once clear and not mean. The clearest indeed is that made up of the ordinary words for things, but it is mean ... On the other hand, the diction becomes distinguished and non-prosaic by the use of unfamiliar terms, i.e. strange words, metaphors, lengthened forms, and everything that deviates from the ordinary modes of speech'.

[56] Cf. Rhet. 1404b 1–4: 'Language to be good must be clear, as is proved by the fact that speech which fails to convey a plain meaning will fail to do just what speech has to do. It must also be appropriate, avoiding both meanness and undue elevation'.

[57] Cf Poet. 1458a 22f with Rhet. 1404b 10–12: 'it is therefore well to give everyday speech an unfamiliar air: people like what strikes them, and they are struck by what is out of the way'.

[58] Rhet. 1404b 18f.

METAPHORICAL TRUTH

who speaks well on the one hand allows that which by comparison with ordinary usage is strange, as it were to come to mind by itself, so that it does not obtrude, and, on the other hand, speaks clearly and plainly.[59]

3. *Discovering* metaphors is not for everyone, however. Aristotle makes an interesting qualification here which deserves particular attention because the grounds on which he makes it offer insights into the function and nature of the metaphorical.

Metaphors must be successful. If they are to succeed, similarity must be discerned since 'a good metaphor implies an intuitive perception of the similarity in dissimilars'.[60] This cannot be learned from others, however; it is 'a sign of genius'.[61] The ability to perceive similarities and the resultant creativity in forming metaphors are distinctions given us by nature. In the end, these distinctions come from an intuitive sense of analogy, a taste for correspondence. By 'taste' we are to understand something like the capacity for aesthetic judgement. The exercise of this capacity to perceive the correspondences of being presupposes a human nature which, for its part, corresponds to these correspondences. This Aristotle calls εὐφυΐα, a nature which corresponds to nature. One has to be born to the task of perceiving correspondences and forming successful metaphors.

In a successful metaphor, consequently, language corresponds to the correspondence which has always pervaded that which is. 'Metaphors ... must be fitting,' says Aristotle, and their fittingness comes from analogy: 'they must correspond to the thing signified'.[62] When we remember that Plato calls analogy 'the fairest bond', since it alone 'makes the most complete fusion of itself and the things which it combines',[63] we may measure the extent to which for Aristotle a metaphor formed in accordance with the structural laws of analogy

---

[59] Rhet. 1404b 35f: 'a good work can produce a style that is distinguished without being obtrusive, and is at the same time clear'.
[60] Poet. 1459a 7f.
[61] Poet. 1459a 6f. Cf. Rhet. 1405a 8–10. Rhet. 1410b 7f mentions the skill given by practice as a condition for an appropriate transference, obviously presupposing that it is a question of training.
[62] Rhet. 1405a 10f.
[63] Cf. Plato, Timaeus 31c 2–32a 7: 'The fairest bond is that which makes the most complete fusion of itself and the things which it combines, and

could be a way of turning that which is into language. Every successful metaphor must be iridescent with something of the correspondence which holds the world together in its deepest reaches. What is hermeneutically fascinating about metaphor is the fact that it unites linguistic freedom on the one hand and a semantic sense of actuality on the other, in a way quite unknown to statements which operate with the common significations (ὀνόματα κύρια) alone. Metaphorical language harmonizes in the most exact way the creative potential of language and strict conceptual necessity, bringing together the surprise of linguistic novelty and the familiarity of that which is already known. In this way a gain is always made through metaphor. The horizon of being is expanded in language. And so metaphor is a particular form of the way in which in language we have dealings with that which is. But just because of this, metaphor presupposes a particular sense for that which is, a sense of correspondences. Not every similarity is useful, and so by no means everyone who discovers similarities is also able to form fitting metaphors. One can churn out some dreadful nonsense (and here some of the most recent theological literature is paradigmatic), to say nothing of boundless lack of taste. Aristotle notes that if the analogy is lacking, μεταφορά leads us to relate together quite contrary things, in a way which stands out in a most disagreeable way: ἀπρεπὲς φανεῖται.[64] Anyone feeling called to form

proportion (analogy) is best adapted to effect such a union. For whenever in any three numbers, whether cube or square, there is a mean, which is to the last term what the first term is to it, and again, when the mean is to the first term as the first term is to the mean—then the mean becoming first and last, and the first and last becoming means, they will all of them of necessity come to be the same, and having become the same with one another will all be one'. Here we have a tripartite geometric proportion, in which the mean determines the interrelation of each part and thus each part itself. According to Timaeus 69b 5, God has ordered all things in such a way that they have 'all the measures and harmonies which they could possibly receive'. From the relevant literature on the complex problem of analogy in Plato and Aristotle, see above all E.-W. Platzeck, *Von der Analogie zum Syllogismus* (Paderborn, 1954).

[64] 'Metaphors . . . must be fitting, which means they must fairly correspond to the thing signified; failing this, their inappropriateness will be conspicuous: the want of harmony between two things is emphasised by their being placed side by side': Rhet. 1405a 10–13. Amongst inappropriate metaphors, Aristotle counts those which are ridiculous, too solemn, and too far-fetched: Rhet. 1406b 6–9.

metaphors would do well in discovering similarities to heed the warning against carelessness which Aristotle's teacher put in the mouth of the stranger in the *Sophist*: 'a cautious man should above all be on his guard against resemblances: they are a very slippery sort of a thing'.[65]

The whole point of the formation of metaphors, then, is that they should succeed, that is, that they really should bring to speech that which is, although in doing that they ascribe more to actuality than it actually is. If metaphors are successful in this way, their hearer experiences a repetition of the gain which occurs in the formation of fitting metaphors, which we have described as an expansion of the horizon of being. That which the power of human language has achieved by corresponding to the correspondences in being, namely the event of a gain to being, can now be repeated by everyone who enters into this successful metaphor, as the event of a gain to knowledge. And so Aristotle regards metaphorical language as an excellent learning process for the hearer who is addressed by it, superior to other processes of language because of the easy, playful way in which it takes place. In metaphorical language, that which is to be learnt is passed on to the one who is addressed as it were in a game.

4. Aristotle treats this important dimension of metaphorical speech in more detail in his *Rhetoric*. His starting-point is that all of us naturally find easy learning a pleasure: 'we all naturally find it agreeable to get hold of new ideas easily'.[66] This is entirely comprehensible if, as the first sentence of the *Metaphysics* asserts, 'all men by nature desire to know'.[67] The realisation of a natural impulse gives pleasure so that every process of learning should, in fact, be pleasurable for the learner.[68] The pleasure is heightened, however, if the object which we inevitably desire can be attained in an easy way. The natural human impulse to know prefers, of course, to be realised without unnecessary effort. In this we correspond in our human way to God and nature. For just as 'God and nature create nothing that is pointless',[69] so it is entirely natural that the

---

[65] Plato, Sophist 231a 6–8.
[66] Rhet. 1410b 10f.
[67] Meta. 980a 21.
[68] Rhet. 1371a 31f: 'learning things and wondering at things are also pleasant for the most part'.
[69] De caelo 271a 33.

easiest realisation of a natural desire is intrinsic to that which is desired. The natural desire to know which is inherent equally in all desires that its self-realisation be promoted (which explains, without condoning, a certain impatience on the part of today's theology students with the more or less laborious processes of historical and dogmatic learning: the real point is whether the same end could be achieved more easily). The natural desire wants to attain its goal as quickly as possible. And so methods of acquiring knowledge which 'make us seize a new idea promptly'[70] are to be preferred, for everyone likes to quicken the pace on the road to knowledge.

Easy learning thus caters for human nature. Because by nature we must desire to know, we are 'brought into (our) natural condition through learning';[71] through easy learning we increase the undeniable pleasure of gratifying our natural desire to know.

Knowledge, however, is language which refers to that which is. To know what is the case means to be able to say what is the case. According to Heraclitus, part of perceiving that which is, is demonstrating in language what is the case; and according to Parmenides, thinking cannot be discovered without being which comes to speech.[72] Knowledge is dependent upon language and therefore upon words. Words name things insofar as they signify something. For Aristotle this is carried out in an elementary way by nouns: 'nouns express ideas'.[73] In speech, words (nouns and verbs) are joined together in such a way that in statements of judgment they can bring to speech what is the case. This semantic reference to the object makes language the place of knowledge. Through the semantic function of words, that which is is present in language as knowledge.

There is, however, a further use of words, which adds new knowledge to that which is already known. In such linguistic usage, that which is *becomes* present as knowledge. In certain cases an expansion of knowledge can only occur through a new use of

---

[70] Rhet. 1410b 21.
[71] 'Wondering implies the desire of learning . . . while in learning one is brought into one's natural condition': Rhet. 1371 a 32–4.
[72] Cf. E. Jüngel, 'Zum Ursprung der Analogie bei Parmenides und Heraklit' in *Entsprechungen. Gott—Wahrheit—Mensch* (Munich, 1980), pp. 52–102.
[73] Rhet. 1411 b 11.

words. Words such as these which of themselves allow us to increase our knowledge, making easy learning possible, are those which we consequently most enjoy and find most agreeable: 'those words are the most agreeable that enable us to get hold of new ideas'.[74] Since, however, the words commonly used for signifying things are already familiar to us in their function of signifying or referring, this effect can only be achieved by an unfamiliar word or by an unfamiliar use of words. For Aristotle, metaphor is the best means of producing this effect. Why?

Metaphor is neither a familiar process of naming (and thus not a familiar word), nor a completely strange expression used only by a few. It is neither an ὄνομα κύριον nor a γλῶττα, but rather is a strange word coming up against the word normally used. And so it should be neither completely out of the way and foreign (ἀλλοτρία) nor too common (ἐπιπόλαιος); rather it should set before our eyes (πρὸ ὀμμάτων ποιεῖν)[75] that which it brings to speech. This it achieves above all by using expressions of energy (of effective movement), and expressions that give life to those things which are lifeless and without soul.[76] For the person addressed in this way, metaphor becomes a word which plays between familiar and unfamiliar use of words; mediating between two familiar phenomena (like, for example, the relation of evening to day and that of old age to life), this playful word also mediates new knowledge to the one addressed (by speaking of the evening of life, or the day growing old). In a metaphor such as 'the evening of life', the one addressed is faced with a correspondence between what are at first sight two completely distinct and dissimilar horizons of meaning (life and day). But thereby the insight emerges that old age and evening have a common function: they both bring to an end the whole of which they are the final part. This can serve as an example of the increase in knowledge which is gained in a playful way through a metaphor formed according to analogy. 'Easy learning' is accomplished

[74] Rhet. 1410 b 11f. The full passage runs: 'We all naturally find it agreeable to get hold of new ideas easily; words express ideas, and therefore those words are the most agreeable that enable us to get hold of new ideas. Now strange words simply puzzle us; ordinary words convey only what we know already; it is from metaphor that we can best get hold of something fresh' (Rhet. 1410 b 10–13).
[75] Cf Rhet. 1410 b 32–5: metaphors 'ought to set the scene before our eyes; for events are to be seen in progress rather than in prospect'.
[76] Cf Rhet. 1411 b 24–33.

through other modes of metaphorical speech in a similar way. Aristotle takes his example from Homer, who called age 'stubble' for both are withered.[77] Beyond a broadening of perception through the joining of two different horizons of meaning, metaphor contains knowledge of a logical state of affairs which, if it is to be expressed in language, makes it necessary to develop a more general concept. To this extent, μεταφορά carries with it a tendency to form logical concepts. Metaphor can either imply (in the case of metaphor formed by analogy) knowledge of the identity of relations, or (in all the other three cases of ἐπιφορά) the knowledge of *genus proximum* (the related genus) and *differentia specifica* (the specific species). Usually, however, this tendency to form concepts is not pursued by the hearer of the metaphor and, on the other hand, Aristotle positively forbids the use of metaphors in making definitions.[78] For all that, the recognition of what is common to different things or what is similar in dissimilar things, shines forth as the real increase in knowledge which metaphor mediates.

This can only happen, however, when the metaphor is understood by the one to whom it is addressed. If metaphor is to facilitate easy learning, it must itself be no less easily understood. This is another reason why 'metaphors must be drawn ... from things that are related to the original thing, yet not obviously so related—just as in philosophy also an acute mind will perceive resemblances even in things far apart'.[79] A metaphor formed in this way will succeed, which means with respect to the hearer that it achieves what Aristotle demands of convincing rhetorical syllogisms: without being trivial, they must be immediately transparent or at least be understood soon after they have been stated.[80] Metaphor is disclosure language, both for the one who creates it (the speaker) and for the one who is addressed by it (the hearer). At the same time it is convincing language to the hearer,

[77] Cf Rhet. 1410 b 14f, with *Odyssey* XIV.214.
[78] Cf Anal. post. 97b 37f.
[79] Rhet. 1412 a 11–13. Cf Rhet. 1412 a 20–22: 'because the hearer expected something different, the acquisition of the new idea impresses him all the more. His mind seems to say, "Yes, to be sure; I never thought of that"'.
[80] Rhet. 1400 b 28–33. Cf Rhet. 1410 b 20–6: 'We see, then, that both speech and reasoning are lively in proportion as they make us seize a new idea promptly. For this reason people are not much taken by obvious arguments ... nor by those which puzzle us when we hear them stated,

formulating a discovery in such a way that it mediates both that which is discovered and the event of discovery itself.

However high the value which Aristotle without doubt accords to metaphor, it is limited from the outset by his definition of metaphor as a merely rhetorical figure and function of language. Metaphor has no business in the dialectical concern for correctness. In that context one needs the ὄνομα κύριον since the clarity of language is thereby safeguarded. And so metaphor is not suited for the process of definition. A definition must be based on something clear (τὸ σαφές), and so that which is to be defined cannot be defined either by metaphors or by something named through the use of metaphors.[81] The unsuitability of metaphor for statements in which we are concerned for correctness can also be seen in the fact that in disputing about truth, metaphors can make the opposite of truth unfalsifiable. One who is uncertain about the truth can misuse a metaphor by making irrefutable the word which is itself not true.[82] And so metaphor belongs to the realm of sophistical conclusions. It plays between reality and appearance. And if it establishes itself as reality rather than appearance, then metaphorical appearance triumphs over reality.

5. Aristotle's understanding of metaphor was generally followed, as we reminded ourselves at the outset. The interpretation of metaphor as a non-literal mode of speech belonging to rhetoric became generally accepted. We now draw together the presuppositions of this interpretation.

Language normally has enough words to express univocally all the states of affairs in the world. This is done in sentences, which make statements by combining words. The usual place of a word in the context of language as a whole and in the relation of language to world is given in language use. Language use shows what words mean. Moreover, it also shows that there are many words which function in our statements as the 'normal words' for states of affairs. They signify something. Their function of signification is based on the fact that their semantic sense (the so-called content of the word)

but only by those which convey their information to us when we hear them stated, provided we had not the information already; or which the mind only just fails to keep up with'.

[81] Cf. Anal. post. 97 b 31–8.
[82] Cf. Soph. elench. 176 b 14–25.

coincides with their meaning (their referential relation to an object), so that the speaker of a word associates with it the same information value as the hearer of the same word. The horizon of sense and the horizon of meaning coincide because the word has a context of being in the sentence which corresponds to the linguistic context, both for hearer and speaker. Many of these words are, however, capable of being used in another way. Over against their original, proper use, they come to have a different meaning, though their sense remains unchanged: they now signify a different object. In this kind of metaphorical use of words, sense and meaning diverge; the original meaning is suspended, so that another new meaning can take its place. The sentence 'Achilles is a lion' certainly calls to mind the lion in the wilderness; at the same time, we know Achilles is no such lion. Metaphorical predication of this sort presupposes consent between the speaker who forms the metaphor and the hearer to whom the metaphor comes with no warning, a consent which is not simply the so-called proper use of language. The latter always presupposes consent (*consuetudo*) between speaker and hearer that a certain word with a certain sense carries a certain meaning and so brings to speech a certain state of affairs. Metaphorical language, however, gives the speaker a linguistic advantage (a semantic *voluntas*) over the hearer. For in forming a metaphor the speaker breaks out of the normal use of language by establishing a new combination of words which initiates a new relation of meaning. The hearer does not yet know the new linguistic and ontological contexts of the word which is familiar in its old meaning. Nevertheless the speaker is confident that the word will be accepted in its new linguistic context, since if the metaphor succeeds, the relation of the old and the new ontological contexts of the word will make it plain. The relation of states of affairs controls linguistic usage, so that the speaker can be confident that by his metaphorical use of the word consent with the hearer will again be achieved, indeed, that a new consent will be achieved. This consent has, of course, to be achieved first with the hearer. And it is this event of achieving consent which makes metaphorical speech appealing in a special way. We experience metaphor as agreeable and attractive.

It is, however, precisely the appeal of metaphor which is regarded as deficient form of statement with respect to truth, however legitimate that appeal may be. The only way of really stating what actually is the case is to bring world to speech in univocal words which refer immediately to states of affairs. The language of address is a specifically rhetorical phenomenon and nothing else. Appealing language is a mere linguistic ornament (*ornatus*). Hardly any consideration is given to the fact that that which is appealing attracts because it belongs to the essence of the ontological relation of language (so that unhappy metaphors can be far more painful than erroneous statements). The way in which Aristotle protects διαλέγεσθαι from μεταφοραί speaks for itself. It shows that metaphor is regarded as a luxury which 'rhetorical' speech can afford, but must not be afforded in dialectical speech. We speak with many metaphors, and we like to hear them. Language itself, it seems, loves metaphors. But when it comes to a point where truth is at stake, it can also do otherwise.

Reflection on the character of metaphor is, however, indebted to Aristotle not only for his detailed observations, whose value cannot be overestimated, but also especially for his analysis of the function of metaphor as address. If we do not wish to deny that metaphor is a proper form of speech, we need to have no less an estimation of the character of language as *address* as we do of its character as *statement*. Language as address cannot be simply more alien to truth than language as statement. Aristotle's analysis of the function of metaphor does not release us from this question, but in its own way points right into it.

On the basis of Aristotle's definition of μεταφορά, another point is to be asserted against the understanding of metaphor as a non-literal mode of speech. We have, after all, come across a kind of metaphorical speech which is important even in the strictest form of statements. Whilst metaphor is as a rule a linguistic ornament, there is a set of cases in which, within the terms of the hermeneutical presuppositions assumed, the metaphorical signification of a state of affairs is *necessary*. A *necessary metaphor* of this kind is the remedy in a hermeneutical emergency, in a situation in which normal language use does not represent a particular state of affairs by a *verbum proprium*, so that (at first) an 'ordinary word' for that state of affairs is lacking. In such cases the *verbum proprium* is, as we saw, replaced by a metaphor formed by analogy, which then becomes the usual signification in normal usage. The post-Aristotelian tradition calls this necessary metaphor κατάχρησις (*abusio*, catachresis), thereby expressing both that the usage was derivative and that the derivative usage was the normal one. This metaphorical catachresis is enough to call into question the entire traditional theory of metaphor.

Metaphorical catachresis could be taken as an indication that metaphor could assume the function of a noun acting as an ordinary signifier or even of a concept defined with the aid of such nouns. In some exceptional cases, then, metaphor would assume the function of literal speech. There are, however, reasons to go much further and to question the theory of language, whose premises have as yet remained untouched, by speculating that for the most part words which are thought to be ordinary words were originally metaphors. But since metaphor is a form of language which addresses, along with the reference to such language to the world there would emerge that basic form of language which addresses us in our humanness. The relation of language to the world cannot be separated from the relation of language to the 'I', which can only be addressed as an 'I' insofar as it belongs to a 'we'. It is no accident that the 'lexical area which creates catachresis ... is the area most closely interesting to us: the social realities of family, life and work'.[83] On the other hand it is also noticeable that the 'mental realities' which bear special similarity to us are brought to speech by a 'vocabulary of catachrestic origin' which points to bodily experiences in the world: '*animus* (wind), *sapiens* (tasting), *spiritus* (breath)'.[84] If we understand so-called catachresis out of the basic process of μεταφορά, then it becomes evident that the apparently rigid semantic relation to the object of many, if not all, words, is a fiction, or at least the result of a linguistic history which is equally the history of the world relation of the human person addressed as a person. One could probably interpret Aristotle's thesis that words essentially mean something only by convention as an indication of this fact. The proper locus of words would then by the *movement* of language, which is concrete as presence when it combines words into a unified *statement*, and which moves itself through time as a *linguistic history*. A statement reduces the multitude of possible meanings, which I would like to call the parabolic dimension of language, to that which is most defined; and it is of the essence of definition to hang on, to fix the word used to define with a particular meaning. Possibility is thereby reduced to actuality. Language as address resists this, establishing the power of the possible over against, though not without, the actual. The structure

[83] Lausberg, *Handbuch* §562.
[84] Ibid.

of metaphor enables linguistic and conceptual history, since it is of the essence of μεταφορά to be constitutive of language both synchronically and diachronically.

The hermeneutical and theological relevance of the parabolic dimension of language, which must on no account be treated as a minor matter, has been indicated more than once. In his treatment of Homer's parables, Bruno Snell has shown how deeply reference to the world and the character of language as address interpenetrate in parabolic language, so that 'the story . . . requires the comparison to achieve full expression'.[85] Our calling someone who stands firm in dangerous situations a rock rests upon the fact 'that the inanimate object is itself viewed anthropomorphically . . . It appears, therefore, that one object is capable of casting light upon another in the form of a simile, only because we read into the object the very qualities which it in turn illustrates. This peculiar situation, namely that human behaviour is made clear only through reference to something

[85] B. Snell, *The Discovery of the Mind. The Greek Origins of European Thought* (Oxford, 1953), p. 200. I have drawn attention to the general hermeneutical significance of Snell's reflections for an understanding of the parables in my dissertation *Paulus und Jesus* (Tübingen, 1979), p. 94, n. 7 and pp. 136–8. Snell is also referred to by K. Löwith, 'Die Sprache als Vermittler von Mensch und Welt' in *Gesammelte Abhandlungen. Zur Kritik der geschichtlichen Existenz* (Stuttgart, 1960), p. 222. Löwith rightly remarks that in metaphor 'our experiences of the surrounding world and of our own times illuminate, inform and determine one another. The one reminds us of the other . . . And since our linguistic relation to the world is not limited to the naming of individual objects, everything can be compared with everthing else and set in a mutually illuminating relation to everything else'. The problem analysed by Snell was already described by Nietzsche: 'When someone hides something behind a bush and looks for it again in the same place and finds it there as well, there is not much praise in such seeking and finding. Yet this is how matters stand regarding seeking and finding "truth" within the realm of reason. If I make up the definition of a mammal, and then, after inspecting a camel, declare "look, a mammal," I have indeed brought a truth to light in this way, but it is a truth of limited value. That is to say, it is a thoroughly anthropomorphic truth . . . At bottom, what the investigator of such truths is seeking is only the metamorphosis of the world into man. He strives to understand the world as something analagous to man, and at best he achieves by his struggles the feeling of assimilation' (op. cit., pp. 85f). The weakness of Nietzsche's assertions lies in the way in which he makes his negative evaluation of anthropomorphism hermeneutically absolute. For a full debate here, it would be necessary to go back to Kant's distinction between 'dogmatic' and 'symbolic' anthropomorphism.

else which is in turn explicated by analogy with human behaviour, pertains to all Homeric smilies. More than that, it pertains to all genuine metaphors, in fact to every single case of human comprehension. Thus it is not quite correct to say that the rock is viewed anthropomorphically, unless we add that our own understanding of the rock is anthropomorphic for the same reason that we are able to look at ourselves petromorphically, and that the act of regarding the rock in human terms furnishes us with a means of apprehending and defining our own behaviour. In other words, and this is all-important in any explanation of the simile, man must listen to an echo of himself before he may hear or know himself'.[86] It is equally important for the functioning of language.

[86] Ibid., pp. 200f. It is especially tempting to compare Snell's hermeneutical observations on Homer's parabolic language with Luther's reflections on the metaphorical language of Scripture. Luther wants to understand, for example, sentences like 'Christ is the rock', 'Christ is a vine' or 'Christ is a flower' as literal modes of speech and argues against Zwingli's attempt to use such statements as an argument for the fact that the copula 'is', both in those statements and in the much disputed words of institution 'This is my body', has to be interpreted as 'means'. For Luther the sentences mean exactly what they say: Christ *is* a rock, a vine, a flower. Moreover, it would be logically meaningless to say: 'Christ *means* a flower'. The predicates in these sentences take on a new meaning, so that according to all the grammarians and rhetoricians the word used as a predicate becomes a new word. 'All grammarians say that "flower" here has become a new word and has acquired a new meaning, and now no longer means the flower in the field but the child Jesus. They do not say that the word "is" has here become metaphorical, for Christ does not represent a flower but is a flower, yet a different flower from a natural one' (M. Luther, *Confession Concerning Christ's Supper*, LW 37, p. 172). For Luther, the use of a word can give it a different meaning (reference) without thereby making into an allegory the predication made by the word in its different usage: 'This art (sc. grammar) teaches how a child may make two or three words out of one, or how he may give to a single word a new application and several meanings' (ibid., p. 171). The one word possesses 'a common meaning' (in correspondence with the Aristotelian conception of ὄνομα κύριον which causes a ταπεινὴ λέξις) (ibid., p. 172). The metaphorical use leads to a 'new word'. It is permitted if there is some similarity between the two things designated by the same word: such expressions 'abound in the Scriptures. In grammar one speaks of a trope or metaphor when a single name is given to different things on account of a similarity in both. Though in spelling the name is the same, *potestate ac significatione plura*: in force, usage, and meaning there are two words, an old and a new, as Horace says and as children well know' (ibid., pp. 172f).

IV

1. As we saw, metaphors are the articulation of discoveries. This articulation always stands in relation to what has already been discovered.[87] In a basic sense, what has already been discovered is

Thus Luther contends the idea that metaphorical language is non-literal. Against Zwingli's 'rationalistic' interpretation, according to which 'is' in such sentences is really to be understood as 'means', so that the copula comes to have a different meaning, Luther focusses on the *creative power* of metaphorical language, which is why he insists on taking literally the term 'is' in metaphorical expressions. Summarising Luther's remarks from a hermeneutical point of view, we could say that they affirm the ontological relevance of metaphorical speech, in that through it a new context of being is disclosed, grounded in a gain to language. The new (metaphorical) use of a word gives this word a new meaning and this new meaning brings new being to speech. 'In such expressions we are speaking of an essence, what a person is and not what a person represents, and we coin a new word to express his new essence' (ibid., p. 173). Luther here presupposes that the old common meaning of the word used metaphorically is to a certain extent destroyed: 'No language or logic permits us to say, "Christ signifies the true vine". In this passage no-one can say that the true vine is the wood in the vineyard. Hence the text irresistibly compels us to regard "vine" as a new word, meaning a second, new, real vine, and not the vine in the vineyard' (ibid., p. 174). Metaphor profits from the possible non-being of the world as we conceive of it, in that it suspends it (the natural vine), in order newly to bring to speech the being of the world. This is of course only possible since new being is only expressible in parables of the old. And so Luther understands metaphor as the realization of the parabolic nature of language. Again, Luther here presupposes that being is itself parabolic (analogical), that there is that which is parabolic within things themselves ('on account of the similarity in both', ibid., p. 172). The parable within that which is thus makes speech in parables possible: 'He who speaks in parables makes common words into pure tropes—new and different words. Otherwise they would not be parables, if he used common words in their original sense' (ibid., p. 175).

[87] K.-O. Apel was thus right to defend against Wittgenstein the 'metaphorical appearance' which comes from 'metaphorical hypostasization' as being 'indispensable to the progressive expansion of the human consciousness in the history of thought'. Cf. his 'Die Frage nach dem Sinnkriterium der Sprache und die Hermeneutik' in *Weltgeschichte* 4 (1968), p. 26. Apel's plea accords with Blumenberg's remarks referred to above. As a hermeneutical test, we should try to imagine our language without metaphors: it would shrink to the domain of that which has already been talked through from every angle, of the 'meaningless'—meaningless 'for the reason that this domain no longer offers any stimulus to any kind of creative

the human person as discoverer. As discoverers, we discover ourselves as being in the world and claimed by the world. That the world lays claim to us is already, however, a transference. I am claimed by a demand directed to me, by an experience of being addressed, so that if the world lays claim to me I already see myself as a person addressed. We find ourselves, it seems, as those who are addressed in this way: only so do we—and only we—have a world. For to be addressed by something is to perceive something as what it is. In this lies the difference between the world and a mere conglomeration of that which is: we let ourselves be addressed and claimed by the world, in accord with our 'already-being-addressed'. Language which expresses us and our world (or, more precisely, the statements with which we signify ourselves and our world) draws its sense from the fact that we let ourselves be addressed and claimed by the world, on the basis of our already-being-addressed by a complex of that which is the case. Linguistic statements reflect the world, which for its part reflects our being-addressed insofar as we let ourselves be addressed by it.

The specific metaphors of our language which are richly present in all language use and yet which must always be created afresh, are a reminder of what we would call the metaphorical essence of language. What takes place in language always takes place as language, in that along with our world we find ourselves *transferred into language* if we undertake to relate to our world *in language* and *to transfer* one to another in language. Language is controlled by an anthropomorphism which is anything but anthropocentric, because and to the extent to which it is metaphorical. We exist as a passing over from being into language, a passing over which itself belongs to being as a *gain to being*.

Speculation? Mysticism? The converse would be philistinism. An inadequate sense of actuality? On the contrary: an attempt to conceive of actuality out of the encounter of possibility and necessity, and to sharpen our sense of the actual out of a sense of that which is necessarily possible.

processes, least of all to utterances which point to the unexplored and the unexperienced' (E. Biser, 'Sprache und Person. Zur Signatur des antipersonalen Sprachtyps' in G. Ebeling et al., ed., *Festschrift für Ernst Fuchs* (Tübingen, 1973), p. 71). The thoroughly metaphorical structure of language contains the possibility of innovation, by which both science and poetry live.

The gain which we value as an expansion of our horizons through successful metaphors and whose effect in intensifying our existence can only be disputed by those who regard discoveries as existentially irrelevant—this gain reminds us of a movement which benefits being itself and in which we ourselves as those who are addressed have our ontological locus.

2. These reflections on the metaphorical structure of language lead us back to Nietzsche's thesis that truth is fundamentally nothing other than a 'moveable host of metaphors, metonymies, and anthropomorphisms'.[88] Nietzsche intended the thesis to be derogatory, to debase truth. But the insight which it contains could be turned in another direction and on good grounds to be taken positively. Beda Allemann has sought to do this by setting Nietzsche's insight into the metaphorical structure of truth against his scepticism. Allemann criticises Nietzsche for 'defining the fundamental process as one between object and words', so that words can be understood purely as 'signs which inevitably distort reality'.[89] Over against this, Allemann finds 'the condition of possibility of language ... in the fact that words can enter into relation with one another without being separated from their meanings. Here, in the area in which processes between words are enacted in the setting of a word sequence, the fundamental transference takes place. In this process the meaning of words which is already to hand is actualised and thereby more closely specified, so that a meaningful relation is produced. The decisive metaphorical quality of language seems to me to lie in this process'. Only when we set aside the understanding of words as isolated signs with meaning are we able to perceive that μεταφορά is the fundamental process of language, and accordingly to speak of the 'fundamental metaphorical quality of language'.[90] This does not preclude us from following Nietzsche in understanding the transfer of being into language as μεταφορά or from acknowledging a fundamental metaphorical quality in truth. Instead of debasing truth to metaphor, however, we need to recognise μεταφορά itself as *the event of truth*.

Nietzsche's polemic in his thesis is directed against an

[88] Nietzsche, op. cit., p. 84.
[89] B. Allemann, op. cit., p. 42.
[90] Ibid.

understanding of truth orientated to the correspondence of a word with the state of affairs which it signifies and which, accordingly, absolutises these words as concepts making them into truths. He objects to the idea that every word owes its origin to 'a unique and entirely individual original experience' which nevertheless 'simultaneously has to fit countless more or less similar cases—which means, purely and simply, cases which are never equal and thus altogether unequal'.[91] In just this way, the word becomes a concept: 'Every concept arises from the equation of unequal things'.[92] By 'discarding ... individual differences', we construct an equality which does not really exist. What functions as a concept is, in reality, 'a *qualitas occulta* (an occult quality)'.[93] Devaluing concepts in that way, Nietzsche thinks that he has exposed truth as an illusion: 'truths are illusions which we have forgotten are illusions; they are metaphors which have become worn out and have been drained of sensuous force'.[94] Concepts as 'the *residue of a metaphor*'[95] and truth as forgetfulness of the fact that metaphor is metaphor—so Nietzsche argues against concepts and against truths, for 'the hardening and congealing of a metaphor guarantees absolutely nothing concerning its necessity and exclusive justification'.[96] It only guarantees the 'repose, security and consistency' of the human person who, in forming metaphors is active 'as an *artistically creating* subject'; for in forming concepts we forget that we are creative subjects, setting ourselves apart from reality as '"self-consciousness"'.[97] We use our understanding of truth to deny the anthropomorphic element in language, thereby denying that we are artistically creative subjects. In order to be truthful, we force ourselves 'to lie according to a fixed convention', and even to forget that we are doing so. The human speaker 'lies ... unconsciously and in accordance with habits which are centuries old; and precisely *by means of this unconsciousness* and forgetfulness he arrives at his sense of truth'.[98]

3. In tracing back to a metaphorical event which leads to language

[91] Nietzsche, op. cit., p. 83.
[92] Ibid.
[93] Ibid.
[94] Ibid., p. 84.
[95] Ibid., p. 85.
[96] Ibid., p. 87.
[97] Ibid., p. 86.
[98] Ibid., p. 84.

via the human speaker, Nietzsche sought to destroy the understanding of truth as *adaequatio intellectus et rei*, '(f)or between two absolutely different spheres, as between subject and object, there is no causality, no correctness, and no expression; there is at most an *aesthetic* relation; I mean a suggestive transference, a stammering translation into a completely foreign tongue'.[99] Who would wish to deny that over against the hard world of fact language is quite alien?[100] The transfer of being into language, although itself

[99] Ibid., p. 86. According to Nietzsche, this transference needs 'in any case a freely inventive intermediate sphere and mediating force (ibid.). This reference to the freedom of mediation which is required is the really creative starting-point in Nietzsche's reflections on truth and illusion in an ultramoral sense. From this starting-point, the interpretation of that mediating freedom as 'deception without injury' is to be conceived as a fundamental ontological attitude: 'So long as it is able to deceive without *injuring*, that master of deception, the intellect, is free; it is released from its former slavery and celebrates its Saturnalia. It is never more luxuriant, richer, prouder, more clever and more daring. With creative pleasure it throws metaphors into confusion and displaces the boundary stones of abstractions, so that, for example, it designates the stream as "the moving path which carries man where he would otherwise walk." The intellect has now thrown the token of bondage from itself. At other times it endeavours, with gloomy officiousness, to show the way and to demonstrate the tools to a poor individual who covets existence; it is like a servant who goes in search of booty and pay for his master. But now it has become the master and it dares to wipe from its face the expression of indigence' (pp. 89f).

[100] The anthropological process of the formation of language also points in this direction. According to all that can here be assumed on good grounds, human language formation is constituted by the fact that the sounds uttered by the human self go beyond a simple relation of biological relevance between sound and object in a particular situation, of which animals are also capable. Human sounds can be transferred to other situations, so that they are at the speaker's disposal independent of the situation and can be reproduced at will. Here we clearly come across a basic process of transference between two domains which are foreign to each other. What takes place is something like an annihilation of a particular given situation, and the particular relation of subject to fact which can only be repeated in the same situation. This annihilation is the condition of possibility for a language in which the signification of facts by sounds can proceed independent of a particular speaker and a particular state of affairs. A language which is open to the plurality of situations (and thereby to the phenomenon of the situation as such) can only arise once this restriction to the particular situation has been destroyed. In this respect, mention should be made of the analogy of the character of human language as address. The fact that the speaker is one who is addressed implies, insofar as the one who is addressed replies in turn to the one who addresses, a difference of situation

existent, is a special event. It is the event of truth, in which that which is *lets itself be discovered*, and, *as that which is discovered*, enters into connection with *that which has already been discovered, standing over against the (human) discoverer*, and *corresponding to the discovery (of the discoverer)*.[101] As this transfer of being into language, the event of truth is an absolute metaphor. Thus we have to distinguish between (1) the event of truth as μεταφορά (namely as the turning into language of that which is), which accordingly is thoroughly determinative of language; (2) the thoroughly metaphorical structure of language, which is especially evident in particular metaphors and parables, but which constitutes the essence of spoken language as the interplay of human persons and world; (3) particular metaphors in language, which could be said to recapitulate in a particular case both the metaphorical structure of language and truth as the event of μεταφορά, and could therefore be called reminders of the metaphorical structure of language and truth.

in which the reply is more than the execution of an order which repeats what has been heard. In the distinction of being-addressed and answering, language is an event of communication, occurring as the interplay of being agreed, reaching agreement and disagreeing. We indicate this fact by calling the human person a 'linguistic being', one not merely addressed with respect to something or to the person's affective reaction to that something, but rather one who is addressed with respect to the person's self (and thus to everything to which that person is related). In this way the person can answer not only truly or falsely but also *freely*. The person's 'right' answer is more than just the opposite of a false answer; it is a free answer, in which the one who answers can stand apart from the present situation and correspond to another situation. Free response is the condition of possibility for true statements. For it is precisely this freedom from being restricted to the situation, from a restriction which does not admit that the situation is just that—*a* situation—which allows us to suspend the relation of being addressed and answering, and to understand the apophantic statement (which abstracts from the speaker) as a paradigm of language as such. The structure of the statement then becomes the basic model of the formalization of everyday speech, in which in one way the freedom of sounds from restriction to the situation takes place. Another way in which this freedom takes place is the opening up of the situation by a proper handling of everyday speech.

[101] On the definition of truth out of the event of 'discovery' or 'uncovering' (*Entdecken*), see M. Heidegger, *Being and Time*, pp. 262–9. Over against the definition which he gives there of 'being true' as a mode of human existence, a definition in which 'being-uncovering' is identified with 'being true' (ibid., p. 263), we explicitly called truth an event in which being *lets itself* be discovered. For the importance of this difference, we may refer again to Heidegger, e.g. to his work 'On the Essence of Truth' in *Existence and Being* (Chicago, 1970), pp. 292–324.

METAPHORICAL TRUTH

Metaphors in language preserve the movement of being into language by continuing this movement within language and expanding both our language and our relation to being. They participate in truth, by leading the actual beyond its actuality without asserting anything false about it. And precisely because they lead the actual beyond its actuality, they specify and emphasize this actuality. So metaphor does say more than is actual, and yet precisely in so doing it is true. The appearance of metaphor is not deceptive; rather, it preserves the address-character of language by which alone we are made capable of discovering ourselves and thereby the world.

4. The address-character of language, however, also contains a temptation to untruth, in the same way that slavery is also potentially present in freedom. The dimension of address can indeed lead to false statements. One can say more than is actual without thereby corresponding to the being of actuality. Every possibility that is yet to be actualised can wear thin as deception and untruth when the deceptive appearance replaces the metaphorical appearance. Precisely because it addresses, then, language is ambivalent. All sophistry trades on this ambivalence.

One way of moving from this ambivalence to univocity would certainly be what Nietzsche described in his caricature as the eradication of the metaphorical power of language in favour of concepts which live from definitions. According to Aristotle's rule, metaphors are forbidden in making definitions. But this cannot be carried through completely if we wish to avoid formalized systems of signs.[102] But if we remain conscious of the fact that a good number of concepts are customary metaphors stripped of their metaphorical power, a language which is alert to its own ambivalence will demand control of a conceptual language which deals only in statements and consciously inhibits the element of address. There is no direct route from myth to logos, from symbol to concept, from μεταφορά to ὄνομα κύριον, from address to statement. This dialectic reflects the way in which the event of truth contains a variety of relations between that which is discovered, the act of discovery, the discoverer, that which has already been discovered, the discovery itself and—not least—to that which has not been discovered.

[102] On this, cf. C.F. von Weizsäcker, *Die Einheit der Natur* (Munich, 1972), pp. 82f.

The languages of argument and narration should not contradict each other. Though it may not be initially necessary, metaphorical truth eventually needs a *collegium logicum* (logical connexion). On the other hand, we may expect that a language which reflects on the structure of its statements and cultivates its tendency to self-control, will affirm that the address-character of language is essential to it. But then one will accept another way of moving from the ambivalence of language to univocity, namely the right use of its ambiguity. The successful metaphor, whose univocity can be sharper and more precise that we would like, cannot and need not be proved. Its power and its worth are axiomatic.

V

The language of faith is metaphorical through and through. 'God' is a meaningful word only in the context of metaphorical speech, and immediately becomes meaningless if the *connexio verborum* (combination of words) is not understood metaphorically. Even the statement 'God is God', which avoids metaphors, says nothing at all if it does not also say *in what way* God is. And it is this which theological metaphor enables us to say. It leads to *analogia nominum* (analogy of names), without with there is no proper talk of God.

Theological responsibility towards the language of faith leads immediately to the problem of metaphorical predication. Several aspects of our previous discussion can be illuminated in a particular way; in what follows, we shall refer to at least two of these. First, we shall deal with the question of the *possibility* of metaphorical language about God within the horizon of the Christian faith, and second, we shall conclude our reflections with some remarks on the address-character of theological metaphors and thus on their anthropological relevance.

1. First, we have to start from the premiss that for the Christian faith, we only speak of God if at the same time we speak of a fundamental difference between God and the world. A statement about God which presented him as and only as a part of, the unity of, or the ground of the world would not be a statement about the God in whom we believe. Biblical insights—such as that it profits nothing to gain the whole world and lose one's relation to God, one's soul—point in another direction. Or again, it would be

equally erroneous to think of God and bring him to speech as an ideal, perfect world, as, that is, the world's double. There is only one path open to faith, between 'Spinozism' and 'Platonism'; this path theology has to choose as its own path of thinking, though it may learn from Spinoza and Plato. For insofar as it reflects upon the Christian faith, theology has to conceive of God as the one who *came* to the world in Jesus Christ and as such does not cease to *come* to the world. Christian theology may not set aside the task of preserving this tension in its thinking; because of this, it has to insist both that God became insurpassably worldly in a man and that, as such, he will have us believe in himself as the one who comes to the world. God would be thought of as part, and only part, of the world if his identity with the man Jesus were not understood as the *event* of his identifying, of his coming to the world. Faith expresses this tension by confessing Jesus *as* true God and God *as* true man. The statement quoted at the beginning, 'This man was the Son of God' is such a confession, whose homological character is grounded in the fact that God is not a predicate of the world. God comes to the world when he appears within it.

If language about God is only appropriate if it speaks of the fundamental difference between God and the world, then the question arises: how is such language possible? Our language is worldly language, and has only worldly words which refer to and are predicated of worldly beings. All predication is worldly; even the word 'God' belongs to worldly language and therefore—as Luther showed in his exposition of the first commandment—can only say that it transcends the horizon of the world from within that horizon: 'That to which your heart clings and entrusts itself is, I say, really your God'.[103] And obviously this can be an idol, a piece of the world. Consequently, no word which speaks of God can of itself designate the difference between God and the world. It

---

[103] M. Luther, *The Large Catechism* (*BC.* p. 365). It is just this problem which indicates the proper place of 'natural theology', though here we can of course only make mention of this. In our present context, the problem of 'natural theology' consists in the fact that the word 'God' and all its equivalents participate in the 'metaphor' of being into language, whereas God's coming to speech, conceived as revelation, both presupposes and ruptures this 'metaphor'. This is because, whilst God comes to speech in the same way as worldly being, he nevertheless comes to speech as one who is distinguished from all worldly being, and so by comparison comes to speech *ex nihilo*.

must be transferred from other states of affairs. The difference between God and the world, and, indeed, God himself, can only come to speech metaphorically. God is only properly spoken about when we speak of him metaphorically. All non-metaphorical language about God is not even figurative language about him. This is the truth (and the plausible truth, on the aristotelian premiss that definitions should not make use of metaphors) of the otherwise deeply problematic statement: *deus definiri nequit* (God cannot be defined).

But if we are only able to speak of God metaphorically, then a foreign term must be added by use of analogy, so that we can apply to God a word used to designate worldly things. God must be named catachrestically. Yet even here we face problems. For unlike God, all states of affairs named by metaphorical catachresis belong to the world, and as such are more or less known to the one who wishes to name them. Indeed, it is only on this basis that we can name them by comparison. God, however, is to be named in his difference from the world, as the one who is absolutely unknown on a worldly basis. The strange word in this case would have to be transferred to an equally strange state of affairs, whose strangeness is total; and in that case, the possibility of theological metaphor would founder, and we would have to pass over God in silence. Before trying to unravel this problem, we should clarify it a little more for ourselves on the basis of what has already been established.

Metaphor characteristically relates together two horizons of meaning which are represented in a statement by two words. Strictly speaking, metaphors are not words but statements,[104] in which the meaning of the grammatical subject and of the metaphorical predicate collide, forcing one of two words to change in meaning; this must, of course, be successful. Achilles is a lion because 'lion' in this metaphorical statement, without losing its meaning, no longer designates the (to speak metaphorically) king of the wilderness, but rather the brave warrior named Achilles. We have been taught by Aristotle that this is a case of the transference of a strange word which must make itself plain in its very

[104] Cf. F. Vonessen, 'Die ontologische Struktur der Metapher', *Zeitschrift für philosophische Forschung* 13 (1959), p. 402: 'It is the whole sentence and not simply the word' which 'acquires its direct or metaphorical meaning, its function in the sentence, only from the judgment as a whole'.

strangeness. By appropriating the strangeness of the strange word, the one who understands the metaphor is afforded access to a new dimension of being which a statement working with clearly defined concepts would close off. In a non-metaphorical statement, the 'world' of the lion and the 'world' of the warrior are fundamentally distinct by the difference in nature, even if the warrior is out hunting lions. Metaphorical predication makes this difference in nature into a hermeneutical tension, which makes linguistic communication between the two worlds possible, so that the 'strange world' of the lion is able to reveal aspects of Achilles and his behaviour in a new way. The one who is addressed with a metaphor must 'unite' the world of Achilles with that of the lion whilst retaining the distinction between them. The result is a tension within which something new is gained. Something of the being of the lion is attributed to Achilles, but in the new use of the word 'lion', the lion with his being no longer has a place. The *is* in the sentence 'Achilles is a lion' does not indicate an identification of Achilles and the lion, but nevertheless says something about the being of Achilles, something essential. Metaphor specifies *in what way* Achilles is. Metaphor thus defines the way in which being is.

We can only participate in the linguistic process of metaphor if we know what a lion is and who Achilles was. We do not as a rule need to be told that a lion is. But who the individual Achilles was has to be narrated. Achilles must already have been introduced as a brave warrior, he must already have been put in the limelight, if the metaphorical predication 'Achilles is a lion' is to be meaningful. As metaphor clarifies the way in which being is, it indicates that being is historical.

This means that in order to be able to speak metaphorically, we have to *narrate* so that familiarity can be established. Metaphors are the climaxes of a narrative for which we have been prepared by the narrative itself, which for its part can again imply metaphorical language. Metaphors remind us by saying something new.[105] The new thing which metaphors bring about includes the recapitulation of the story that was told from a very specific point of view. And so with respect to the one who is addressed, metaphors are, as it

---

[105] On the importance of memory for narration and innovation, see J. B. Metz, 'Erinnerung' in *Handbuch philosophischer Grundbegriffe* (Munich, 1973), pp. 386–96, and other relevant statements from the same author.

were, clusters of time.[106] In metaphor, that which has happened in a story is present in such a way that as a result something new can be said. Losing its old meaning, the word that is used metaphorically comes to have a new meaning, selecting one aspect of its sense to be constitutive of this new use.[107] In this way, a metaphorical statement has a new information-value over against a non-metaphorical sentence with the same intention.

Turning to the question of the possibility of theological metaphor, we may conclude from what has been said that familiarity with God has first to be established. God must first be made known if he is to become a meaningful subject of metaphorical predications as the only predications appropriate to him. Such a making known of God, which must in addition always state the difference between God and the world, can only take place in metaphorical speech. In this way we find ourselves in a circle, for clearly all that this does is repeat the necessity that God, in this particular respect at least, must be already known and familiar. If we are to escape from the circle, it is above all important that God himself makes human familiarity with himself possible. And, indeed, the Christian faith lives from the experience that God has made himself known, that he has established familiarity with himself. That this experience coincides with the logically unique possibility of avoiding the circle does not nullify its validity.

Thus, God's difference from the world is not merely to be negatively declared and defined, but rather trusted in as a positive state of affairs; and this can only happen if God is the one who

[106] It appears to be a different matter in the case of lyric poetry, which sets up metaphors without introducing them by narration. The reason for this, it seems to be, is that the lyrical metaphor takes over the function of narration. Lyrical metaphors are concentrations of time, but as narrations they are speech-events which do not so much recapitulate as liberate. The hearer must *say to himself or herself* what the metaphor says.

[107] This presupposes—following recent critics of Russell and Wittgenstein—that nouns possess not only meaning (reference) but also sense, so that the sense which is established in a sentence is the unity of sense of words that make sense. We need not discuss whether such words would also have sense if they never entered a sentence, or whether they are able to have their own sense only on the basis of the sense-making unity of a sentence. If words also *mean* something outside the sentence, then they ought also to possess a certain sense, since it is impossible to see how they could refer without having sense. But this question is logically highly complex!

METAPHORICAL TRUTH

comes to speech in the same way that he is the one who comes to the world. This coming to speech is then narrated *in* language, a language which would be, as it were, a priori metaphorical language. In such language God allows himself to be discovered as the one who comes. Language about God is thus eminently the language of discovery. But if God is discovered as the one who comes the world, and in this way as the one who is distinguished from the world, then both the world and the worldly act of discovery are themselves *newly discovered*. God is a discovery which teaches us to see *everything* with new eyes.

Such a discovery could, however, be full of terror. For terror and shock also let us see everything with new eyes. The discovery which leads to familiarity with God could certainly be the discovery of a *mysterium tremendum* (fearful mystery). Obviously one can be familiar with terror also. Is God also to be feared? Is to have discovered him more terrible than not to have discovered him? Is the God who becomes manifest simply a magnification of the terror which an encounter with the God who hides himself would mean? For the sake of God, this must not be said. The undeniable 'background' of religious terror, familiar also in biblical language about God's revelation, is more properly understood as the inevitable *remembrance* of *lack of familiarity* with God who is trustworthy.[108] Since familiarity with God is brought about by God himself, it exists only as trust, trust in God. The trust which leads to familiarity with God is acquired trust, human trust acquired from God. Trust is, nevertheless, explicitly a free act; trust cannot be forced. Hence the 'trust and faith of the heart'[109] which, according to Luther, makes both God and idol, can only prevent itself from producing an idol if the trust and faith are captured for freedom and therefore in freedom. Hence metaphorical talk of God seeks us out at that point where we can gain the freedom to trust in God. God lets himself be discovered in such a way that in the event of discovery trust in God can arise. This, however, presupposes a word of address.

[108] Even lack of familiarity, when one is familiar with it as a lack, can come to speech metaphorically. This may be the place of the *veiling* function of metaphor which some linguists stress, though this can be overemphasised if this veiling function is deduced from the spirit of taboo. On this, cf. the discussion of the thesis of H. Werner, *Die Ursprünge der Sprache* (Berlin, 1919) in Bühler, op. cit., pp. 351ff.

[109] M. Luther, *The Large Catechism* (*BC* p. 365).

2. In the critical analysis of Aristotle from which we started, we have made clear the character of metaphor as address, and out of that have clarified the address-character of all human language. Because it is essentially metaphorical predication, language about God is also language of address. The word 'God' is, even as a cry which utters the metaphorical *connexio verborum* (combination of words) only in silence, a word of address. It is either an address, or it does not speak of God. Accordingly, we ourselves are to be regarded from a theological point of view as those who have been and are addressed. Defined theologically, we are those who, having always been addressed by God, are, on the basis of this being-addressed, always newly to be addressed.

Of course the fact that 'God' is a word of address and that we are beings addressed by and still to be addressed by him by no means leads to the conclusion that every use of the word 'God' as an address is theologically adequate. In the domain of address, the possibilities of 'taking the name of God in vain' are multiplied. With good reason Luther pointed out and combatted 'abuse ... in spiritual matters, which pertain to the conscience'[110] as the worst form of misuse of the name of God. Everything depends upon addressing the hearer in the right way, as one who is addressed by God. Thus the event in which we are addressed in God's name is decisive for the proper formation of theological metaphors. That event is the event in which God once for all came to the world and came to speech as the one who addresses us: the event of the life, death and resurrection of Jesus Christ, the event of the justification of sinners. In this event free choice of theological metaphors has both its ground and its limits.

That is why we may not offer what is 'suitable' by worldly standards as a catachrestic name of God. For if in discovering God we also learn to discover afresh the act of discovery, we must be especially careful to consider as expressive of God those things which, to the 'eyes which see and yet do not see', appear to contradict him. The being of the God who comes to the world could all too easily be conceived as the being of a divinity defined as possessing to the *n*th degree the world's excellences and as lacking all its deficiencies. Formation of theological metaphors on the basis of this kind of *via eminentiae* (way of eminence) and *via negationis*

[110] Ibid., p. 372.

(way of negation) dominated the Christian tradition—much to its detriment. Over against this, the being of the God who comes to the world is to be brought to speech out of the history of the God who has come to the world. Intrinsic to this history as its decisive moment is the cross. The freedom of metaphorical speech is a freedom for the word,[111] set free by the history in which the cross is the distinguishing feature, and thus not an arbitrary freedom. If it wishes truly to express God, it must not orient itself by criteria offered by an understanding of the world abstracted from this history.[112] God corresponds to himself—even, especially, in contradiction. Thus the cross of Jesus Christ is the ground and measure of the formation of metaphors which are appropriate to God. Every theological metaphor must be compatible with the cross of Jesus Christ. Christians, however, believe the cross to be the world's turning-point (*Wende der Welt*).[113] As such it concerns the whole world. This makes it clear that the *strange words* which are transferred to God may be taken from any context, as long as they can be appropriated by faith in the crucified.

If the cross, as the world's turning-point, is the foundation and measure of metaphorical language about God, then such language itself has the function of bringing about a turning around, a change of direction. God cannot be spoken of as if everything remained as it was—which, of course, does not mean that everything which does not remain as it was is therefore new or even eschatalogical.[114] Metaphor is a word turned into something new. Its most proper function is realised in language about God.

In their function of addressing us, cross and μεταφορά meet in another respect of the greatest theological significance. As the world's turning-point, God cannot be conceived to be a worldly necessity. Precisely because he is the saviour who turns the world around, God is more than necessary. The same can be said of theological metaphor. Like parables, metaphors cannot be deduced.

[111] For the category of 'freedom for the word', reference should be made to the works of Ernst Fuchs.
[112] Cf. O. Dreyer, *Untersuchungen zum Begriff des Gottgeziemenden in der Antike* (Hildesheim, 1970).
[113] For this phrase, see F. Gogarten, *Jesus Christus Wende der Welt* (Tübingen, 1966); ET *Christ the Crisis* (London, 1970).
[114] Often the exact opposite is the case: something can become obsolete and grow out of date for the reason that it is not allowed to remain as it was.

That which has to be said metaphorically can be said in various ways.[115] This is especially true of language about God. The language of faith, if it takes its identity seriously, is directed by a freedom which can hardly be surpassed. For its identity is the word of the cross as a word which liberates and which can only be preserved in liberty.

Here, however, we also encounter the reason why the language of faith does not allow actuality to dictate what it has to say to us about actuality. How else could it say that Jesus is God's Son, that his death on the cross is the turning-point of the world? Such statements 'deceive' actuality, much as the course of history 'deceives' each present. This does not mean that actuality is passed over or missed. Rather, it is enhanced. But this has consequences for actuality. Theological metaphor enters into actuality in such a way that it encounters not only a horizon of meaning other than its own, not only another 'world' (as the world of Achilles encounters that of the lion). Rather, it enters the actuality of the world (insofar as the world assumes the metaphorical quality of being predicated of God) in such a way that the world is confronted with *the possibility of its own non-being*, from which alone new being can arise. One who speaks about God speaks to the hearer of the fact that the non-being of both the hearer and the world is a possibility overcome by God alone. This is the essence of all *religious* language. *Biblical* language, which we also call the language of faith insofar as

[115] It is not necessary to call Achilles a lion. He could also have been called a panther or an eagle (Homer also uses these metaphors). But it was fitting to call Achilles a lion. Such successful metaphors will persist. For their part they make history and become irreversible, although originally one could have spoken differently. Amongst these transferences which were originally free but which became irreversible through their excellence, we may above all count the basic religious metaphors and also the basic metaphors of the Christian tradition. 'Son of God', when used in connection with Jesus of Nazareth, is one of these predications which have become irreversible. Other metaphors may be superseded by new ones. Working out criteria for metaphors which endure and those which are replaceable would be one of the many tasks which a theological theory of metaphor would have to tackle. So far, however, such a theological theory of metaphor remains a desideratum for which the necessary preparatory work has not been undertaken, either by systematic or practical theology (whose proper province it is). J. B. Metz's call for a narrative theology deserves strong support, although in my view it is unfortunate if it is taken as an alternative to argumentative theology.

we translate it into our own words, is distinct from religious language only in this one—radical—respect: it tells of the possibility of non-being not simply as that which *can only be overcome* by God, but as that which *has been overcome* by God. In this, the language of faith proclaims the existence of a *new creation*.

This story of salvation is gathered in kerygmatic and homological metaphors (as clusters of time and eternity) whose root metaphor is the identification of the *risen one* with the crucified man Jesus. Insofar as this root metaphor, as an expression for an event, can only make this event comprehensible within the context of the history of the God who comes to the world, the root metaphor needs to be interpreted through further christological and theological metaphors. Thus the metaphor 'Son of God' refers us to the origin, and the metaphor 'Kyrios' (Lord) to the present and future, of the history whose telling is nothing other than letting God come to speech. When this happens, God reveals himself in the context of the world as its mystery. For God is the mystery of the world in that he has overcome the non-being of the world as the one who comes to it.

In theology, a mystery is that which for God's sake in every case must be *spoken*. The biblical texts claim to do this. According to what has been said about the hermeneutical and theological relevance of metaphor, the criterion for legitimating this claim is speech 'in which we expect of each other and grant to each other, so to *distance* ourselves from the world, that all can experience in the world that which is greater than it (Gal 6.2ff)'.[116] With the world and in the world, theological metaphor creates space for God.

It may be useful to present the most important of our reflections on the theological relevance of metaphor in a systematic way through a series of theses. In these, some trains of thought will recede and others will be extended somewhat further.

1. Metaphorical language is neither non-literal nor equivocal language, but a particular mode of literal speech and in a particular way language which specifies.
2. One dimension of metaphors as literal, specifying language is that of address. Metaphors address and ought to do so. This distinguishes them from statements of definition which do not address but only say what is the case.

[116] E. Fuchs, *Hermeneutik* (Tübingen, 1970), p. 174.

3. As a particular mode of literal, specifying language, the function of metaphor is comparable to that of definition insofar as it brings something to speech as something—though with the difference that metaphor brings a state of affairs to speech with the aid of a totally new state of affairs, thereby through language setting in motion what the definition states. Metaphor is language which liberates, whereas the definition limits and secures. Both are means of stating more precisely that which is.

4. Metaphorical language specifies by working with the dialectic of familiarity and strangeness. It makes both a state of affairs and a pattern of language use strange by employing an ususual word to signify a state of affairs in an unusual way. At the same time, it presupposes that this familiarity will be *assimilated into* the familiar world, so that the familiar world will be *expanded*.

5. Metaphors expand the horizon of being by going beyond fixation upon actuality with that which is possible, in this way *intensifying* the being of that which is.

6. Metaphors are events of immediate learning. They teach playful learning.

7. It is not the word used in an unusual way which is metaphorical, but rather the predication accomplished with the help of a word used in an unusual way.

8. In a metaphorical statement, a word functioning as a predicate is used in such a way that in this instance it loses its usual relation to the state of affairs which it signifies (i.e. its usual meaning), although the meaning which is lost is still presupposed. In the sentence 'Christ is a vine' we are not to think of the vine in the vineyard, and yet in another sense we must have it in mind. The word used metaphorically in a metaphorical predication is, in Luther's phrase, a 'renewed word'.

9. The dismantling of the common meaning of a word used in a metaphorical predication occurs in favour of a new meaning for this word, on the basis of the selection of one aspect of the sense that is normally attributed to the word in the semantic unity of a sentence. The change of meaning leads to a hermeneutical tension within the metaphorical statement, from which the grammatical subject profits: its being is specified.

10. Since metaphorical predications work with the strangeness both of the state of affairs about which a metaphorical statement is made and also of the word with which a metaphorical predication

is accomplished, they presuppose familiarity with both this state of affairs and the original meaning of the word. If this familiarity is not present in a natural way, it must be created through narration. Metaphors expand and specify the narrated world.

11. Metaphors are reminders of the thoroughly metaphorical structure of human language. Human language is structured in a thoroughly metaphorical way, in that through it we exist as *those who have been addressed*, as those who, on this basis, let ourselves be addressed by *that which is* (that which is the case) *as world*. Along with this world which addresses us, we transfer ourselves into language, and within language transfer one into the other.

12. The thoroughly metaphorical structure of language is rooted in truth as event, in which world is transferred into language so that that which is lets itself be discovered. Truth as the letting-itself-be-discovered of that which is occurs when that which is discovered is connected with that which has already been discovered, facing the discoverer, in correspondence to the discovery itself.

12.1. Clearly the discoverer is also part of what has already been discovered, insofar as that person has discovered him or herself (or been discovered) to be one who has been addressed, and insofar as the person discovers him or herself in the process of discovery to be a discoverer.

12.2 To discover means to take something to be true. In language that which is perceived is taken to be true. The essence of truth as a letting-itself-be-discovered and the essence of language as a process of discovery emphasise the fact that truth and language are *perceptible*. Truth and language are concrete.

12.3. The correspondence between the discovery and that which is discovered, in the sense of an *adaequatio intellectus ad rem*, is ontologically possible only on the basis of the connection between that which is discovered and that which has already been discovered, on the basis of the overagainstness of the discoverer and that which is discovered, and so on the basis of the event in which that which is lets itself be discovered.

12.4. The possibility of that which is letting itself be discovered (as world) is grounded in the turn of that which is into language as an event in which its being is augmented. To be true is more than simply to be.

13. The metaphorical structure of language, which is rooted in

truth as the event of the transference into language of that which is, implies freedom of choice in words, which is the freedom of the speaker. This freedom of language is conditioned by the interplay between the ourselves and the world, in which we understand ourselves cosmomorphically and the world anthropomorphically. In this interplay between ourselves and the world, the concrete (sensuous) power of truth becomes effective.

14. The freedom of metaphorical language in no way excludes the desire for a conceptual language in which this freedom is controlled and which makes it possible to articulate the correspondence of discovery and that which is discovered.

15. Like all religious language, the language of the Christian faith is thoroughly metaphorical. The relation of faith to religion is finally decided in the use of metaphor, though not in the metaphorical use of words.

16. The language of the Christian faith shares with religious language the characteristic of stating actuality in such a way that an increase of being comes to speech.

17. This gain in being, which for its part must be demonstrable in experience of actuality, cannot be stated in a language which seeks to picture actuality by replacing it with concepts. Equally, however, such a conceptual language is required as a control.

18. The gain in being asserted by the Christian faith, which is primarily to be proclaimed as the justification of the sinner, certainly exists as an 'actual' potential of this world through the life, death and resurrection of Jesus Christ. Nevertheless, it must come to speech in a language which lets this gain become an event for those who are addressed.

19. A language which brings to expression more than the actual and yet equally engages with actuality is in a fundamental sense language of address. As language which states, the language of faith is language of address. Its character as statement and its character as address can only be distinguished methodologically. Narrative is one fundamental process which brings together address and statement. Another process of this kind is kerygmatic proclamation; a further example would be confession.

20. As language which makes a gain to being become an event, religious language is metaphorical. As language about the God who comes to the world and who has come to the world in Jesus Christ, the language of the Christian faith is metaphorical in a particular way.

METAPHORICAL TRUTH 71

21. In the language of Christian faith, the function of theological metaphor is to address the hearer in such a way that he or she is able to bring together the context of their experience and the possibility of non-being—a possibility which not only can be overcome by God but also has been overcome once and for all by God in the life, death and resurrection of Jesus Christ. From this comes an *experience with experience* which must be made credible in the context of previous experiences as a gain to being.

22. The particular difficulty of Christian language about God comes from this event of a gain to being, since it has to talk of a God who does not belong to the being of the world and yet precisely as such comes to this world, into the context of worldly being. And so we must talk of God in such a way that with the means of this world, space for God is made in this world, space which he claimed when he came to the world in Jesus Christ. Metaphor is structurally adequate to this task.

23. In that God gains space in the world through the means of the world by coming to speech, the horizon of this world is expanded in such a way that the world's actuality (its problems, conflicts, and values) can be more sharply grasped. The language of faith sharpens our sense of actuality by addressing us with more than is actual. Structurally, this takes place in metaphorical speech.

24. The gain to being brought about by metaphorical language about God expands the horizon of the world in such a way that we may speak of the renewal of the world. A theological metaphor can only have this effect, however, because of the renewing power of the Spirit of God. The hermeneutical end-point of theological metaphors is thus *invocation of the Holy Spirit*, in which it is *God* who is now *addressed metaphorically*.

25. Working out a theological theory of metaphor is an urgent desideratum for both dogmatics and practical theology.

ANTHROPOMORPHISM

A fundamental problem in modern hermeneutics

> *'He who formed the eye, does he not see?'* [Ps 94.9]

The problem raised by anthropomorphic language about God is as old as critical reflection upon human language about him. It is, moreover, a problem which is not simply raised by the biblical texts. Admittedly the undeniable lack of embarrassment with which both the Old and New Testament writers talk κατα ἄνθρωπον (anthropomorphically) raises hermeneutical questions about the appropriateness of such language. And, it seems, the Bible itself takes appropriate measures to counter its unembarrassed anthropomorphism. The Old Testament's prohibition of images (Gn 20.4), whilst it hardly has its origin in the problem of anthropomorphism, certainly has consequences for it. In the New Testament, too, questions in contexts other than that of anthropomorphism, such as the question of the righteousness of God in choosing Jacob but rejecting Esau (Rom 9.6–19) lead to insights into the infinite qualitative distinction between creator and creation, which critically expose the all-too-human character of language about God: 'who are you, a man, to answer back to God?' (Rom 9.20).

For all that, the hermeneutical critique of anthropomorphism does not really have its roots in the Bible. As a rule the biblical texts do not seem to be aware of the problem, for they talk in an entirely unconstrained way of God who 'comforts like a mother', who 'loves and hates', who has a 'strong arm', 'hands', 'powerful breath', and even a 'beloved Son', thereby calling himself 'Father'. If we are reminded in the Bible of the human character of our language about God, it is for reasons quite different from hermeneutical misgivings about the appropriateness of anthropomorphic language about the divine.

ANTHROPOMORPHISM

It is in the earliest Greek philosophy that anthropomorphic language is perceived as a cause of offence. As is well known, Xenophanes clearly formulated the problem raised by the stories of the gods in Homer and Hesiod:[1] 'mortals believe the gods to be created by birth, and to have their own (mortals') raiment, voice and body'.[2] Over against this, Xenophanes—knowing full well that 'as for certain truth, no man has seen it, nor will there ever be a man who knows about the gods'[3]—requires us 'to praise God with decent stories and pure words'.[4] The criterion for such 'pure words' should be Xenophanes' own verse about the 'one God' who, as 'among gods and men the greatest', is 'not at all like mortals in body or in mind'.[5] Ever since Xenophanes, theology has involved critique of anthropomorphism. Indeed, the very earliest occurrence of the word 'theology', Plato's inquiry after the 'norms of right speech about the gods' (τύποι περὶ θεολογίας), is found in such a context.[6]

The problem of anthropomorphism is, therefore, older than Christian theology and its hermeneutic. It was, of course, inevitable that in taking up other questions and problems from pre-Christian metaphysics, Christian theology should also assume this problem. Here, however, we will not look further at this matter, but rather turn to a specifically modern problem in anthropomorphism. For at the outset of the modern era, critique of anthropomorphism contributed a good deal to the rise of the so-called historical-critical method of biblical exegesis. The first part of the following reflections takes the form of an historical recollection of the thinker whose significance for the self-understanding of the modern era can hardly be overvalued, even though through him a number of the attitudes of the pre-Christian metaphysical thinkers experience a notable revival. The second part counters the first and offers systematic reflections on the specific character of anthropomorphic talk of God.

[1] 'Both Homer and Hesiod have attributed to the gods all things that are shameful and a reproach among mankind: theft, adultery and mutual deception': Freeman, p. 22, fr. 11.
[2] Ibid., p. 22, fr. 14.
[3] Ibid., p. 23, fr. 34.
[4] Ibid., p. 20, fr. 1.
[5] Ibid., p. 23, fr.23.
[6] Republic 379a.

I

1. Spinoza—of whom, according to Lessing, people talk 'just as if he were a dead dog',[7] and whom no less a person than Schleiermacher called 'that saintly outcast'[8]—is known to exegetical theologians above all by his *Theologico-Political Treatise*. The real intentions of this occasional work, written in the interests of 'freedom of judgment' and 'public peace',[9] can only properly be appreciated when we keep in view its connection with Spinoza's great work, his *Ethica ordine geometrico demonstrata*. In particular, we need to take note of the connection between the method of the *Theologico-Political Treatise* as a foundational document of 'historical-critical hermeneutics'[10] and the geometrical method of the *Ethics*. For when we do this, it becomes apparent that the so-called historical-critical method of biblical interpretation is the twin sister of the geometrical method by which Spinoza constructed a thoroughly consistent metaphysical system in his *Ethics*. Moreover, it also becomes apparent that both that metaphysical system and the historical-critical interpretation of Scripture which is bound up with it must judge anthropomorphic language about God to be a mode of speech which is not adequate to the being of God and so one which deserves radical critique.

2. There is a familiar Reformation ring to the hermeneutical rule in the *Theologico-Political Treatise* that 'our knowledge of Scripture must . . . be looked for in Scripture only'.[11] And the Reformation tone can also be heard in Spinoza's view that the divinity of Holy Scripture

---

[7] G. E. Lessing, 'F. H. Jacobi über seine Gespräche mit Lessing' in *Werke* VIII, ed. H. G. Göpfert, (Munich, 1979), p. 569.
[8] F. D. E. Schleiermacher, *On Religion* (Richmond, 1969), p. 84.
[9] Cf. B. de Spinoza, *A Theologico-Political Treatise*, trans, R. H. M. Elwes (New York, 1951), p. 6. (Elwes' nineteenth century translation is generally inadequate, and I have frequently altered it after consulting the Latin (in B. De Spinoza, *Opera. Werke. Lateinisch und Deutsch*, vol I, ed. G. Gawlick, F. Niewöhner (Darmstadt, 1979). For the sake of convenience, however, page references are given to the Elwes translation—TR.)
[10] H.-J. Kraus, *Geschichte der historisch-kritisch Erforschung des Alten Testaments von der Reformatie bis zur Gegenwart* (Neukirchen, 1956), p. 57; the second revised and expanded edition (1969, p. 64) has 'historical-literary hermeneutics'.
[11] *Theologico-Political Treatise*, p. 100.

can only be proven from Holy Scripture itself.¹² On closer inspection, however, these echoes of the Reformation turn out to be virtually the opposite of what Luther, at least, intended in the thesis that Scripture, speaking as the Word of God, is *sui ipsius interpres* (self-interpreting).¹³

Indeed, Spinoza substantiates the view that the divinity of Scripture can only be proved from Scripture by an argument which is in opposition to the Reformation doctrine of the *particula exclusiva* '*sola scriptura*' (the exclusive particle 'Scripture alone'). For Spinoza, the divinity of Scripture, proved from Scripture alone, consists in the fact that Scripture teaches true moral precepts (*vera documenta moralia*), and 'by such means alone can its divine origin be demonstrated'.¹⁴ However, it is also true that precisely these moral precepts can also be proved independently of Scripture through commonly-held axioms (*ex notionibus communibus*),¹⁵ indeed, they must be proved solely with the aid of the natural light of reason.¹⁶ By contrast, a merely moral interpretation of Scripture fails on Luther's reckoning to grasp what it is that makes Scripture into the Word of God: the gospel of the justification of sinners,¹⁷ i.e. that which concerns Christ.

For Spinoza, then, *sola scriptura* certainly means that Scripture should be interpreted out of itself, but in such a way that the agreement between Scripture and those moral truths knowable by reason alone should prove the divinity of Scripture. *Sola scripura* is a purely formal principle of biblical interpretation, which has the function of hindering us from defining the *meaning* of scriptural statements out of an alien context. The *meaning* of Scripture is to be drawn from Scripture alone. But Scripture may not determine the *truth*.

¹² Ibid.
¹³ M. Luther, 'Assertio omnium articulorum per bullam Leonis X. novissimam damnatorum', *WA* VII.97.23
¹⁴ *A Theologico-Political Treatise*, p. 100.
¹⁵ Ibid.
¹⁶ It is just this which is the task of Spinoza's *Ethics*.
¹⁷ See, for example, Luther's 1516 lectures on Galatians (on Gal 1.8f): 'those words of men are so concerned with outward behaviour and so devoid of faith that no greater benefit could be rendered to faith than if once and for all they were thoroughly and totally done away with' (*LW* 27, p. 178). Over against this, the Word of God is 'a word of grace and forgiveness' (ibid., p. 164, on Gal 1.1).

76   THEOLOGICAL ESSAYS

3. This becomes particularly clear when we examine Spinoza's hermeneutical method. Here he says that we are to admit no principles or data for the interpretation of Scripture and the setting forth of its content other than those taken from Scripture and its 'history' (*historia*).[18] Thus if Scripture is rightly to be understood, an *historia Scripturae* (history of Scripture) is the hermeneutical postulate which must be fulfilled. What cannot be established with the greatest clarity from such a 'history' ought not to be claimed as scriptural teaching.[19]

What Spinoza understands by *historia Scripturae* can be illuminated, first, by the requirements which it must fulfil, and, second, by the fact that Spinoza seeks to understand the *historia Scripturae* at which he is aiming by analogy from the *historia naturae* (history of nature) which he presupposes as common knowledge. First of all we examine the requirements which an *historia Scripturae* must fulfil.

Spinoza identifies three such requirements.[20] An *historia Scripturae* must investigate the origins of the biblical writings, and in particular the specific characteristics of the Hebrew language which is presupposed by the New Testament writings as well. Next, it must order the contents of each biblical book under headings, and distinguish the obscure or ambiguous passages from those which are clear. Finally, an *historia Scripturae* must inquire into the historical circumstance (*casus*) in which each book arose, the 'fate' (*fortuna*) of its transmission (i.e. its textual history), and the gathering together of the various holy scriptures into a corpus (the formation of the canon). Once we have an *historia Scripturae* which satisfies these requirements, we may also investigate what the Holy Spirit and the prophets wished to *teach*.

In looking at the second requirement, Spinoza emphasises that in exposition of Scripture we are concerned with the *meaning* of linguistic statements drawn from their context (*sensus ex contextu orationis*), and not with their *truth*. Spinoza explicitly warns against prematurely asking the question of the truth of a text and thereby

[18] Cf. *Theologico-Political Treatise*, pp. 99f.
[19] 'The universal rule, then, in interpreting Scripture is to accept nothing as an authoritive scriptural statement which we do not perceive very clearly when we examine it in the light of its history' (ibid., p. 101).
[20] Ibid., pp. 101-3.

prejudging its meaning,[21] somewhat along the lines 'what ought not to be cannot be'. The question of the truth of things must be suspended in exposition of Scripture.[22]

Spinoza's *historia Scripturae* is clearly a description, a descriptive investigation of the Bible, and so ἱστορία (history) in the old sense of the word as it was used by Herodotus. However, the *historia* which Spinoza requires has an order to it, clarifying that which is earlier on the basis of that which comes after it. From this comes a genetic nuance in the meaning of the concept which leads to the modern concept of history (*Geschichte*). But the concept of history (*historia*) takes this nuance in its meaning from the geometrical method of thinking which is assumed in the *Theologico-Political Treatise*, a method which begins with that which is *in itself* prior (and not simply that which is prior according to our cognition). The hermeneutical method of biblical exegesis which Spinoza postulates in the *Treatise* is only one example of general scientific procedure, as Spinoza himself indicates in his remark that this method requires no light other than that of 'natural reason'.[23] Spinoza dismissed with biting irony the view that for true understanding to take place there has to be special illumination by a supernatural light which is given by God to believers only.[24] This is all the more noteworthy since Spinoza certainly makes parallel 'what the Bible and what the Holy Spirit wish to teach'.[25]

4. It has been said that 'the principles of an historical-critical

---

[21] 'We are at work not on the truth of passages, but solely on their meaning ... In order not to confound the meaning of a passage with its truth, we must examine it solely by means of the signification of the words, or by a reason acknowledging no foundation but Scripture' (ibid., p. 101).
[22] Cf. E. Hirsch, *Geschichte der neueren evangelischen Theologie* I (Gütersloh, 1949), p. 268: 'The question of the content of the Bible and the question of its truth fall apart. Exegesis and inquiry into the truth become different things'. Hirsch's manifest aversion to Spinoza the Jew betrays itself in the next sentence, which is problematic from many points of view: 'A hundred years was to pass before theology—independent of Spinoza—acknowledged that such a separation of the historical and the systematic tasks was inevitable, and sought to find a responsible form of such separation, free from Spinoza's native cynicism'.
[23] *Theologico-Political Treatise*, p. 113.
[24] Cf. ibid., pp. 113-5.
[25] Ibid., p. 99.

hermeneutic were formulated for the first time by Spinoza'.[26] If that is correct, then it is all the more important to ask what fundamental methodological decision lies behind this first formulation of the principles of an historical-critical hermeneutic. The answer is surprising. The historical-critical method owes its origin not to the observation of a fundamental difference between historical being and the natural order, nor to the discovery of the independence of history, but to the application to Scripture of methods appropriate to the interpretation of nature. Spinoza declares explicitly that 'the method of interpreting Scripture does not widely differ from the method of interpreting nature—in fact, it is almost the same'.[27]

In this connection Spinoza's introduction of the concept of *historia Scripturae* as a parallel to that of *historia naturae* becomes clear. Scripture should be expounded out of its history in the same way that nature is expounded out of the *historia naturae*.[28] And for its part the *historia Scripturae* should develop after the manner of the *historia naturae*.[29]

Spinoza was not the first to use the concept of *historia* to refer to different fields. Bacon, who associated *historia* with the intellectual faculty of memory—in the same way that he associated imagination with poetry and reason with philosophy[30]— distinguished between natural history and civil history (in which ecclesiastical history and literary history were also to be counted).[31] Moreover, *historia* had reference in all cases to individuals limited by space and time, of whom *historia* speaks by the memory.[32]

[26] H.-J. Kraus, op. cit., p. 57. Spinoza's *Theologico-Political Treatise* is indeed 'already a kind of stocktaking of the whole development' which precedes him. 'He assimilates completely the results so far achieved in all areas' and 'sets them in the context of the modern critique of religion' (K. Scholder, *Ursprünge und Probleme der Bibelkritik im 17. Jahrhundert. Ein Beitrag zur Entstehung der historisch-kritischen Theologie* (Munich, 1966), p. 165).
[27] *Theologico-Political Treatise*, p. 99.
[28] Cf. ibid., p. 104.
[29] Cf. ibid., p. 99.
[30] F. Bacon, *The Advancement of Learning* II.1, in *The Works of Francis Bacon* I, ed. J. Spedding, R. L. Ellis, D. D. Heath (London, 1860), p. 292. According to Bacon there are only 'these three emanations of the three faculties of the rational soul' (ibid., p. 293).
[31] 'History is either natural or civil. Natural history treats of the works and deeds of nature; civil history of those of men' (ibid., p. 293).
[32] Ibid., p. 292.

Since it is related to individuals and remembers the first impressions of individuals, Bacon makes *historia* identical with experience, whilst philosophy, which is concerned with abstract notions, is identified with the sciences.[33]

Bacon's classifications are of especial interest in our context since he also applies them to theology. Theology, too, is composed of three parts which correspond to the three rational faculties of the soul: sacred history, divine poesy (parables) and commands and dogmas as a kind of *philosophia perennis*.[34] Prophecy is thereby classed with *historia* since the divine *historia* has this prerogative over human *historia*, that it can narrate future events too. *Historia* is thus essentially narrative.[35]

If we apply Bacon's categories to Spinoza, the *historia Scripturae* which he proposes is a variety of civil history. But more important than such classifications is the way in which Bacon's categorization indicates that history narrates individual occurrences, natural or human, whereas reason (*ratio*) constructs and arranges notions abstracted from the data presented in such a manner. Spinoza can say that in just the same way that 'the interpretation of nature consists in the examination of the history of nature, deducing from there definitions of natural phenomena',[36] so 'Scriptural interpretation proceeds from a faithful history of Scripture, inferring the intention of its authors as a legitimate conclusion from its fundamental principles'.[37] History is thus the necessary preliminary work for doctrine set out by the geometric method. Nevertheless, Spinoza considers the difficulties of working out such an *historia Scripturae* to be so great that he holds accurate interpretation to be in most instances impossible.[38] Yet he does hold that a right understanding of Scripture as a whole is possible, insofar as everything which pertains to salvation and is necessary for

---

[33] 'I consider history and experience to be the same thing, as also philosophy and the sciences' (ibid., p. 293). Cf. p. 292: 'Philosophy discards individuals; neither does it deal with the impressions immediately received from them, but with abstract notions derived from these impressions'.

[34] 'Theology therefore in like manner consists of either sacred history, or of parables, which are a divine poesy, or of Doctrines and Precepts, which are a perennial philosophy' (ibid., p. 293).

[35] Ibid.

[36] *Theologico-Political Treatise*, p. 99.

[37] Ibid.

[38] Cf. ibid., p. 112.

blessedness can be known with certainty.[39] Everything else—which is, we note, the greater part—is 'more curious than profitable'.[40]

5. That Scripture is largely irrelevant to truth is for Spinoza bound up with the particular hermeneutical character of accommodation, which constitutes the origin of anthropomorphic talk of God. Histories and revelations make up the greatest part of Scripture. But both the miraculous natural events which are chiefly narrated in the histories, and also the revelations of the prophets, are conformed or accommodated to the judgment, i.e. the outlook and opinions, of those who express them. As such they may be identified with the aid of the natural light of reason, but not understood and verified.[41]

(a) On the one hand, Spinoza attaches the highest importance to the fact that Scripture frequently treats matters which cannot be deduced from the principles of natural illumination.[42] On the other hand, he emphasises strongly that the method of interpretation which expounds Scripture only from Scripture demands no other light than that of natural illumination, whose essence and strength it is, by a method of comparison, to deduce and infer that which is obscure from what which is known or presupposed to be known.[43] So he requires that the method by which we ascertain the teaching of Scripture drawn from its *historia* must be in accord with natural

[39] 'It is most plain that we can follow with certainty the intention of Scripture in matters relating to salvation and necessary to blessedness' (ibid., p. 113). Of course, we are not here to think of salvation mediated through the death of Christ and of the blessedness of the forgiveness of sins. It is only a matter of human obedience realised as love of neighbour.
[40] Ibid.
[41] 'Scripture often treats of matters which cannot be deduced from principles known to reason, for it is chiefly made up of narratives and revelation. The narratives generally contain miracles, that is . . . narratives of extraordinary natural occurrences adapted to the opinions and judgment of the historians who recorded them; the revelations also were adapted to the opinions of the prophets . . . and in themselves surpassed human comprehension' (ibid., p. 100).
[42] Ibid.
[43] 'I do not doubt that everyone will see that such a method only requires the aid of natural reason. The nature and efficacy of the natural reason consists in deducing and proving the unknown from the known, and in carrying premises to their legitimate conclusions, and these are the very processes which our method demands' (ibid., p. 113).

ANTHROPOMORPHISM

illumination so characterised—a method, therefore, such as is used in the explication of nature out of its *historia*.[44] Spinoza describes this method as a procedure which first investigates what is most common and universal to all nature (*universales et toti naturae communes*), and from there gradually proceeds to the less universal. In this way, we have first of all to work out from the *historia Scripturae* what is the most general, that is, the basis or foundation of the whole Scripture—namely, the existence of the one almighty God, who is alone to be worshipped, who cares for all and who above all loves those who revere him and love their neighbours as themselves.[45] From 'this universal doctrine of Scripture, we must then proceed to the other doctrines less universal ... which ... have regard to the general conduct of life ...; whatever is obscure or ambiguous at such points in Scripture must be explained and defined by its universal doctrine'.[46]

(*b*) This method of clarifying by proceeding from the general or the evident to the less general and the less evident trades upon a material premise which Spinoza has already stated at the beginning of the *Treatise*. He there defines prophecy and revelation in such a way that they include natural knowledge[47]—not simply *notitia dei naturalis* (natural knowledge of God) which belongs to natural theology, but rather all natural knowledge, which for Spinoza is as such knowledge of God. For 'although natural knowledge may be called divine' or prophetic, 'its professors cannot be called prophets'.[48] For prophets *interpret* revelation in such a way that they are believed on the basis of authority, while philosophers *explain* revelation in such a way that it can be known with the same certainty with which it was previously known by them. Consequently, whilst philosophers function so that those whom they address become philosophers themselves, those whom the prophets address ought not to and could not become prophets themselves and attain the same

---

[44] Cf. ibid., p. 104.
[45] Cf. ibid.
[46] Ibid.
[47] 'Prophecy or revelation is sure knowledge revealed by God to man ... From this definition it follows that prophecy really includes natural knowledge' (ibid., p. 13).
[48] Ibid., p. 14.

certain knowledge through their own knowing.[49] They remain dependent upon the interpretation and authority of interpreting institutions. 'They' here means the common people who according to Spinoza are eager for the extraordinary and the strange but look down on the gifts of nature and place too little value on the natural knowledge shared by all. In order to live a live pleasing to God, they want and need religious authorities—but not a Spinoza.[50]

(c) The revelations which come to speech in the Bible are for Spinoza a deficient mode of revelation with regard to the transmission of their cognitive value—the philosopher never tired of pointing out that 'the authority of the prophets has weight only in matters of the conduct of life and true virtue, and that their other doctrines affect us little'.[51] Indeed, Scripture 'demands from us nothing but obedience, and censures disobedience but not ignorance'.[52] Accordingly, faith is not dependent upon explicitly true dogmas, but only upon such dogmas as are necessary for obedience to the commands to love God and one's neighbour.[53] Over against this, natural knowledge is directly related to truth and certainty, which it also seeks to mediate. In view of the definition

[49] 'He alone is an interpreter of God, who interprets the decrees which God has revealed to him to others who have not received such revelation, and whose belief, therefore, rests merely on the prophet's authority and the confidence reposed in him. If it were otherwise, and all who listened to prophets became prophets themselves, as all who listen to philosophers become philosophers, a prophet would no longer be the interpreter of divine decrees, inasmuch as his hearers would know the truth, not on the authority of the prophet but by means of actual divine revelation and inward testimony' (ibid., p. 269, n. 2).

[50] Cf. ibid., p. 11: 'I do not ask the multitude, and those of like passions with the multitude, to read my book'.

[51] Ibid., p. 8.

[52] Ibid., p. 176.

[53] 'It follows that faith does not demand that dogmas be true as that they should be pious, that is, such as will stir up the heart to obedience ... Thus it is not true doctrines which are expressly required by the Bible, so much as doctrines which are necessary for obedience, and to confirm in our hearts the love of our neighbour, wherein ... we are in God, and God in us' (ibid., pp. 187f). In Luther's 1520 treatise on *The Freedom of a Christian*, one can read that to which this conception is opposed: 'By faith he (the believer) is caught up beyond himself into God. By love he descends beneath himself into his neighbour. Yet he always remains in God and in his love' (*LW* 31, p. 371). For Luther, however, faith lives from the truth of the Word of God.

ANTHROPOMORPHISM

which Spinoza himself gives (*rei alicujus certa cognitio a Deo hominibus revelata*, certain knowledge of something revealed to us by God), natural knowledge must be designated revelation in the full sense of the word. And therefore natural knowledge does not rely on accommodation, which is constitutive of prophetic language. The prophets received their revelation in the form of words or images (*verbis vel figuris*).[54] And these, along with the signs which accompanied them, were in each case adapted to the capacity and current outlook on life of the recipients of revelation, since they were aimed at their imaginative capacity. Consequently the certainty which is characteristic of prophetic revelation is not a mathematical but, as Spinoza expresses it, a moral certainty.[55]

By contrast, mathematical certainty is characteristic of natural knowledge, which is therefore in the fullest sense revelation of God. It is not accommodated to the individual limitations of the knower, and may therefore act as a critic of the prophets' anthropomorphic way of speaking. Like his whole system, Spinoza's hermeneutic lives from the presupposition that the human mind objectively contains the nature of God within itself; consequently it is able to form concepts which teach the nature of things and right conduct in life. To this extent, the nature of the human mind, understood in this way, is the first cause of divine revelation.[56] In an ironic parallel to the doctrine of the verbal inspiration of Holy Scripture, Spinoza states that the nature of God himself and of his decree as it were dictate natural knowledge to us.[57] And they do so to the extent to

[54] 'A perusal of the sacred books will show us that all God's revelations to the prophets were made through words or images, or a combination of the two' (ibid., p. 15).

[55] 'As ... the certitude afforded to the prophets by signs was not mathematical ... but only moral, and as the signs were only given to convince the prophet, it follows that such signs were given according to the opinions and capacity of each prophet ... and so that the signs varied according to the individual prophet. So also did the revelation vary ... according to individual disposition and temperament and according to opinions previously held' (ibid., pp. 29f).

[56] 'Seeing then that our mind subjectively contains in itself and partakes of the nature of God, and solely from this cause is enabled to form notions explaining phenomena and inculcating morality, it follows that we may rightly assert the nature of the human mind (insofar as it is conceived in this way) to be a primary cause of divine revelation' (ibid., p. 14).

[57] 'God's nature, insofar as we share it, and God's laws dictate it (natural knowledge) to us' (ibid., p. 14).

which we participate in the nature of God. God himself is not therefore to be sought and found by human thinking primarily through analysis, whether of thinking (Descartes), or of objects (Aristotle), or of Holy Scripture. To the extent to which the human intellect knows clearly and distinctly, it is dictated to by God and nature. And this dictation does not happen through signs, words and images, but in a way which best corresponds to the nature of the mind[58]—evidently Spinoza is thinking of the intuition of mathematical knowledge.

(*d*) Thus natural knowledge, if it is set out systematically, can begin with God himself, for it has already discovered him as the immanent cause of all things, including the mind which knows clearly and distinctly.[59] 'Tschirnhaus reports the following dictum of Spinoza: "Scholasticism began with objects; Descartes began with thinking; I begin with God". The basis of this argument is evident. If God is that which is *of itself prior*, then we must begin with him . . .'[60] This is all the more valid in that for Spinoza the order and connection of ideas themselves is the same as the order and connection of things.[61] God is that which is of itself prior, since he is the *only* substance which Spinoza defines as that which is in itself and conceived through itself, i.e. as that substance which has no need of the concept of another thing in order to be conceived.[62] But if God has no need of the concept of another in order to be conceived, then all anthropomorphic talk of God must fall short of

[58] 'All that we clearly and distinctly understand is dictated to us . . . by the idea and nature of God; not indeed through words, but rather in a way far more agreeable to the nature of the mind' (ibid., p. 14).
[59] 'God is the immanent cause of all things': Spinoza, *The Ethics*, ed. S. Feldman (Indianapolis, 1982), p. 46. Cf. ibid., pp. 7of: 'Hence it follows that the human mind is part of the infinite intellect of God; and therefore when we say that the human mind perceives this or that, we are saying nothing else but this: that God . . . has this or that idea'.
[60] W. Schulz, 'Der begriffene Gott. Das System Spinozas und seine Bedeutung für die neuzeitliche Metaphysik', *Neue Rundschau* 88 (1977), p. 545.
[61] 'The order and connection of ideas is the same as the order and connection of things . . . for the idea of what is caused depends on the knowledge of the cause of which is the effect' (*Ethics*, p. 66).
[62] 'By substance I mean that which is in itself and conceived through itself; that is, that the conception of which does not require the conception of another thing from which it has to be formed' (ibid., p. 44).

him. Inevitably it makes God finite, spatial and temporal, thereby falling short of true knowledge of God. For according to Spinoza, truth 'as such transcends time . . . and here the real meaning of the turn to the mathematical method is manifest in its inner necessity. If we speak of God and start from the definition of God . . . which we must do since God is prior—then we may not use anthropomorphic conceptions'.[63] And so in his *Ethics*[64] Spinoza exposes and criticises as anthropomorphism which falls short of God's being an idea that is absolutely fundamental to biblical talk of God, namely that intellect and will belong to God's nature, and that God acts with particular ends in view. The mathematical method, which 'is not concerned with ends',[65] prohibits anthropomorphic talk of God. It prevents us from ascribing or imputing to God those attributes which make men perfect unless unless we wish to ascribe to men the attributes which make the elephant or the ass perfect.[66] God's divinity excludes humanity. Spinoza makes the point very sharply against the New Testament in a letter to Oldenburg: 'The doctrines added by certain churches, such as that God took upon himself human nature, I have expressly said that I do not understand; in fact, to speak the truth, they seem to me no less absurd than would a statement that a circle has taken upon itself the nature of a square'.[67]

6. This historical reminiscence of some ideas of the thinker who is to be regarded at the very least as one[68] if not the father of the

[63] W. Schulz, op. cit., p. 545.

[64] 'I shall show . . . that neither intellect nor will pertain to the nature of God' (*Ethics*, p. 44). Cf ibid., p. 58: 'But in seeking to show that Nature does nothing in vain . . . they seem to have shown only this, that Nature and the gods are as crazy as mankind'.

[65] Ibid, p. 58.

[66] 'In philosophy, when we clearly perceive that the attributes which make men perfect can as ill be ascribed and assigned to God as the attributes which go to make perfect the elephant and the ass can be ascribed to man; here I say these and similar phrases can have no place, nor can we employ them without causing extreme confusion in our conceptions': Spinoza, letter 23 (Van Vloten's numbering; Spinoza to Blyenbeergh, 13 March 1665) in R. H. M Elwes, ed., *The Chief Works of Benedict de Spinoza* II (New York, 1951) p. 347.

[67] Ibid., p. 299, letter 73 (Spinoza to Oldenburg, n.d.).

[68] Cf. T. Hobbes, *Leviathan* III.33: 'The light therefore that must guide us in this question (the interpretation of Scripture), must be that which is held out unto us from the Books themselves: And this light, though it

historical-critical method, has made clear that this hermeneutic of biblical language about God, whose *meaning* it seeks to investigate, does not really acknowledge *truth*. That is to say, it only acknowledges truth insofar as the biblical texts are in agreement with the truth already known through the natural light of reason independently of biblical language about God. The historical-critical method came into being as a twin of the mathematical method. Thus part of the intention of the historical-critical method is to keep God free from all historical determinateness as a being known without the medium of human language. And so for Spinoza, as the historical-critical hermeneutic is used, it refers to the geometric method as the only appropriate way of talking of God. Insofar as this hermeneutic allows itself to make 'positive' statements about God, these statements are obtained through a procedure which converges with the geometric method. In brief: *the historical-critical method of interpreting Scripture is fundamentally a method which serves the prevailing interest in the unhistoricality of God.*

This dominating interest in the unhistoricality of God is particularly manifest in the critique of anthropomorphism which is bound up with this method. Spinoza's historical-critical hermeneutic specifically aims to identify all the historical limitations of human talk of God, so that it can go on to criticise them as anthropomorphisms and render them innocuous. Anthropomorphic talk of God is thereby regarded as an accommodation of revelation to the recipient of revelation; and it is not, as one might think, the self-revealing God who is the subject of the accommodation, but rather the one who knows him or herself to be the recipient of revelation (whilst remaining ignorant of the fact of being the subject of this accommodation). The recipient's individual determinateness and particular social and historical situation stamp what he or she knows to be communicated in revelation. *Quidquid recipitur, secundum modum recipientis recipitur,* whatever is received is received according to the mode of the recipient. For all that, the individual, social and historical determinateness of the *modus recipiendi* should, insofar as it can be known as such, be transcended, or, to the degree to which this transcendence is not possible, be regarded as a criterion for the irrelevance of that which is communicated. Historical being

> shows us not the writer of every book, yet it is not unusefull to give us knowledge of the time, wherein they were written'.

in its particularity has no proper significance for that which is appropriate as revelation. It can only be explained on the basis of more general data and general principles, and so becomes clear only to the extent to which the particular is robbed of its particularity. The true is the general. And as the general, the true is the criterion of both itself and falsity.[69] Hence all anthropomorphism is shown to be talk of God which falls short of his being.

7. Some centuries later the historical-critical hermeneutic inaugurated by Spinoza manifested its undeniable outcome. After initial difficulties getting going, it made its own way more and more, controlling and improving itself by constant self-criticism. And finally it appears as if an entire age has become 'historical-critical'. Thereby indeed the problems bound up with this hermeneutic and its methodology are handed down as it were by heredity, one of these being the hermeneutical discrediting of anthropomorphism. It should be part of the ethos and self-understanding of the historical-critical hermeneutic to be increasingly sharply conscious of these problems and to revise itself sufficiently so that the acknowledged problems can be overcome. To the degree to which new problems are thereby introduced, the next question but one may and must be that of the redundancy of that hermeneutic.

If in what follows, we only offer a systematic discussion of the immediate question of how we can achieve a positive hermeneutical view of anthropomorphic talk of God, this is certainly not in order to dismiss the historical-critical hermeneutic on account of its congenital defects,[70] but in order to help it acquire that hermeneutical vitality which can be attained not by a decrease but only by an increase in historical-critical awareness of the problem. 'The critical historian needs to be more critical',[71] if in view of the problem of anthropomorphism Scripture is at last to become *sui ipsius interpres*.

[69] 'Indeed, just as light makes manifest both itself and darkness, so truth is the standard both of itself and falsity' (*Ethics*, p. 92). Propositions §§ 40–44 in the second part of the *Ethics* could be read together as a short summary of the problems with which we are concerned.

[70] On the impossibility of such a procedure, see G. Ebeling, 'The Significance of the Critical Historical Method for Church and Theology in Protestantism' in *Word and Faith* (London, 1963), pp. 17–61.

[71] K. Barth, *The Epistle to the Romans* (London, 1933), p. 8.

II

'People rant so much against anthropomorphism and forget that Christ's birth is the most significant anthropomorphism'.[72] Kierkegaard's remark in his journal is not simply a witty aphorism: it goes to the heart of the hermeneutical problem raised by the anthropomorphisms of the Bible. We will first of all sketch this briefly in connection with Hartmut Gese's tradition-historical study of the Christological statement in the creed 'born of the Virgin'. Then we will set out the anthropomorphic structure of all human language. Finally, the general hermeneutical reflections will be tied into the preceding biblical discussion and made theologically fruitful.

1. In his analysis of the Old Testament origins of the phrase *natus ex virgine* (born of the virgin) as it is applied to Jesus, Gese comes to the following conclusion: 'In the *natus ex virgine* God's dwelling in the world becomes an event in an unsurpassable, final way'. In view of its tradition-history in the Old Testament, the phrase could 'hardly be more seriously misunderstood' if it were interpreted along the lines of a 'docetic disembodiment and sublimation'. 'The meaning of the tradition is not Jesus' being lifted out of the human, but the opposite, the descent of the Holy One into this world'. Once the New Testament's statements and their reception in the church's creed are set in the context of the Old Testament tradition, it becomes clear that the biblical texts testify to the 'revelation of God's coming into the world' as a 'process' which reached its final end with the death of Jesus.[73] What Gese calls a 'process' could perhaps better be described as the history of God's coming-to-speech. The biblical texts understand themselves, more or less, as testimony to this history. In them there *comes to speech* the fact that God *comes to the world*.

---

[72] S. Kierkegaard, *Journals and Papers* I (London, 1967) §280. On the theological justification of anthropomorphism, see H. M. Kuitert, *Gott in Menschengestalt. Eine dogmatisch-hermeneutische Studie über die Anthropomorphismen der Bibel* (Munich, 1967); F. Christ, *Das Problem des Anthropomorphismus bei Schleiermacher* (dissertation, Protestant Theological Faculty, Tübingen, 1981).

[73] H. Gese, 'Natus ex virgine' in *Von Sinai zum Zion. Alttestamentliche Beiträge zur biblischen Theologie* (Munich, 1974), p. 46.

A biblical hermeneutic has to draw the consequences of this for appraising the function of anthropomorphic talk of God. If in the biblical texts there comes to speech the fact that God comes to the world, and if the history of God's coming to the world reaches its end in the man Jesus and in his history in the world, then the anthropomorphic character of human talk of God cannot be factually false. The formal character of the biblical texts as anthropomorphic language about God has to be seen as an expression of their material content. That of which they wish to speak lies close to a deliberate anthropomorphism. But note: *deliberate* anthropomorphism. For in the same way that the God who comes to the world, by his very entering into it brings about a crisis in the world and changes it from its very foundations, so also within language a distinction is made between language which expresses God and language which contradicts him, such that words which bring God to speech are used in a way which changes their meaning. This is most clearly expressed in the Johannine ἐγώ εἰμι (I am) sayings. It needs to be borne in mind that, like all words which speak of God, all anthropomorphism has *metaphorical* or *analogical* value.[74] In this respect, the choice of words is deliberate. We should start from the fact that the authors who signal their intention to speak in the biblical texts were thoroughly self-conscious of this after their fashion. Keeping this proviso in mind, we nevertheless say that if Scripture has the right to be its own interpreter (*sui ipsius interpres*), anthropomorphism is theologically justified.

2. Anthropomorphism is not simply warranted on a biblical basis, however: it is absolutely unavoidable, for all human talk is at least implicitly anthropomorphic. We turn to explain this by reflecting on the basic anthropological character of language.[75] Our train of thought takes up a suggestion from Immanuel Kant.

In his *Prolegomena*, Kant develops a question from the *Critique of Pure Reason*, the question 'whether we may ... think of this being, which is distinct from the world, in *analogy* with the objects of experience'. Kant's answer is 'only as object in *idea* and

[74] See the essay 'Metaphorical Truth' in the present volume.

[75] It is good in this context to remember that earlier centuries used the term *anthropology* to speak of what from the seventeenth century would technically be called *anthropomorphism* (the word is newly coined in Leibniz, though it is anticipated in Epicurus).

not in reality ... Nay, more, we may freely, and without laying ourselves open to censure, admit into this idea certain anthropomorphisms'.[76] In explaining this hermeneutical concession in the *Prolegomena*, Kant links what he has to say to Hume's critique of theism, testifying of him that 'all his dangerous arguments refer to anthropomorphism'. For according to Hume, talk of God is 'of no value, and cannot serve as any foundation to religion or morals'. On the other hand, theism cannot avoid the very anthropomorphic talk of God which makes it 'self-contradictory'.[77] Kant associates himself approvingly with what he calls Hume's 'very powerful objections' in rejecting uncritical '*dogmatic* anthropomorphism' which applies to God attributes drawn from human perception of the world, so that our 'experiential knowledge' expands to such an extent that instead of God we know 'nothing but world'.[78] However, Kant distinguishes *dogmatic* anthropomorphism from *symbolic* anthropomorphism, holding the latter to be hermeneutically permitted. In symbolic anthropomorphism, 'we limit our judgment merely to the relation which the world may have to a Being whose very concept lies beyond all the knowledge that we can attain within the world. For we then do not attribute to the Supreme Being any of the properties in themselves, by which we represent objects of experience, and thereby avoid dogmatic anthropomorphism; but we attribute them to his relation to the world, and allow ourselves a symbolic anthropomorphism, which in fact concerns language only, and not the object in itself'.[79] Following the scholastic tradition, Kant calls this 'symbolical' anthropomorphism 'knowledge ... *by analogy*', understanding 'analogy' to mean not 'as is commonly understood, an imperfect similarity of two things, but a perfect similarity of relations between two quite dissimilar things'.[80] Anthropomorphism in this sense of *analogia proportionalitatis* (analogy of proportionality) makes possible language which determines God 'with respect to the world and with respect to ourselves, and more we do not require'.[81]

[76] I. Kant, *Critique of Pure Reason* (London, 1949), p. 566.
[77] I. Kant, *Prolegomena to any future Metaphysics* §5 (Chicago, 1929), p. 128. Cf. D. Hume, *Dialogues concerning Natural Religion* IV.
[78] Ibid., p. 128.
[79] Ibid., pp. 128f.
[80] Ibid., p. 129.
[81] Ibid., p. 130 (ET slightly amended—TR).

ANTHROPOMORPHISM

Kant's thoughts on anthropomorphism can be carried further in two directions. First, there is his helpful insight that the problem hitherto presented by anthropomorphic language about God can be approached fruitfully with the aid of the older doctrine of analogy. Theology, too, can follow Kant's judgment and say that, in view of the possibility which this gives of bringing God's relation to the world to speech through inner-wordly relations, 'more we do not require'—though in a quite different sense. Over against Kant, the chief business of theology is, with the biblical texts, to bring to speech God's coming to the world. To this end, an insight into the *relational* character of anthropomorphic talk of God, through which we determine God 'as regards the world and as regards ourselves', is a hermeneutical gain.

This is to be linked to Kant's remark that symbolic anthropomorphism 'concerns language only'. Here also we must oppose Kant with Kant, in that the distinction which he maintains between language and the object appears problematic. Both linguistic and ontologically-oriented philosophy are more cautious in their judgment in this matter.[82] Kant's assertion that symbolic anthropomorphism 'concerns language only' can be taken further, in that it makes clear that language is the medium of knowledge in which all along a relation to the human person is given. In language, not only God but everything is referred to 'with respect to the world and with respect to ourselves'.

3. Anthropomorphism is not peculiar to religious language alone. Indeed, anthropomorphic language about God is the most intense expression of the fact that in all that it says language also implicitly expresses the human person. From this starting-point, the view that explicit anthropomorphism is a particularly gross form of figurative and therefore non-literal mode of speech, overlooks the essence of language. The charge that anthropomorphic language makes the human person into the criterion is therefore mistaken, even though there is a certain truth in it, since language all along presupposes the

[82] Cf., for example, H.-G. Gadamer's hermeneutical thesis that 'being is language, i.e. self-presentation': *Truth and Method* (London, 1975), p. 443. For analytical philosophy I refer to the excellent study by I.U. Dalferth, *Religiöse Rede von Gott* (Munich, 1981). This work represents a successful combination of insights in fundamental theology and analytic competence—something not so far achieved in the field of theology.

human person as criterion. Heidegger remarks pertinently that 'neither the proponents of regular anthropomorphism nor its opponents ask the decisive question of whether this criterion is not necessary and why it is so'.[83]

The answer suggested by hermeneutical reflection upon the linguistic character of the human person runs that, prior to all our speaking, we are all along those who are *addressed*. Human persons are beings responsive to themselves. But as such, we are also responsive to everything which is other. In this sense, the human person is ζῷον λόγον ἔχον (a linguistic being). And so when language states something, it is always related to the one who on his or her part also expresses this relation when he or she states something. And so anthropomorphism is an essential characteristic of language.

This basic anthropomorphic character of language would, however, be radically misunderstood if it were conceived in such a way that in language we related everything to ourselves in a thoroughly egocentric way, *making* ourselves into the measure of all things. If the idiom of 'measure' is to be retained at all, we have to say that *language* makes us into the measure. But this happens in such a way that we are able to *look away from* ourselves and thus as it were to traverse the world and measure it against ourselves. In language the one who is responsive to self is turned to self and its world in a way that enables that person to transcend self and so be a human person. To be responsive to oneself does not mean to be fixed and set in one's own *actuality* but to be aligned to the *possibility* of a world. Insofar as we are in this fundamental sense responsive to ourselves, we are—in the very midst of the most generalised abstractions—'the criterion'. Even in pure formalization or in planning a purely technical language, where everything human appears alien, the human person still remains the criterion against which everything is measured. And we are this as we look beyond self. Hence in explicitly anthropomorphic language about God, 'God is not debased to the level of man, but on the contrary, man is experienced in what drives him beyond himself'.[84]

4. This general hermeneutical argument concerning

[83] M. Heidegger, *Schelling's Treatise on the Essence of Human Freedom* (Athens, Ohio, 1985), p. 163.
[84] Ibid., p. 164.

anthropomorphism has now to be linked to the theological argument set out earlier, which presupposed that the biblical texts bring to speech God's coming to the world, thereby justifying the anthropomorphism which they employ. In looking at how to understand these texts, an historical-critical hermeneutic has to execute a dual task. It has to give greater weight than has hitherto been accorded to the claim of the texts to be understood, and to the nature of the human person who seeks to understand.

It is the claim of the biblical texts to speak *secundum dicentum deum* (according to God's speaking). Insight into the nature of human persons tells us that everything of which we speak is brought to speech *secundum recipietem hominem* (according to human reception). This insight prohibits us from following Spinoza in characterising the accommodation of revelation to the individual, social and historical particularity of the one who speaks of God as a defect, which has to be rectified 'by the geometric method'. For the geometric method is itself to be identified as a form of the vision through which human persons, responsive to themselves, are enabled to look beyond themselves and traverse the world. As we externalise ourselves in language we express our own capacities in everything that we say; this is not, however, a defect but the condition of the fact that we able to speak at all, and so of the fact that we are beings who are addressed.

The uncontestable principle *quidquid recipitur, secundum modum recipientis recipitur*, consequently, does not contradict the claim of the biblical texts to speak *secundum dicentem deum*. Rather, an historical-critical hermeneutic has to keep in mind both the basic character of language as address and also the fact that God addresses human persons in particular events; in this way, the truth which comes to speech *secundum modum recipientis hominis* (according to the mode of human reception) is to be called truth not *in spite of* but *in* its historicality. The biblical texts bring the *concretissimum universale* to speech, in that they face us in our particular time and space with God who comes to the world. They did this in their own time and now await interpretation in different times by persons of those times.

5. In that the biblical texts testify to God's coming to the world as a history, the history of God's coming to speech, and in that this history has its greatest and most significant anthropomorphism in

the birth of the man Jesus, anthropomorphic talk of God is subject to a hermeneutical criterion which makes it necessary for us to distinguish between suitable and unsuitable anthropomorphisms, between those which are responsible usage and those which are not. Indeed, by this criterion we are critically to distinguish within Scripture itself between that which leads to Jesus Christ and that which does not. This does not, of course, mean that we must insist like Plato upon a regulated 'right speech about the gods'. But we will certainly have to insist that the gospel of the God who comes to the world in Jesus Christ is that address against which every statement which involves the name of God must allow itself to be measured. And that means that talk of God and talk of ourselves belong together in the dialectical way in which they exist alongside each other in the gospel.

First, then, anthropomorphic talk of God is only appropriate and responsible Christian language if it expresses the *freedom* of the God who *comes* to the world. Any anthropomorphism which transforms the freedom of the divine advent into a necessity does not match up to the concrete distinction between God and the world, and so—as Kant remarks pointedly—brings to speech 'nothing but world'. The incontrovertible hermeneutical power which belongs to anthropomorphism should not be misused so that we make religious use of God. It is worth emphasising that such religious use regularly assumes the form of a political anthropomorphism.

Anthropomorphic talk of God is, second, only appropriate and responsible Christian language if it expresses the *liberation of the human person* through the God who comes to the world in Jesus Christ and comes definitively to speech in the λόγος τοῦ σταυροῦ (word of the cross). Any anthropomorphism which transforms the freedom of the sinner to which the gospel bears witness into religious slavery or religious (i.e. pseudoreligious) self-liberation, thereby overturns the Easter joy which refers us at one and the same time to God and to ourselves—by referring us to the *humanity of God.*

THE WORLD AS POSSIBILITY AND ACTUALITY

The Ontology of the Doctrine of Justification[1]

I

Some of the words of our language stand out clearly as having a surplus of meaning, so that they can be used or abused in a more meaningful way than other words. In using such words we lay upon them the burden of saying more than they are able to say.

The 'whole', for example, is more to us than the sum of its parts. The parts of a broken vessel would be an obvious case in point. But it is questionable whether the whole of a human life is always more than simply a part of the sum of its parts: those whom the gods love die young, and those who outlive their own years often provoke the judgment that in the end less (than the whole) would have been more. So we ought to question whether the end is always that which makes something into a whole. There are sums of parts which do not constitute a whole at all. And it could be wholly unjustified to postulate that a life or history is in the end a whole, as little warranted as the assertion that the true is the whole (a proposal which certainly holds for truth itself—a half-truth is no truth at all—but which, formulated in a general way, gives to the notion of 'the whole' an unwarranted surplus meaning: truth could also be a torso).

Words which are obliged to say more than they are able to say seem, as it were, to freeze and harden into concepts which make a claim that is, as a rule, self-justified. Such concepts appear to state what really matters. 'Actuality' (*Wirklichkeit*) is one of these words. Amongst comparable words it makes a claim with which they cannot compare. Although the concept of the actual is anything but univocal, it resounds with a claim to ontological prevalence which we cannot fail to hear even in its most ordinary usage. When

---

[1] For the whole of what follows, see H. W. Wolff, 'Jahwe und die Götter in der alttestamentliche Prophetie', *Evangelische Theologie* 29 (1969) pp. 397–416. I also refer with gratitude to G. von Rad who, in part of the discussions following the paper, verified the systematic starting-point of the following reflections on the phenomena of the Old Testament.

used as an addition, it increases the meaning of a predicate ('this is really (*wirklich*) outrageous', 'really good', etc., analogous to the Greek ὄντως). Taken by itself, 'the actual' or 'actuality' does not have a comparative and needs no predicate—presupposing that we do not ask what in fact is 'actual', what in truth 'actuality' is, and hence what true 'actuality' is. But even if we are willing to ask or prepared to argue about true actuality, 'actuality' appears to be something which our language cannot transcend; 'actuality' seems quite self-evidently to state what really matters in every case.

Nor are matters any different when the one and only actuality is replaced by several actualities—the actuality of life, the actuality of the world, the actuality of faith, the actuality of God, my actuality or the actuality of whomsoever. By claiming to state what really matters in every case, however, one of these actualities can deny that another 'really' matters. One actuality calls the other's actuality into question, as, for instance, the actuality of the world and the actuality of God seem to call one another into question. Nevertheless, even where actualities dispute about what is actual, the concept of the actual in no way loses its surplus of meaning. All that happens is that something is hindered from identifying itself with the claim of the concept and thereby making itself absolute.

Following the logic of our use of language, then, it seems reasonable to understand the 'actualities' which struggle with one another as actuality, and accordingly to define 'actuality' out of the 'dispute about the actual': actuality is the dispute about what is actual.[2]

Here, however, 'dispute' is not to be understood as a *human* engagement in struggle, in which one human understanding of actuality enters into dispute with another. It is, of course, true that the dispute about the actual has its chief location in humanity, and that from the very beginning humanity is part of this dispute and so part of actuality. But from time immemorial, 'dispute' has been the father of all things (πόλεμος πάντων πατήρ),[3] and very early on humanity began to think of the existence of things as coming to be and passing away in the form of a legal dispute about that which is actual: 'they give justice and make reparation to each other for their injustice, according to the arrangement of Time'.[4]

[2] Similarly G. Ebeling, *Word and Faith* (London, 1963), pp. 380ff.
[3] Heraclitus in Freeman, p. 28, fr. 28.
[4] Anaximander in ibid., p. 19, fr. 1.

THE WORLD AS POSSIBILITY AND ACTUALITY

Clearly, to understand actuality as a dispute about the actual is a circular process. But the circle is not a vicious circle of thought; rather it is a factual circle of being, which is conceptualised by thinking of actuality as a dispute about the actual. It is best to acknowledge this circle, for only then are we on the track of the problem which lies within the claim bound up with the concept. One of the 'blunders' of metaphysics has been its failure to acknowledge this circle, its attempt to pass over it in ideas or to expunge it by logical thinking, as if it did not exist or only existed as a mistake. All this has worked with the metaphysical premise that the laws of thinking are the laws of being; 'it is the same thing to think and to be'.[5] Thinking, as it is, cannot endure this circle. Consequently, it is expunged from being, and thereby the *problem* which would disclose itself to a more careful and attentive inspection, the problem of what actuality is, is passed over. In so doing, we fail to latch onto the strange state of affairs that in actuality (conceptualised as the struggle about actuality) a dimension of being is decisive which uncritical use of the word 'actual' (a use, that is, which neglects the circle) passes over: *the possible*.

From the beginnings of metaphysics, actuality has been given ontological priority over possibility. In this way, possibility was pushed out of place by actuality. Being was and is identified with actuality. 'This does not only accord with our everyday use of language, which does not talk of "that which is" but rather of what is "real"; it also fits in with conventional shades of philosophical meaning ... according to which the "possible" is not "real" being but only its rudimentary form, so that only that which is actual is complete being'.[6]

II

Aristotle shaped this idea into a metaphysical first principle. His declaration that it is clear and obvious that 'actuality is prior to potentiality'[7] was of incalculable significance for the history of thought (and here, indeed, it would be appropriate to say: for the

---

[5] Parmenides in ibid., p. 42, fr. 3 with n. 2.
[6] N. Hartmann, *Zur Grundlegung der Ontologie* (Meissheim, 1948), pp. 66f.
[7] Meta. 1049 b 65; cf. 1072 a 9.

history of being). This affirmation of the ontological priority of actuality over possibility (both in formula—λόγῳ—and in substance—οὐσίᾳ—and in time—χρόνῳ) pushed thinking, that which is thought and that which was made therefrom in a direction which has come to determine the world. Aristotle's decision was one with consequences such as few other events have had. It is, therefore, appropriate to make it a matter for reflection. Here I limit myself to the issues most significant for our inquiry.

Aristotle does not think of the ontological priority of actuality over possibility simply as an ontic precedence of the actual over the possible. Rather, the priority of actuality consists in the fact that the possible is defined as the possible by reference to actuality. Aristotle certainly rejects the opinion of the Megaric school that only the actual is possible and that that which is not actual is not possible,[8] that being possible is 'to be conceived as a modal moment included within and presupposed by actuality'.[9] Against this theory Aristotle objects that on such a view, for example, a person would not be a builder unless that person were engaged in the activity of building,[10] or again, that that which stands will always stand and that that which sits will always sit.[11] For if this were the case, then 'that which is not happening will be incapable of happening'[12] and that which is could not have come into being. Over against this, it has to be acceptable that a thing have the possibility of being and yet not be, or that something have the capacity to walk without actually walking, or that that which is not walking still have the capacity to walk.[13]

Of course, not everything that does not walk is capable of walking. *The criterion for the possibility of walking* is the *excluded*

---

[8] Meta. 1049 b 29f.
[9] N. Hartmann, *Möglichkeit und Wirklichkeit* (Meissenheim, 1949), p. 12. Hartmann commends the Megaric thesis as 'the introduction of a strong notion of possibility' surpassing Aristotle's proposal, since according to this concept of possibility there are not many possibilities but only one, 'namely that which becomes actual; everything else is quite impossible'. This 'statement is paradoxical, flatly contradicting the usual concepts. If it is true, it must also be truly revolutionary' (pp. 12f.).
[10] Meta. 1046 b 33f.
[11] Meta. 1047 a 15f.
[12] Meta. 1047 a 11f.
[13] Meta. 1047 a 21ff.

THE WORLD AS POSSIBILITY AND ACTUALITY 99

impossibility of walking. The impossibility of walking can, however, only be excluded by the *actuality* of walking. Hence: 'a thing is capable of doing something if there is nothing impossible in its having the actuality of that of which it is said to have the capacity'.[14] It is in this sense that 'evidently potentiality and actuality are different',[15] if one does not want to exclude becoming and temporal change. But despite this proviso about the Megaric identification of possibility and actuality, Aristotle's concept of possibility is completely oriented to that of actuality. For the possible is related to the actual as (a part of) that which is not to that which is. Being cannot properly be attributed to the possible. Only that which is actual can properly be said to be.

Things which *are* not are certainly possible, but do not exist 'because they do not exist in fulfillment'.[16] Thus ἔστι (to be) can only be said of those things which can also be described as fully realized, as actuality. In the end, being and actuality are identical.[17] Possibility, on the other hand, is qualified by a sign 'not'. It is, of course, of decisive importance that this 'not' is not a *nihil negativum* (negative nothingness), for the actuality of this world arises from its possibility not as from nothingness but as from a 'not yet' which as such participates in being even though it is not yet. Insofar as the actual is the particular actualization of the possible, the possible is qualified by a 'not yet'. This 'not yet', which distinguishes the possible from the actual, constitutes the ontological priority of actuality.

This is not contradicted by the fact that from a temporal perspective the actual is always derived from its possibility whose actualization it is (as grain comes from seed).[18] For though the possible *strives* to be actualized, it is always actualized by something which has already been actualized and which belongs to the same species as that which is to be realized: 'For from the potential the actual is always produced by an actual thing ... there is always a first mover, and the mover already exists actually. We have said ... that everything that is produced is something produced from

[14] Meta. 1047 a 24ff.
[15] Meta. 1047 a 18f.
[16] Meta. 1047 b 1f.
[17] Cf. Meta. 1050 b 2.
[18] Meta. 1049 b 21.

something and by something, and in the same species as it'.[19] So actuality is the origin and goal of all that comes into being, and possibility exists for the sake of actuality.[20] Possibility stands in a teleological relation to actuality.

However, in his account of the ontological priority of actuality, Aristotle accords an unsurpassable significance to the act—as the ultimate end of the act of actualization, whether outside it or inside it.[21] Actuality exists for the sake of the act, so far as it is not itself an act. Hence the noun 'actuality' is derived from 'act', and concerns the act's completion. 'For the action is the end, and the actuality is the action. Therefore even the *word* "actuality" is derived from "action", and points to the fulfilment'.[22] According to Aristotle, our understanding of the structure of the world and of the divine which rules the world, is oriented to this complex of act and actuality. The ontological primacy of actuality leads consequently to the primacy of the act, for whose sake everything passes into being. The aristotelian world loves the act, and in love for the act it is the world.

It is, moreover, only consistent that the act, for whose sake that which is exists, should be in its purest form that actualizing act which is in itself pure actuality without any possibility: a perfect unity of act and actualization.[23] This unity is a 'thinking on thinking', νοήσεως νόησις.[24] The thinking which thinks itself is free from all possibility (which would make the continuity of its thinking wearisome);[25] and the same is true of God the unmoved mover of all, the 'unmovable first mover'.[26] Since this God is free of all possibility, he is the act for whose sake the world exists and out of love for whom the world is what it is. The world is moved by love for this perfect act. Thus God himself does not love. The perfect act of thinking on thinking is the unmoved and unloving God of the world who 'alone truly is, and out of love for whom all that is exists'.[27]

[19] Meta. 1049 b 24–9.
[20] Meta. 1050 a 9.
[21] Cf. Meta. 1048 b 18–35; Eth. Nic. 1040 a 1ff., b 4ff.
[22] Meta. 1050 b 21ff.
[23] Cf. W. Bröcker, *Aristoteles* (Frankfurt, 1957), p. 218.
[24] Meta. 1074 b 34f.
[25] Meta. 1074 b 28.
[26] Meta. 1074 a 37.
[27] W. Bröcker, *op. cit.*, p. 226.

III

It is evidence of the potency of Aristotle's understanding of actuality that it determined not only philosophy and life in the world which it advocates, but also Christian theology, in a way which still affects us and which, indeed, is hardly ever questioned even today. Although the concepts of δύναμις and ἐνέργεια, *potentia* and *actus*, possibility and actuality, have been emphasised in different ways over the course of the centuries, nevertheless, 'they always contained the teleological-constitutive element. The roots of this lay too deep in the Western mode of philosophising for a fundamental revision of the modal concepts to be able to make any headway'.[28] Attempts at such a revision as a rule came to grief because with Aristotle they still presupposed that 'the possible' is a category formed by reference to the category of 'the actual'.[29] The aristotelian doctrine of the priority of actuality over possibility was not really called into question. Yet it is just this doctrine which made the possible into a 'half-being over against that which is', in the sense of a 'not-yet-being' which is still to be; 'in the aristotelian world, the possible is a kind of ghostly being'.[30]

This understanding of possibility as mere potentiality did, however, lead to a certain position contrary to Aristotle, namely the assumption that 'there must be much more possibility in the world than there is actuality, since out of the present stage a multitude of "possibilities" for the future stand open, only one of which will subsequently become actual'. That which has become actual was now understood 'as a kind of selection from a much broader range of possibility'.[31] But this understanding of actuality as 'selection' still asserted the claim of actuality to be prior. And even if the world were understood as a process, a process which in the very beginning asserted itself—or was asserted by a god—as *this* world over against the multitude of possible worlds, and in the course of which the world is to form itself in its actuality out of 'open possibilities'—nevertheless, it is still actuality (for example, the actuality of the acting person) which is the standard by which the possible is measured.

[28] N. Hartmann, *Möglichkeit und Wirklichkeit*, p. 7.
[29] Even Hartmann's own work falls into this problem.
[30] N. Hartmann, *Möglichkeit und Wirklichkeit*, p. 5.
[31] Ibid., p. 7.

We need to be clear about the significance of the aristotelian understanding of actuality in order to grasp the meaning of the fact that, broadly speaking, Christian theology, too, has remained deeply bound to it. Even when it began to orient itself differently (following Luther, for example, in critical dialogue with philosophy on the basis of the genuinely theological task of evangelical biblical interpretation), nevertheless it continued to be covertly and unconsciously determined by basic tendencies in this understanding of actuality. The ontological priority of actuality over possibility was hardly ever—and never thoroughly—called into question. The concept of actuality has retained an emotive force which secures it a place of highest importance among theologians, too, even among theologians quite opposed to each other. Karl Barth's *Church Dogmatics* is at least *cognitively* determined by the primacy of actuality (of God in the actuality of his revelation) over the question of its corresponding possibility and especially over the general question of possibility (of divine revelation as such). Friedrich Gogarten declares the actuality of faith to be the most important problem of theology.[32] Gerhard Ebeling's theology revolves around actuality in very great measure, taking as its theme 'Faith and Unbelief in Conflict about Reality (*Wirklichkeit*)' rather than about possibility.[33] As I see it, only Ernst Fuchs and Jürgen Moltmann have, in very different ways, called into question from a theological point of view the ontological priority of actuality over possibility, the one under the influence of Martin Heidegger and the other under the influence of Ernst Bloch. With his 'ontology of the not-yet', however, Bloch still asserts the priority of the 'coming actuality'. Obviously in this philosophy there is objectified a convergence in the history of ideas between the aristotelian starting-point and particular apocalyptic-messianic expectations, in which actuality is surpassed by actuality. Whilst in the 'ontology of the not-yet' theology finds the most ingenious interpretation of its traditional eschatology, at least in its formal aspects this represents only a modification of apocalyptic expectations in the scheme of 'already-not yet'. To say 'not yet' is to think 'but then . . .' And, in good apocalyptic fashion, he asserts the primacy of actuality as Aristotle conceived of it.

[32] Cf. F. Gogarten, *The Reality of Faith* (Philadelphia, 1955), p. 10.
[33] Cf. G. Ebeling, op. cit., pp. 374–85.

Theology must at all costs acknowledge how deeply in its 'already-not yet' eschatology it is bound to this understanding of actuality. We need to realize that an interpretation of Jesus' proclamation of the Kingdom of God and of Paul's doctrine of justification which remains wholly within the 'already-not yet' scheme puts new wine into old wineskins. For whilst Jesus' proclamation of the Kingdom of God and the theology of Paul make use of apocalyptic conceptual material (though it is already critically selected!), they represent a complete metamorphosis of both the apocalyptic material and also the world view inaugurated by Aristotle. With Ernst Käsemann and others I am of the opinion that eschatology played a decisive role in early Christianity. But the eschatology which was decisive in this way *came into being* with Christianity, and so is essentially *Christian* eschatology and is to be understood as such out of itself. That it was formulated in the language of its time and is only historically accessible in this form is self-evident; but this can only spur us on to understand it critically (*sachkritisch*) out of its factual origin—however difficult this may be.

In order to achieve such an understanding of the origin of the eschatology which sprang up with the Christian community, it is essential that we undertake a theological dismantling of the primacy of actuality as conceived by Aristotle. Such a dismantling cannot be accomplished from a position of the ontological or eschatological 'not yet', however; rather, without abandoning the distinction between present and future, it would have equally to argue against the conception of the 'not yet' which has been all too innocuous in Christian understandings of the eschaton. The *necessity* of this theological dismantling of the ontological primacy of actuality over possibility is best seen by laying bare the theological starting-points from which it could be carried out. These theological starting-points can be nothing other than the basic conditions for Christian theology. For *dismantling* can only be theologically necessary when it also accomplishes the *construction* of that which is theologically necessary.

Before attempting to lay out the starting-points for a theological dismantling of the ontological primacy of actuality which came to dominate from Aristotle onwards, I wish to draw attention to a self-evident truth, that such a *theological* dismantling will in no way change our world, which owes itself to the priority of actuality over possibility which is to be dismantled. Although Christians do have the task of changing the world, not only in deed but also in concepts, it is first of all important to define the place which theology occupies in the responsibility which it alone is called to assume before its own object. Only then may we ask both how, coming from this place, theology may follow its path in the world which is to be altered, and also what kind of path theology has to follow in the world, to which it belongs totally, though not unreservedly.

IV

The necessity of a theological dismantling of Aristotle's affirmation of the priority of actuality in the sense of an energy and entelechy which actualizes the possible, is Christologically grounded. The Christological grounding of this necessity becomes clear in the doctrine of justification, the proper development of which would be an essential contribution to the dismantling task. If I begin here by referring to Luther, I am nevertheless presupposing that 'we do not honour the doctrine of justification simply by repeating it',[34] but only by undertaking a responsible contemporary development of a concept of that which was brought to speech by Paul and worked out by Luther.[35] That the doctrine of justification is in this sense an indispensable criterion of proper theology, that as such it is in every way the *articulus stantis et cadentis ecclesiae* (the article by which the church stands or falls) which can only be disavowed by a 'church' which does not wish to stand and which ignores its own foundation (1 Cor 3.11)—all this constitutes an indispensable affirmation, to dispute which is to dispute the entire possibility of theological knowledge.[36]

Luther objected on more than one occasion to the aristotelian thesis that a person becomes righteous by doing right (i.e. by doing that which is righteous). 'We do not become righteous by doing

[34] H. Conzelmann, 'Die Rechtfertigungslehre des Paulus: Theologie oder Anthropologie?', *Evangelische Theologie* 28 (1968) p. 390. Cf. E. Wolf, 'Die Rechtfertigungslehre als Mitte und Grenze reformatorischer Theologie' in idem., *Peregrinatio* II (Munich, 1965), pp. 19–21.
[35] Cf. E. Jüngel, *Die Freiheit der Theologie* (Zürich, 1967).
[36] Cf. Luther's statement 'Take away assertions and you take away Christianity': *The Bondage of the Will, LW* 33, p. 21.

THE WORLD AS POSSIBILITY AND ACTUALITY 105

righteous deeds but, having been made righteous, we do righteous deeds'.[37] Or: 'We are not, as Aristotle believes, made righteous by the doing of just deeds, unless we deceive ourselves; but rather—if I may say so—in becoming and being righteous people we do just deeds. First it is necessary that the person be changed, then the deeds (will follow)'.[38] Already in his lectures on Romans of 1515/16, Luther insisted on drawing a distinction between the philosophical or juridical and the biblical use of the concept of *iustitia* (righteousness). Whilst philosophers and lawyers understand righteousness as a quality of the soul,[39] in biblical usage righteousness depends more upon the imputation which God effects than upon actuality: 'the "righteousness" of Scripture depends upon the imputation of God more than on the essence of the thing itself ... he alone has righteousness whom God mercifully regards as righteous because of his confession of his own unrighteousness and because of his prayer for the righteousness of God, and whom God wills to be considered righteous before him. Therefore ... we are righteous only by the imputation of a merciful God through faith in his word'.[40]

We can only properly appreciate Luther's polemic against the aristotelian understanding of the righteous person when we see it in the context of his positive assertion of the justification of the sinner through faith in the justifying Word of God (*per fidem verbum eius*). As soon as we attempt to do this, however, it becomes clear that to call into question the aristotelian view of how persons become righteous is also to call into question the aristotelian understanding of actuality. 'We become just by doing just acts', declared Aristotle;[41] here he presupposes that since ethical virtues are not innate in us by nature, they do not exist in us as a possibility before they exist in actuality. Rather, we are righteous in so far as we

[37] Luther, *Disputation Against Scholastic Theology*, LW 31, p. 12.
[38] M. Luther, letter to Spalatin, 19 October 1516, LW 48, p. 25. This contrast with Aristotle is also set out in Luther's comments on Ps 85.13 in the *First Lectures on the Psalms. II: Psalms 76–106*, LW 11, pp. 173f., in a kind of immanent critique of Aristotle.
[39] Over against those things which belong to us by nature, as, for example, sense perception which, as a natural endowment, is *temporally* prior as a possibility to the act in which it is actualized: Aristotle, Eth. Nic. 1103 a 26ff.
[40] M. Luther, *Lectures on Romans*, LW 25, pp. 274f.
[41] Eth. Nic. 1103 b 1.

continue to act righteously. For 'states arise out of like activities'.[42] This understanding of 'being righteous' as human ἕξις (that is, as a disposition of the human self which it gains for itself in a particular respect, through which it is actually capable of something) realized through repeated performance of ontologically equivalent acts, presupposes the understanding of actuality we have described above. The human person realizes his or her actuality, and in so doing is actual. A person is actual insofar as that person creates actualities which as such are then possibilities for newly intensified acts. By skilful playing of the lyre, one becomes a lyre-player, an artist on the lyre, who then has the possibility of playing the lyre skillfully; bad lyre playing, by contrast, makes one a bungler. Equally, 'by doing the acts that we do in our transactions with others, we become just or unjust'.[43] The difference between the righteous person and the unrighteous is nothing other than a difference in their acts. By them, we determine ourselves for righteousness or unrighteousness. On this basis, the move from acting righteously or unrighteously to being righteous or unrighteous is ontologically seamless. We are what we make of ourselves.

By contrast, Luther's antithetical assertion that we only come to *act* righteously once we *become* and *are* righteous, lays before us a problem which can only be solved by abandoning the aristotelian understanding of actuality: how can a person *become* righteous prior to that person's deeds?

'*Prius necesse est personam esse mutatam*', it is first necessary that the person be changed. The necessity of a *change of being* which is asserted here presupposes that Luther does not regard the unrighteous person as one who can equally determine him or herself to be righteous or unrighteous, for then it would be the *liberum arbitrium* (free will) which determined itself to act righteously or unrighteously. For Luther, however, the unrighteous person is one who is already unrighteous, that is, a sinner who, lacking the free will which belongs to God alone, cannot make him or herself righteous through any human act. As a sinner, this already-unrighteous person is one whose being is the radical negation of the being of the righteous person, not simply logically but ontologically. This means, however, that there is the most radical

[42] Eth. Nic. 1103 b 21.
[43] Eth. Nic. 1103 b 14ff.

antithesis between the unrighteous and the righteous person, which can only be adequately stated as that nothingness which we have to consider as the antithesis of creation. The *persona mutata* (changed person) is only properly understood as *ex nihilo creata* (created out of nothing). It is just this which Paul meant when he described the justifying God as the one who gives life to the dead and calls into being the things that are not (Rom 4.17).

If we take this description seriously—and theology has to take it seriously—then we face the conclusion that the justified person is linked to his or her sinful self by nothing but the creative Word of God. Apart from this Word, nothingness holds sway between the *homo peccator* (sinner) and the *homo iustus* (justified person). Indeed, the *homo peccator* has to be lost in this nothingness, if and when God declares a person to be righteous. Formulated anthropologically, this means in Pauline terms that the old (outer) person perishes, whereas the justified (inner) person is daily renewed (2 Cor 4.16; cf. 5.17). Luther considered this state of affairs to be the work of God grounded in the essence of God, in saying that 'it is the nature of God first to destroy and tear down whatever is in us before he gives us his good things'.[44] For 'God destroys all things and makes us out of nothing and then justifies us'.[45] In these statements, God alone is set forth as the *causa efficiens* ('efficient cause', as Luther says in good aristotelian fashion) of justification. These statements are, indeed, the inevitable consequence of the Pauline doctrine of justification. That this consequence is not to be understood metaphysically is made clear by the consideration that the sinner's being reduced to nothing is the revelation of God's wrath, which, according to Rom 1.18–3.20 consists in the fact that God gives the sinner up (παρέδωκεν) to the sinner's self and sins, in that by the law God binds the sinner to sin and death. The law of sin and death accomplishes the divine work of destroying and reducing to nothing, in that it lets the sinner be. Under the illusory appearance of being, the sinner celebrates nothingness. Sin is relationlessness, loss of relation. The sinner is, to put it simply, a person without relations, with no relation to God or to self. Lack of relation to God is what is meant by the theological concept of the nothingness which, under the illusory appearance of being, is not *more* but *less*

[44] M. Luther, *Lectures on Romans*, *LW* 25, p. 365.
[45] M. Luther, *Die zweite Disputation gegen die Antinomer*, *WA* 39/I.470.7f.

than the *nihil negativum* (negative nothingness) from which in the beginning God created all things. As the loss of relation it is as it were the more pronounced form of this *nihil negativum*: *nihil nihilans* (the nothingness which negates).⁴⁶ And precisely because it is this mode of nothingness, not only nothing at all but also in its very nothingness a nothingness which *negates*, it cannot be recognised as nothingness, but is rather celebrated under the illusory appearance of being. And so Luther is correct to say: 'by faith alone we must believe that we are sinners, for it is not manifest in us'.⁴⁷

The sinner's relationlessness and the judgment of God's wrath upon the sinner which takes place in and with sin is not revealed, however, as sin is enacted but only as it were in retrospect, within the brackets of the revelation of the righteousness of God in the gospel.⁴⁸ Only in the one who knew no sin and yet was made sin for us (2 Cor 5.21) is the sinner revealed in relationlessness and sin. That Jesus Christ was made sin for us by God means that the *destruere et in nihilum redigere* which is enacted in and with our sin is revealed in Jesus Christ, as he and he alone dies the accursed death which we live. Jesus' death on the cross is grace, since it reveals that in the midst of life we are in death. He makes manifest the nothingness which the sinner celebrates under the illusory appearance of being. Or at least Jesus' death on the cross reveals this when we allow it to speak for itself (that is, according to the law).

However, Jesus' death on the cross by no means only speaks for itself. It speaks in the *gospel* as the word of the cross. And precisely as the word of the cross, the gospel is the proclamation of the lordship of the risen one. More precisely: the gospel proclaims that the risen one lives as the crucified. And in this the death of Jesus comes to have its real meaning, namely, as the event of the love of God (Jn 3.16). Jesus' resurrection from the dead promises that we shall be made anew out of the nothingness of relationlessness, remade *ex nihilo*, if through faith in the creative Word of God we allow ourselves to participate in the love of God which occurs as the death of Jesus Christ. In this sense, Christian existence is *existence out of nothingness*, because it is all

⁴⁶ I.e. as it were the (logically impossible) unity of the contrary and contradictory opposite to being.

⁴⁷ *Lectures on Romans*, p. 215.

⁴⁸ On this, see my book *Paulus und Jesus* (5th ed., Tübingen, 1979), p. 29.

along the line existence out of the creative power of God who justifies. The Christian is accompanied by this nothingness in the double form revealed in Jesus' death and resurrection: as the *end* of the old and the *beginning* of the new, as a reminder of the judgment enacted in the sinner, and as the promise which surpasses judgment in the same way that grace has surpassed sin (Rom 5.20). *Media vita in morte sumus*, in the midst of life we are in death; but even more *media morte in vita sumus*, in the midst of death we are in life.[49]

V

One of the tasks of a thorough development of the doctrine of justification is to interpret the event of our justification not simply with regard to its Christological grounding and its anthropological meaning but also with regard to its *ontological* implications. This is not because theology wants to have jurisdiction of a proposed ontology, but rather because the ontological implications of the event of justification are constitutive moments of the 'kingly rule of Jesus Christ', of the world-relation of the Kingdom of God. As such moments, these ontological implications have a *critical function* within the world and its self-understanding. Theology has to set out this critical function within the world's current historical self-understanding. On the basis of what has so far been established, we shall now try to make a suggestion in the area of ontology.

The decisive ontological implications of the event of justification are to be grasped through the notion of *creatio ex nihilo*. This notion makes it necessary for us to think of nothingness, over against the aristotelian conception of actuality. According to this conception, the world does not contain nothingness. What was understood as 'coming to be' and 'passing away' are 'misleading concepts' in so

[49] M. Luther, *Lectures on Genesis 21–5*, *LW* 4, p. 116. Cf. F. Gogarten, op. cit., pp. 128f. We should dispute Gogarten's assertion that wrath and death on the one hand and salvation and life on the other hand 'are like each other. The wrath and death are unbounded, and the mercy and life are likewise unbounded' (ibid., p. 127, referring to Luther, *WA* 40/III.577). Wrath and death have been limited by salvation and life, in that they have been overcome. Faith lives from this overcoming; and faith does not create it, any more than faith could unite the two contraries unless they had already been united in Jesus Christ.

far as they 'contain non-being'.[50] Our present understanding of actuality, still best represented by the actual accomplishment of modern science, takes possibilities (in the sense of change) into account as the not-yet of an actuality to come; it is therefore only really oriented to the distinction between the actual and the not-yet-actual. Doubtless it thereby encounters a decisive dimension of the world.

Theology participates totally in this dimension. Because of this, it does not exclude *any* relevant method of inquiry, but will rather do what it can to promote the improvement and development of such methods of grasping actuality. Sociology and cybernetics will certainly not be the last discoveries which theology will do well to discover, not only because of their scientific make-up but also because of the usefulness of what can be discovered through them. To close our eyes here would be irresponsible.

But it would be even more irresponsible if theology did this indispensable *opus alienum* (alien work) for its own sake and not for the sake of theology's *opus proprium* (own work)—that is, if theology held *one* decisive dimension of the world to be the *only* and all-decisive dimension. For thereby theology would abandon thinking of the world as creation. But theology cannot cease to think of the world as God's creation; indeed, this is its primary responsibility above all others, and everything else that it does must be done in service to this.

The absolutizing of actuality and the distinction between the actual and the non-actual as the measure of the world is subject to fundamental critique from the event of justification, a critique which understands the world not only as בְּרֵאשִׁית but—out of the resurrection of the dead—as creation out of nothing. Theology must establish that the radical nothingness of Good Friday is the other dimension of the being of this world. This is not in order that we may indulge in some profound ontology of nothingness, but rather that we may think of God as the creator and of his creation as justified. Theology does this by establishing the distinction between the possible and the impossible as incomparably more fundamental than the distinction between the actual and the not-yet-actual. Where the distinction between the possible and the impossible is made, we are concerned with truth (as opposed to actuality). The

[50] N. Hartmann, *Zur Grundlegung der Ontologie*, p. 60.

distinction between the possible and the impossible is incomparably more fundamental because it concerns the distinction between God and the world. And in the distinction between God and the world we are not concerned primarily with actuality, but with truth. Of course, God and the world are not distinguished in such a way that the world is identified with the possible and God with the impossible. Rather, distinguishing the possible from the impossible is a matter for God—whereas the world, denying the fact that it is created, constantly identifies the possible and the impossible, thereby as it were making the impossible an actual state of affairs.[51] The most solid expression of the actuality which results from identifying the possible and the impossible is the phenomenon of religion, whose gods are impossible actualities, 'bungling actors' (Isa 2.8, 10.10f.; Ps 96.5, 97.7, et al), 'beings that by nature are no gods' (Gal 4.8). However, we need to grasp more profoundly *how* it is that in the distinction between the possible and the impossible we are concerned with the distinction between God and the world. And starting from this distinction, we need to arrive at an understanding of both God and the world.

1. *God*

If we say that distinguishing between the possible and the impossible is a matter for God, we cannot mean this in the sense that it is already established what is possible and what is impossible, so that God simply distinguishes retroactively what is already possible from what is already impossible. If this were the case, then God would be a secondary phenomenon, and hence not God. Nor, on the other hand, can we define God as the one who makes possible the impossible and then lets it be actual as 'miracle'. For this would not be a miracle, but simply a piece of magic brought about by sin. Once again, though on different premises, God would be a secondary phenomenon, which could certainly confuse possibility and impossibility but would precisely thereby show its priority to God. If distinguishing between the possible and the impossible is a matter for God, then God's divinity must be actualised in such a way that the act of distinguishing determines what is possible and

---

[51] Barth's definition of sin as an 'impossible possibility' is concerned with this phenomenon. But it would be better to speak of an impossible *actuality*.

what is impossible. This means that only this act constitutes that which is possible as possible and that which is impossible as impossible. In this sense, God is to be conceived as the one who makes the possible to be possible and the impossible to be impossible. As the one who does this, as the one who distinguishes the possible from the impossible, God distinguishes himself from the world. And in that he distinguishes himself from the world, God lets the world be actual.

On the other hand, we would have little grasp of the distinction between God and the world if we set God in and for himself over against the world. For then God's being would be thought of as another world: a more primordial and better world, but for all that still another world. In this case, the distinction between God and the world would be nothing other than a distinction *between two worlds*. And one could then—in the same way that one could render absolute one dimension of the world—play 'the actuality of God' off against 'the actuality of the world' (and vice-versa), or try to harmonise the one actuality with the other. In each case, either God would be thought of as being like the world, or the world would be thought of as being like God.

Over against this, God is to be thought of out of the event of justification as the one who in the very act of distinguishing himself from the world relates himself to it. In this way he is, and remains, God. He has shown himself to exist in this way in the indissoluble unity of the death and resurrection of Jesus. Because of this, there is no true proclamation of the cross which does not take place in the power of the resurrection, and even less is there true proclamation of the risen one which does not proclaim him to be the crucified. The Easter message, the gospel, is the word of the cross. Out of this word, we have to say that God himself is the one who makes the possible to be possible and the impossible to be impossible, and in this distinction between possibility and impossibility lets the world be actual. Beyond the distinction between possibility and impossibility, God himself is equiprimordially both, or, to say the same thing, God *is* and his being is in becoming.

2. *Towards the world*

The fact that God relates himself to the world in the act of distinguishing himself from it leads not only to an understanding of

THE WORLD AS POSSIBILITY AND ACTUALITY

God, but also to an understanding of the world. For on the premise which we have worked out (that God distinguishes himself from the world in distinguishing the possible from the impossible), God relates himself to the world by making the possible to be possible and the impossible to be impossible. This abstract formulation immediately becomes concrete when we think back to the event of justification. For this event makes it clear that the divine distinction between the possible and and the impossible is an event of the Word of God which leads the world back to nothingness and makes it anew out of nothingness. Making the possible to be possible and the impossible to be impossible is the business of the *Word*; in the event of the Word, God both distinguishes himself from and relates himself to the world. In the face of the actuality which perpetuates that which is real and which, even in 'making the future' only changes what is actual, the event of the Word of God lets the possible become possible and hands over to perish that which has become impossible. This means: by distinguishing between the possible and the impossible, the Word of God occurs as a word of promise and judgment.

3. *The world*

For our understanding of the world, this means that its being occurs as history, and that this history is constituted, not by the distinction of the actual from the not-yet-actual, but by the distinction between the possible and the impossible, by the Word of God. From this perspective it becomes clear that the traditions of Israel could be subject to constant re-interpretation without such new interpretations being simply alterations of past actuality. Insofar as it could claim to be accompanied by an כֹּה אָמַר יְהוָה the past actuality becomes a quite new possibility as it is newly interpreted. And so it is in Israel's *covenant history* that the world shows that it is *creation*. The world is creation insofar as God's Word, in distinguishing the possible from the impossible, distinguishes being from nothingness: 'Astonishment over the fact that Israel exists and does not not exist is Israel's fundamental experience throughout its entire history'.[52]

---

[52] J. M. Robinson, 'Heilsgeschichte und Lichtungsgeschichte', *Evangelische Theologie* 22 (1962), p. 139. On this problem, cf. G. von Rad, *Old Testament Theology* II (New York, 1965), pp. 99–112, 297–300.

This astonishment means that every step within history has become possible (that is, has been made possible by God's Word) as a step out of nothingness into history. Accordingly, for Israel coming to have history means coming to have a *future* within history. The promise which constitutes the being of the world as history implies that history is gained as it is snatched from nothingness.[53] This means, further, that the promise stands 'in a demonstrable contradiction to the historic reality (*Wirklichkeit*)'.[54] This has its grounds in the indissoluble unity of grace and judgment manifested in Christ, according to which *ex nihilo facere* (to make out of nothing) implies *in nihilum redigere* (to reduce to nothing). Moltmann rightly refers to Jer 23.29 as a criterion for the event of the Word of God: 'is not my word like fire, says the Lord, and like a hammer which breaks the rock in pieces?'.[55]

When justification takes place, there also occurs a divine 'No' which reduces the sinner's actuality to nothingness, a 'No' which is for the sake of the creative divine 'Yes'. Since the justified person owes his or her new being to the Word of God which reduces the actual to nothingness and creates *ex nihilo*, that person hopes in nothing other than God's Word, 'so that it be the purest faith in the most pure God'.[56] And in doing just this, the justified person hopes for the world, not as hope for any particular future worldly actuality, but only as hope in God's creative Word.

(a) From a theological point of view, 'hope in' a particular future worldly actuality is the exact opposite of the kind of hope in God alone which hopes for a future for the world. The future *actuality*

[53] On this, cf. my essay 'Der Schritt des Glaubens im Rhythmus der Welt', in *Unterwegs zur Sache* (Munich, 1972), pp. 257–73.
[54] J. Moltmann, *Theology of Hope* (London, 1967), p. 118.
[55] Cf. verse 39. Verse 29 is not concerned with a criterion by which to distinguish true from false prophecy, as the context suggests. Verse 29 is independent from a literary point of view, and is directed at those who hear, not those who speak, the Word of God, as G. Quell has shown in *Wahre und falsche Propheten* (Gütersloh, 1952), pp. 166ff. However, against Moltmann I would object that the promise does not provoke an 'incongruence with being' but rather an incongruence in actuality, which, on the contrary, does not pronounce 'the future of a new reality (*Wirklichkeit*)' but the future of a new being: cf. Moltmann, op. cit., pp. 118f.
[56] M. Luther, *Operationes in Psalmos*, *WA* 5.196.18—contra Moltmann!

of the world is not a matter of *hope*; it is *made*. It belongs to the context of worldy action; it is a matter of calculation and cannot do with hopes any more than we can work with hope in constructing an aeroplane or in pursuing historical-critical inquiry into the past. The future actuality of the world is something which can be made. As such it does not originate immediately from the word of promise, but from the work of the diviner, who, according to Kant, truly represents 'things imminent in future time', if he 'himself creates and continues the events which he announces in advance'.[57] The desire to call this makeable future actuality an object of Christian hope is an exact modern parallel to the conception of hope as 'certain expectation of rewards proceeding from merit',[58] against which Luther once fought. For if human acts aim at objects which can be hoped for, then those acts (not so much individual as corporate) come to acquire the status of merits, since hope would be founded on those very acts.

(*b*) Over against this kind of hope in the future actuality of the world which is always grounded in the world's actuality, the justified hope in God alone for themselves and for the world. In such hope believers are righteous, for in it faith becomes an event which alone in this world participates in God's distinction between the possible and the impossible. It is this participation which is meant when it is said that all things are possible to the one who believes (Mk 9.23). By faith in the word of the cross, the world, through those who believe, comes to share in the divine distinction of the possible from the impossible. And in this sharing through those who believe—and hence through the Christian community—in the distinction in which God relates to the world, the world exists as God's creation, beyond the dimension of actuality. Where the absolutizing of the dimension of actuality is overcome, as there occurs conformity to the reference of being back to nothingness which is accomplished in the being of Jesus Christ, the world is more than its own habitus; it is creation. The actuality of the world is the indispensable *vita activa* (active life) without which we would not be actual. But as creation, the world is equally the irreplaceable *vita passiva* (passive life), without which it would not be possible 'to

[57] I. Kant, *The Conflict of the Faculties* (New York, 1979), pp. 141, 143.
[58] *WA* 5.163.34

conform ourselves to the image and example of Christ, our King and Lord, who began with the active life but whose life was consummated in passion'.[59] Over against this 'consummation in passion' there is only the love of God. This is the meaning of his cry.

What has been set out so far has yielded a theological understanding of actuality. In essence, the consequence of what has been proposed is the dismantling of the claim that actuality is prior to possibility, since the distinction between the possible and the impossible—and thus the distinction between God and the world—is *more necessary* than that between the actual and the not-yet-actual. In actuality that which is already actual is at work as an act, which as such always proceeds from the past. To put the point more sharply, in actuality that which is passing into the past is active. As such it has a certain value and its own necessity. But in the distinction between the possible and the impossible, being is distinguished from nothingness. Such a distinction comes out of the future. For nothingness has as little past as does the creative distinction of being from nothingness. When the possible is distinguised from the impossible in such a way that the possible becomes possible and the impossible becomes impossible, then there occurs something like an origin—whether it be an origin in the beginning or at the end: in both cases it is God's freedom as *love* which makes the possible to be possible. In the very concept of creation it is essential to set God's love over against his omnipotence. God's omnipotence concerns actuality, God's love concerns possibility. God's love concerns the being which is in becoming.

1. It follows that possibility can no longer be defined out of the concept of actuality, whether in the sense of a power, tendency or inclination towards the actual or in the sense of a factor in the being of actuality. Rather, possibility and actuality are factors in being, such that that which God's free love makes possible has ontological prevalence over that which God's omnipotence makes actual through our acts. For as the future of the world which exists historically, possibility is by no means 'mere possibility', but rather is that which is actuality's ultimate concern. As future, possibility is the concrete way in which the world is determined by nothingness,

[59] *WA* 5.166.12f.

THE WORLD AS POSSIBILITY AND ACTUALITY 117

out of which God's creative love lets being *become*. What can be made of the future on the basis of past and present, does not belong to the dimension of possibility; rather, as that which is not-yet-actual, it belongs to the dimension of actuality. What can be made does not *become*, in the strict sense of 'becoming *ex nihilo*'. We make actuality out of that which is actual. We change, we transform. In this way, we make the future. God, however, is not one who transforms; he is the creator, who allows possibility to move towards actuality. But this possibility arises from the divine distinction between the possible and the impossible, arises, that is, *ex nihilo*. The world's possibility is not within but external to its actuality. And its being is external to its futurity.

Nevertheless, this external, future possibility must *address* actuality if it is to be more than pure abstraction from the actual. The indispensable *concretion* of the possible is the *event of the word*. In this event, that which God's love makes possible from outside, and not from a future which arises out of the past, is the ultimate concern of the world's actuality. In the event of the word we discover, in Moltmann's phrase, 'future ... in the past and possibilities in what has been'.[60]

2. If in the event of the word the possible is the ultimate concern of actuality, then the question arises how the possible verifies its possibility (and its distinction from the impossible) in actuality. For possibility, which unconditionally concerns actuality as a future which results from outside and from nothing—from no tendency in the actual—is open to suspicion of being irrelevant to or even altogether impossible for actuality. This problem of verification seems to be the main preoccupation of contemporary theology. And, indeed, it is in fact sufficiently complex to be a considerable embarrassment to any solid theology. How can the possibility which is actuality's ultimate concern verify itself as such, without either losing its freedom from determination by actuality or ceasing to be a real concern of actuality?

If it is actuality's *ultimate* concern, then it cannot be forced to conform to the conditions of actuality in order to be verified. If this were the case, verification would change possibility into actuality. This happens, for example, when the world-relation of

[60] Op. cit., p. 269.

the Kingdom of God is understood to concern actuality as a revolutionary postulate or as a sanctioning of the present order. In both cases, possibility is made into actuality; like everything which is actual, it is a *conditional* and not an absolute or ultimate, concern of actuality. On the other hand, if we stress that possibility is not determined by actuality we are in danger of renouncing any kind of verification. And then possibility would not concern actuality at all, however much it ought to be its ultimate concern. Because it is unconditioned by actuality, the externality of possibility, its futurity which does arise from the actual, gives it an authoritarian appearance which seems to demand submission rather than verification. But although it is a claim which is actuality's ultimate concérn from outside and from out of the future, God's revelation is misunderstood if it is thought of in this authoritarian way. The misunderstanding is based on a fatal confusion of the authority of the possible with its caricature, the sham authority of the authoritarian.

3. For all that, it is important to speak of possibility as possessing a measure of authority. Over against actuality, possibility is not simply 'mere possibility', as our use of language might suggest. Rather, in its distinction from impossibility it is powerful; and the power of the possible is its authority. If we understand possibility not as powerless but as powerful, not as weak but as strong, then we can also—following Bultmann—understand the Pauline definition of the gospel as 'the power of God' to mean that the gospel is God's possibility 'for salvation' to the one who believes. Formally speaking, the power of the possible consists in being distinguished from the impossible in such a way that even in actuality it makes impossible the impossible. This power is the authority of the possible as it is revealed in the authority of the gospel. It differs from pure authoritarianism by giving *itself* (and not something else) to be understood.[61]

Its claim expresses itself in langauge which really concerns actuality. Ernst Fuchs invented the category 'speech event' for this, though the effectiveness of this category in understanding has been widely misunderstood. Which speech events, one might ask, verify

[61] The authoritarian makes something understood (e.g. 'march!') without making the *authority* of the command understood. It allows for no 'reasoning'.

THE WORLD AS POSSIBILITY AND ACTUALITY 119

possibility distinguished from impossibility as being actuality's ultimate concern? In which speech events do we attain a true correspondence between the claim of possibility and the language of actuality?

(a) The most immediate answer would probably be: in assertions. Possibility can only and must be asserted in actuality. In the face of actuality, faith has to assert what God's love has made possible. It was with good reason that Luther defended against Erasmus faith's joy in assertion.[62] What is actual does not, of course, need to be asserted: it asserts itself. But in the dimension of actuality, the claim of possibility is properly expressed by human assertion; possibility must be asserted. However, it must be asserted as distinguished from impossibility. If assertion in the authority of the possible is not to be a purely authoritarian claim, then along with the assertion of the possible, the distinction between the possible and the impossible (i.e. in the terms of our investigation, God himself) has to become relevant for actuality.

This may be the case if the assertion of the possible in actuality were to ask nothing impossible of actuality. In this way actuality would be satisfied, but without undermining the fact that possibility is not determined by actuality. The possible is in itself distinguished from the impossible and therefore corresponds to itself when its claim corresponds to actuality in a way which demands nothing impossible of actuality. If this assertion of the possible is to be actuality's ultimate concern, however, it must at the same time be an assertion of a *claim* and the *granting* of that which transcends actuality and moves it back into possibility, without being conditioned by actuality. This means that the *claim of the possible* can only be asserted as a *granting of freedom*. The authority of the possible is the authority of given freedom.[63]

[62] M. Luther, *The Bondage of the Will*, LW 33, pp. 19–24.

[63] It is significant that Luther interprets Christ's lordship in this way, out of his office as redeemer, and thus in a wholly non-authoritarian way: 'Let this be the summary of this article, that the little word 'Lord' simply means the same as Redeemer, that is, he who has brought us back from the devil to God, from death to life, from sin to righteousness, and now keeps us safe there'. By contrast, precisely because the devil rules in an authoritarian way, he is no lord: 'Before this I had no Lord and King but was captive under power of the devil. I was condemned to death and entangled in sin and blindness': *The Larger Catechism* (Philadelphia, 1959), p. 58.

(b) As that which elicits freedom, the assertion of the claim of possibility is an event within actuality. We can only elicit freedom in actuality, however, when a *space for freedom* is made in actuality, a space in which trust in that which is possible can arise. However, making space for freedom means critically differentiating between specific actualities within actuality: for example, between good and bad acts, or between human and inhuman forms of government. Only where actuality is not an undifferentiated unity does there arise that without which freedom cannot exist. If it is to elicit freedom, then, the assertion of the claim of possibility must take place in speech events which lead us to differentiate actuality, so that there arises that space for freedom in which trust in the possible can occur. Such trust needs *time* to occur. The speech events which lead us to differentiate actuality must, accordingly, grant time. The time which they grant is *de facto* a space for freedom.

Clearly speech events which grant time for trust or space for freedom cannot be limited to momentary decisions, nor can they be characterised by the structure of a command.[64] If we were to define them, it would be as speech events which *plead*. A plea makes a demand without force. Unlike a command, it gives time. It accords freedom which the one to whom a plea has not been made never has. It leads to the differentiation of actuality by possibility. And so pleading ought to be the constitutive element of proclamation. The apostle pleads in place of Christ (2 Cor 5.10) without his words thereby ceasing to demand, and without faith ceasing to be (free) obedience. In a plea, God's love finds its most appropriate expression; and this love reconciles the world to God, having made possible the possible and impossible the impossible, by reducing the latter to nothing and by creating the former anew from nothing.

(c) In his parables, Jesus himself brought to speech possibility over against impossibility as that which is actuality's ultimate concern.

[64] Cf. S. Kierkegaard, *Journals and Papers* II (London, 1970) §1473: 'When a solid is spun about too rapidly, there may be spontaneous combustion. So also when the requirement of the eternal and of ideality precipitously breaks in upon a man and makes its demand upon him—then in despair he may lose his mind. At such a time he might cry out to God: Give me time, give me time. And this is grace—and this is why temporality is called the time of grace'.

THE WORLD AS POSSIBILITY AND ACTUALITY 121

This he did in such a way that actuality was differentiated, space won for freedom, and trust granted. At heart, Jesus' parables are appeals to the hearer, appeals which demand. They *lead* to freedom by walking along a path with the hearers (and not only with each of them individually, but by gathering them into a community through the narrative). This path seeks out the hearers in their everyday world, in their actuality, and then takes them along with it, the different viewpoints and currents of the parable gathering the hearers together towards its climactic point. Here time is granted to the hearer. The Kingdom of God is not proclaimed abstractly, in order to force the hearer to make a momentary decision (over against Bultmann's understanding of the kerygma). Rather, the Kingdom of God takes its time, the time of the parable, in order to seek us out in the world which has been entrusted to us. And so in the parables the Kingdom of God grants us time to find trust, so that we can arrive with understanding at the decision which the parable's climax offers. At the end of the parable, the Kingdom of God has not only led up to that climactic point, to itself; it has also given a 'taste' of itself, has brought itself to speech in parable as parable, and, as a word of freedom, has led to freedom for the word.[65] Hence at the end of a parable it is so difficult to distance oneself from Jesus the narrator. At the end of a parable of the Kingdom of God, unbelief and lack of freedom are really only an 'impossible possibility' (Barth). The hearer has been empowered to make a *right* decision.[66]

Because in such speech events the possible is actuality's ultimate concern, we are forced into a dispute about what is actual. We now have to make distinctions within actuality, we must *act*, we must *decide* according to the necessity of the time constituted by possibility, sometimes, even, decide for a politics (but never for a theology) of revolution. Because we make distinctions within actuality, thereby disputing about what is to be actual, then within our limits we correspond to God who, by distinguishing the possible from the impossible, makes actuality possible and through his Word reveals that πρότερον δύναμις ἐνεργείας ἐστιν, possibility is prior to actuality.

---

[65] Cf. my *Paulus und Jesus*, pp. 135ff.

[66] Parable constitutes analogy as the basic dogmatic form of human language about God, not because parable speaks less clearly but because it speaks more precisely.

VII

We conclude by anticipating an objection to what has been set out.

'I have thought about this too, ... I do not know whether I can put it into words. I thought of the actual; by that I mean the known, and how it came to pass; and I thought of the possible, that which we do not know but can only divine. It makes us sad, with a sadness we conceal from ourselves and others, out of respect for the actual. We banish it to the depths of our hearts. For what is the possible in comparison with the actual; and who would dare speak up for it, knowing he runs the risk of disrespect towards the actual? And yet I often think there is a kind of injustice here—an injustice due to the fact (yes, it is possible in this connection to speak of facts) that actuality takes up all the room and attracts all the admiration to itself. On the other hand, the possible, the unfulfilled, is only an outline, a guess at what might have been. And considering that sort of "might have been", we may easily fear lest we lack respect for the actual—resting, as it must, in good part, upon the perception that our work and all our life are by nature a product of renunciation. But where the possible still exists, if only in the form of longing and intuition, of an adumbration, a whisper of what might have been—that is the sign-manual of destruction, of "pining away".'

Charlotte shook her head. 'I am, and always shall be, on the side of resolution, for holding stoutly to the actual and leaving the "might have been" to shift for itself.'

'Sitting here beside you,' he said, 'as I have the honour to do, I cannot quite bring myself to believe that you have never felt that pull towards the possible. It is so natural, it seems to me: the very preponderance of the real and actual is what tempts us to speculate on the possible, the thing that did *not* happen. The actual gave us great things, and why should it not, with such creative powers? . . .'

Charlotte replied: 'We must highly esteem the idealism which sides with the possible against the actual—despite, or perhaps because of, the greater advantages of the latter. But we must, I think, let it remain a question which of the two is morally superior . . .'.[67]

[67] T. Mann *Lotte in Weimar* (Harmondsworth, 1968), pp. 186–8.

In proposing the priority of possibility over actuality, have we not turned upside down not only ordinary language but even things themselves? One could answer that language opens up other avenues of language use than those which are familiar, that δύναμις and 'capacity' are, even in language, the roots of the 'power' without which nothing is 'actual'. One might also reply that here things are not so much turned upside down as set on their feet again—if one preferred not to ponder whether the world has not been standing on its feet for too long, without making any progress, and whether it might not be high time to turn the whole world upside down in order finally to make some progress. These considerations are not new.[68] But, as we have said, even the past still has possibilities and therefore promises.

[68] Cf. G. W. F. Hegel, *The Philosophy of History* (New York, 1956), p. 365. Here I can only refer in passing to R. Musil's interpretation of possibility as the existential dimension in which the 'man without qualities' exists; the novel of the same title begins the task of dismantling the ontological priority of actuality over possibility.

HUMANITY IN CORRESPONDENCE TO GOD

Remarks on the image of God as a basic concept in theological anthropology

I. *Introductory Remarks*

A *theological* doctrine of humanity can only wish to be 'new anthropology' in a very restricted sense.[1] For in answering the question of what humanity is, theology has to go back to rather old texts without which it is not able to make any theologically binding statements about humanity. At least in one respect, theological statements about humanity are statements of faith, and as such they offer a way of understanding ourselves which came to speech primarily in the texts of the Bible. Accordingly, Christian theology can only provide a *new* anthropology insofar as every theological statement of any particular time must be a new attempt to formulate the Christian understanding of God and humanity established in the Bible, in a way which is binding and comprehensible for that time. In being appropriate to its own time, Christian language about humanity must show that it is appropriate to its own object.

Although theological anthropology is in this way only a *new doctrine* in a very restricted sense, nevertheless with regard to its object it is new anthropology in a radical sense. For the human self-understanding which the Christian faith has to offer and which all theological anthropology has to establish, is concerned in a very special way with the *new humanity*. The Christian faith stands in critical relation to every actuality of human existence, in that it understands humanity *eschatologically* and opens to each person the possibility of an eschatological self-understanding.

'Eschatological' means (a) new in a way which we do not bring about ourselves. In our eschatological self-understanding we are concerned with a new being which we do not attribute to ourselves

[1] This essay first appeared in a series of volumes entitled *Neue Anthropologie* (New Anthropology)—TR.

but which is given to us by God—this is what the Christian faith asserts. And since this new being is given to us by God, it is independent of what we attribute to ourselves. The new being which we attribute to ourselves must nevertheless grow old. The new being which is attributed to us by God is free from the necessity of growing old.

'Eschatological' means (b) new in a way which alone makes the old into the old and leaves it to perish. 'Therefore, if anyone is in Christ, he is a new creation; the old has passed away, behold, the new has come. All this is from God . . .' (2 Cor 5.17f). Theological anthropology is concerned with the new humanity in its distinction from and relation to the actual humanity of which the believer was once part and still is part in one important respect which we ought not to overlook. Hence it is not so much a new doctrine of humanity as a doctrine of the new humanity. In what follows, we will try to sketch out that doctrine under a title which sums up humanity's new being: humanity in correspondence to God. We will confine ourselves to those aspects of the Bible which are most important in laying out the foundations of theological anthropology: we do not here try to exhaust the riches of biblical anthropology.

II. *Formal foundations of protestant anthropology*

Language about the eschatologically new humanity in correspondence to God transcends hermeneutically that which we may ascertain about ourselves through analysis of our existence. We are dependent upon a *secundum dicentem deum*, a word which is to be measured against the God who speaks, which theology calls the Word of God. And so in its hermeneutical peculiarity, language about humanity in correspondence to God already implies a material decision about the being of humanity, according to which we are defined as hearers before we are speakers. Beyond all that we have to and are able to say for ourselves, we are defined ontologically as hearers of a word by which alone our being is constituted. Both ontically and existentially we are to be 'hearers of the word' (Rahner). Necessarily, then, theological language about the eschatologically new humanity transcends human self-experience, since it asks that we experience anew that self-experience. Otherwise it would not be theological language.

Nevertheless, it must still be possible to verify such language within the horizon of analysis of human existence. Precisely because it is *God's* Word which constitutes us as hearers and so makes us capable of speech, precisely because 'God' is the presupposition with which theological anthropology works, every statement in theological anthropology must have universal anthropological *validity* and therefore also universal intelligibility. And so we have to reckon with the possibility of universally valid statements which are universally intelligible only through a highly particular means of access: listening to the Word of God. The ontological character of theological statements can only be grasped through the ontic mediation of the Word of God; we cannot demonstrate that humanity is the creature of God the creator, but only assert this through faith in God the reconciler who justifies humanity as his creature. This assertion must, however, be a statement about *all*, and therefore be universally acceptable—even if faith's presupposition 'God' is left as a mere blank. The fundamental unity of the utmost concreteness on the one hand and the utmost generality on the other, which Christian theology claims for God and for him alone, compels theological anthropology to make statements whose universal validity must be justifiable even if God as the *ens concretissimum* (most concrete being) is left out of the argument. Only the concept of God is capable of such 'theoretical selflessness' which allows us to make anthropological statements, which can only be formulated on their own presuppositions, in such a way that they are anthropologically intelligible to those without God. And so we must be able to formulate every statement in theological anthropology in such a way that it is intelligible and clear without God being named. But we must take care to note, however, that every such statement changes from a statement of the gospel to a statement of the law, from an unambiguous statement of blessing to a statement which is inherently ambiguous. The gain which faith has made with God and in which it rejoices cannot be formulated in a different horizon; in the horizon of the law it is suspended. And so language about the eschatologically new humanity in correspondence to God must—for the sake of God—have an ontological character. Otherwise it would not be anthropological language.

All statements of theological anthropology thus have a particular and rather complex hermeneutical character, which interprets humanity as defined *a priori* from outside itself, even though this 'outside' can only be recognised *a posteriori* (it is only from within the boundaries of human existence that this 'outside' can be discerned as that which determines humanity). The complex hermeneutical character of statements of theological anthropology corresponds exactly to the particular ontological character of human existence of which such statements speak. No anthropology can dispute the fundamental theological insight that humanity is—for good or ill—withdrawn from itself. The *whole* person can only be experienced as such when the *totality* of the person has been transcended. This means that we become whole not from within ourselves or from our own resources, but only from outside ourselves. Part of the truth of the *totus homo*, the whole person, is *nos extra nos esse*, being outside ourselves. If we wish to experience ourselves as whole persons, we must experience *more* than ourselves.

However, theological anthropology speaks of this indisputable necessity as one of law or structure only on the basis of the given possibility of the gospel. It is only because we *can* experience more than ourselves and in this way experience ourselves as whole persons that there is such a thing as theological anthropology at all, or such a thing as a theological definition of humanity. Protestant theology finds such a definition of humanity in humanity's justification by God. 'Paul . . . briefly sums up the definition of man, saying, "Man is justified by faith" '.[2] Language about the eschatologically new humanity in correspondence to God implies that our justification by God has already taken place, although this justification is only 'realized' in faith, since faith alone allows that it has happened definitively in a way which still defines humanity.

And so the particular hermeneutical character of statements of theological anthropology already contains in a formal way what theological anthropology has to say materially. Thus it is advisable already at the formal level to eliminate the main objection against the content of theological anthropology, namely the objection that it is not possible to define human being.

Can humanity be defined? The findings of modern anthropology deny this possibility. Since Lessing at the latest,

[2] M. Luther, *The Disputation Concerning Man*, thesis 32, *LW* 34, p. 139.

humanity appears to be an indefinable synthesis of chance and necessity:

> Man? Where is he from?
> Too base for a god, too good for mere chance . . .[3]

It is significant that the text does not tell us where humanity is *from* but rather from where humanity is *not*: neither created by a god nor fallen from heaven. If God, the *ens necessarium* (the absolutely necessary being, as metaphysics describes him), were its creator, humanity would have had to have been a greater success. On the other hand, the last word to be said about humanity is not the accident of mere conception and birth, a moment of bliss and an hour of agony. For

> A man like you does not remain where chance
> Of birth has cast him: if he so remains
> It's only out of insight, reasons, better choice.[4]

The origin of human existence can be a question neither of mere chance nor of pure necessity. If mere accident were the origin of humanity, the question of our being would be superfluous: we would have no being and would not be worth asking about. But since humanity is 'too good for mere chance', we must ask about ourselves. If, on the other hand, humanity's origin were in some pure divine necessity, no further questions about us need be asked, since our origin would be transparent to us. But since humanity is 'too base for a god', we remain questionable. No answer releases us from the need to keep asking new and further questions about ourselves. In the case of humanity, it is more human to seek the truth than to possess it. The only definite thing seems to be the question-mark which Lessing set against humanity: 'Man?'

Modern anthropological sciences seem to corroborate this state of affairs. It is not by chance that there is a plurality of such sciences. Their more or less disparate plurality indicates that a definition of humanity as a whole seems to have become impossible. Studies of the human body, craniometry, biological typification, ethnology,

[3] G. E. Lessing, *Die Religion. Ein Fragment* in *Werke* I (Munich, 1970), p. 171.
[4] G. E. Lessing, *Nathan the Wise* (New York, 1955) II/5.

genetic and behavioural research, psychological and sociological studies—all these are our specialised scientific attempts to establish something about ourselves. They have been pursued successfully, and today the attempt is sometimes made to integrate them into a philosophical anthropology. There can be no doubt that there has been an enormous growth in specialised knowledge of humanity. But our question about ourselves remains unanswered—unless we push this multitude of positive findings to say more than they really signify. To name a few examples: we know that the ontogenesis of each individual human being is a brief recapitulation of the phylogenesis; that from a physiological perspective human beings are inferior to all animals, since we are as it were unfinished beings, a physiologically premature birth; that the human species is still on the point of developing (increasing in height, bringing puberty forward without shortening the time of maturity); that human beings are culture media for bacteria; that in distinction from the animals we are 'open to the world' (Scheler) and 'exocentric' (Plessner). But we also know that 'killing, roasting and consuming a member of one's own species ... is not ape-like but human behaviour'.[5] What we do not know is who we ourselves are. Certainly the fact that we have developed 'from pre-human forms of life is as little to be doubted ... as the possibilities which lie open to us in the future'; yet for the special anthropological sciences we are 'beings whose origin and destination are equally obscure'.[6] And so can such a being, Plessner rightly asks, 'ultimately be defined?'[7]

If we do not wish to leave the question at this point, there remains the possibility (frequently seized upon today) of making a virtue of necessity and as it were taking at its word our endless question about ourselves. Humanity would in that case be defined as a question which transcends every answer, as radical questionableness. Accordingly, Lessing's ironic couplet would express not only the methodological difficulty of all anthropology but also the radical questionableness which is its proper object.

It is interesting that the modern assertion of the indefinability of

[5] H. Weinert, cited by F. Hartmann, 'Anthropologie I. Naturwissenschaftlich', *Die Religion in Geschichte und Gegenwart* I (Tübingen, 1957), p. 403.
[6] H. Plessner, 'Anthropologie II. Philosophisch' in ibid., p. 411.
[7] Ibid.

humanity, proposed by 'defining' humanity as radical questionableness, ascribes to humanity the unlimitedness which the metaphysical tradition reserved for God. *Deus definiri nequit*, God cannot be defined—so said the metaphysical tradition, which on the other hand knew very well how to define humanity. The modern departure from metaphysics, which still persists, indeed which has perhaps only just begun, is chiefly characterised by the fact that it understands God as a projection of humanity into the infinite, such that God is no longer understood as an indefinable being. And to the extent to which we put an end to the—metaphysical—mystery of God, we become a riddle to ourselves. The indefinability of God is replaced by the indefinability of humanity. *Homo definiri nequit*, humanity cannot be defined—so says the modern era in its various voices.

Detailed anthropological research has made the *totus homo* into an unknown being. It was Aquinas who once said that of God we cannot know what he is but at most what he is not.[8] Today it would seem that we have to say of the whole person that we cannot know what it is but only what it is not.

A questionable virtue can be made of this necessity, however, if the impossibility of an ultimate definition of humanity is replaced by its definition as radical questionableness. This is certainly an elegant solution: on the one hand, the category of radical questionableness does justice to the fact that we only actually know what the *totus homo* is not; on the other hand, this category implies that humanity is essentially open to new questions, and thus it produces some kind of definition of the *totus homo*. To affirm the indefinability of humanity is at the same time to move beyond it. Yet the elegance of this solution does not do justice to the essence of humanity.

That we can and above all must ask questions about ourselves is a characteristic of humanity according to biblical anthropology. But in the horizon of theological anthropology, these questions are neither primary nor ultimate. In Psalm 8, the question about humanity is logically preceded by the fact that God is mindful of us: 'What is man that thou art mindful of him, and the son of man that thou dost care for him?' (for this typically biblical structure of the question of humanity, see besides Ps 85 also Ps 144.3, Job 7.17,

[8] *Summa Theologiae* Ia.3.introd.

Rom 9.20). And regarding the time of eschatological joy, the Johannine Christ promises his disciples that 'in that day you will ask nothing of me' (Jn 16.23). The anthropological consequence of this is that questioning is a derivative phenomenon and that radical questionableness is a myth.

Being is prior to questioning. In order to be able to question, we must hear, we must have heard. Questions arise from answers. Prior to—and also, on the other hand, subsequent to—questioning there are such things as poetry, song, story-telling. Prior to questioning there is instruction (cf. Gn 2.16f with 3.9f). Prior to questioning there is agreement. Ernst Fuchs asserted in a striking way that agreement is the essence of language.[9] It is the interruption of narrative, the cutting short of action, the false note and uneasy, disconcerted wonder (θαυμαζειν[10]) that beget questioning. In these cases, questions have to be asked in order to appropriate and, if need be, to leave behind the disruption.

The view of modern anthropology could be summarised, then, by saying that humanity is a question to which we do not know the answer—or to which we do not *yet* know the answer. This latter view would be that of a 'theological' anthropology fundamentally different from the conception of theological anthropology presented here, which is anthropological only as a function of its theological character, and which offers an interpretation of the eschatologically new humanity in which humanity is an answer to a question which is not yet adequately known. Theological anthropology has then to establish and work out the question to which humanity is the answer.

If humanity is an answer for which the corresponding question has to be found, then the definability of humanity is fundamentally beyond dispute. But if we assert the definability of humanity in this way, we must nevertheless deal with the objection that we are thereby denying what seems to be an assured result of modern anthropology, namely that humanity is fundamentally open to the world. This fundamental openness to the world, implied by humanity's radical questionableness, seems to demand that we regard humanity as indefinable.

Over against this, theology proposes that through the

[9] E. Fuchs, *Hermeneutik* (Tübingen, 1970), p. 177 *et passim*.
[10] Plato, Thaetetus 155d; Aristotle, Meta. 982 b 11–17.

incarnation of God humanity is defined as a being open to God. In this, however, humanity is also defined as open to the world. For—against the theological tradition—the universality of the creator must make us, as those who are open to God, beings who open themselves to the world and to ourselves. The eschatologically new being, by reference to which theology decides what ought properly to be called human being, is that man in whose historical existence God defined himself and, in the act of his self-definition, also defined us: the man Jesus. It is fundamental to a Christian understanding of God and humanity that we neither advance a view of humanity on the basis of a preconceived understanding of God, nor advance a view of God on the basis of a preconceived understanding of humanity—even if it be humanity's indefinability. Rather, judgments about God and humanity can only be made on the basis of one and the same event. For Christian faith, this event is God's identity with the life and death of the one man Jesus, revealed in the resurrection of Jesus Christ from the dead. He is truly divine and truly human, in indivisible unity but in a distinction which is not to be confused. The event of God's identifying with this human life grounds eschatologically the distinction between God and humanity. 'Identifying' does not mean the blurring of all distinctions. Rather, the act of identifying oneself can reveal much more sharply the distinction between the one who identifies himself or herself and the one with whom he or she is identified. The Christian concept of God's identity with the man Jesus is to be understood in this sense, in the sense, that is, of an ontology of the historicality of being. If this is true, however, we have to conclude that humanity is defined by the fact that God defines himself as God in a human person. This is the logical meaning of the doctrine of the image of God in humanity. Everything here depends upon the fact that for the Christian faith the meanings of 'God' and 'humanity' are defined by reference to the person of Jesus Christ. For the *category* of the 'image of God' is identical with the historical *name* Jesus Christ. The person called by that name is humanity in correspondence to God.

However, the person of Jesus Christ signifies a decision about the being of *all* human persons. In him was made a decision about our future, and therefore a decision about the entire history of humanity; and in him, too, was made an ontological decision about the being of humanity.

On the basis of the actuality of this one man who corresponds to God, it is true that the humanity of all human persons consists in corresponding to God. This one man is essential for all. The Christian faith relates all persons to this one man, however, not only ontologically but also existentially, for unlike this one man, all other human persons do not *de facto* correspond to God. There had to be a *new* man, so that humanity could attain its end. But this new man does not exist in correspondence to God solely for his own sake. Rather, in his being a decision is taken about all, in that this one man who corresponds to God *brings into that correspondence* all who do not correspond to God.

Paul calls this event in which we are brought into correspondence with God through the being of Jesus Christ *justification*. Thus Luther (in *The Disputation Concerning Man*) correctly saw that justification is the real definition of human being. Justification by God can be regarded as definitive of human being, since it releases us from the clutches of human action, without denying that the concept of our being includes our actions. To put the matter in a different way: in the event of divine justification, human nature, threatened by itself, is affirmed by God against its constant perversion into abnormality. And so justification is an event of ontological relevance.

In its formal aspect, 'justification' means that it is through the event of divine justice that human beings first become themselves: the *righteousness of God* which occurs in the being of Jesus Christ constitutes our humanity. Justification is thus a *relational* concept. God is righteous in that he makes us righteous. Humanity in correspondence to God is thus defined relationally, in both a passive and an active sense. God's relationship to us is the ground of the fact that we can relate to ourselves. Prior to our relationship to ourselves is the relation which another bears to us. We could not relate to ourselves at all if we did not already exist out of the relation borne to us by another. Ontologically, we are in no way grounded in ourselves. We cannot come to ourselves without already being alongside another.

Nevertheless, *ontically* we wish to ground ourselves in ourselves. We are ruled by the will to self. This is demonstrated in the dominance of the will over the capacity for hearing. The will which cannot hear is the will to self-grounding. Correspondingly, all relations are reduced to a relation to the self as an *inconcussum fundamentum veritatis*, an unshakable foundation of truth. Identity as self-identification is the anthropological postulate of humanity ruled by the will to self.

The Christian faith understands this ontic tendency towards self-grounding as *sin*. For faith, identity as self-identification is the mark of one who is losing him or herself. For according to faith's understanding of the matter, we never find ourselves in ourselves. In ourselves we cannot come to ourselves. We come to ourselves when we come to someone other than ourselves. 'Whoever would save his life will lose it; and whoever loses his life . . . will save it' (Mk 8.35).

By contrast, the justification of the sinner is that event which brings us into connection with something *over against* us. It is crucial that that which is over against us relates itself to us as something which presents itself freely. We can only really go beyond our self-relation if we relate to something over against us which is not immanent to our self-relation. Something which is over against us in this way is present in freedom and creates relations through its own conduct. To put the matter paradoxically: we need something over against us which is not necessary to us. In this sense, God is *more* than necessary to us. For the concrete name of that which is over against us and which freely presents itself is *God*.

The anthropological consequence of this can be stated by saying that part of what constitutes the humanity of the human 'I' is that it receives itself in encountering another. Over against the conventional, rather moralistic definition of human being as a being for others—'the true person exists for the sake of others'—from a theological perspective we need to assert the priority of our relatedness to that which is over against us, freely presenting itself. *The humanity of a human 'I' consists in allowing another to be there for me.* This is what is meant in offering our justification by God as a definition of human being. It does not define us in terms of a (in other respects indisputable) deficiency, but from an event which is to our benefit but which does not arise out of ourselves. In that the being of another is to our benefit, the human creature becomes a human person. In this sense theology calls us *historical* beings. We already have history before we make history.

With this observation, however, we have already passed over into the material foundations of theological anthropology.

HUMANITY IN CORRESPONDENCE TO GOD 135

III. *Material foundations of protestant anthropology*

1. In the Bible, humanity in correspondence to God is called the image of God, *imago dei*. A treatment of the material foundations of theological anthropology has to question the biblical texts about how this being in the image of God is to be understood. In this we limit ourselves to a thoroughgoing exegesis of the decisive biblical statements on the matter. In accordance with the understanding of theological anthropology we have presented so far, the Old Testament text which we consider first must be exposed to the critical authority of the New Testament with its Christological grounding of humanity's being in the image of God. Moreover, from a hermeneutical point of view it is equally clear from what has been said above that every definition of humanity further specifies the notion of God.

The classical reference for the doctrine of humanity in the image of God is Gn 1.26f, supplemented by Gn 5.1, 3 and 9.6. Moreover, Wis 2.23, and Sir 17.3 come into consideration from the wisdom literature. The most important Old Testament commentary on Gn 1.26f is Ps 8.6. Gn 1.26 tells us: 'Then God said, "Let us make man in our own image, after our likeness; and let them have dominion over the fish of the sea, and over the birds of the air, and over the cattle, and over all the earth, and over every creeping thing that creeps upon the earth". So God created man in his own image, in the image of God he created him; male and female he created them'.

An interpretation of this has to start from the fact that the mere existence of humanity is understood as created in the image of God. 'Being in the image of God' is not to be understood—as it is still often interpreted to be—as a quality, honour or distinction appended to the human creature. Rather, humanity's existence is our being in the image of God. Humanity's greatest honour is the fact of existence.

But this existence in which humanity corresponds to God is one of *co-humanity*. Without any doubt the text emphazises the duality of human existence; hence the change between the singular and the plural in the object: God created *humanity* by creating *human persons* as male and female. Here the text is not thinking of the human capacity for reproduction, which is taken up in verse 28 in a specific blessing, and so detached from humanity's being in the image of God.[11] Humanity does not produce its own plurality but rather encounters itself as already in the community of persons. Being in the image of God implies a societary structure for humanity. Humanity comes into existence as a social reality and in this corresponds to God the creator. In terms of the *concept of God*, this must mean that the God to whom humanity corresponds is no solitary God. Rather, God is himself concerned with community; his being is such that he wishes others to participate. Moreover, the consequence for our relation to God of the fact that humanity is created in the image of God as a societary being, is that our God must always be seen as also the God of others. As *my* God he is at the same time *your* God, and so is defined as *Deus pro te*, as 'God for you'.

But if the image of God consists first of all in the most basic fact that each of us exists as the 'I' of a 'Thou', then any suggestion of solipsism is blasphemous. '*Si quis dixerit hominem esse solitarium, anathema sit*: if anyone says that the human person exists alone, let him be accursed.'[12] We cannot relate to ourselves without thereby already relating ourselves to another. And no less importantly, we cannot relate to ourselves unless another already relates to us. Nietzsche's 'azure loneliness', his 'do not mistake me for someone else' is alien to the doctrine of humanity as coming into existence as God's image. Theological anthropology does not acknowledge this concern not to be mistaken for someone else as a human concern. Rather such a concern is deeply inhuman, an ontological self-contradiction, opposed to creation. It is excluded by the definition of humanity as being in the image of God.

We now move beyond this very basic definition to ask what more is meant by the assertion that humanity is God's image.

2. In my view, Köhler brought out a decisive aspect of the understanding of humanity as the image of God in Gn 1.26 and indicated a path for theological anthropology to follow, when he interpreted being in the image of God as consisting in the fact that humanity alone has 'an upright form'.[13] Accordingly, our being in the image of God is shown materially (beyond the most basic fact

---

[11] W. Zimmerli, *1. Mose 1–11. Die Vorgeschichte* (Zürich, 1957), pp. 80ff.
[12] K. Barth, *CD* III/2, p. 319.
[13] L. Köhler, *Theologie des Alten Testaments* (Tübingen, 1966), p. 135.

HUMANITY IN CORRESPONDENCE TO GOD

that we exist and exist with our fellows) in a specific mode of corporeality, in a bodily form. We should not balk at accepting the idea that our innermost nature, our essence, is found in this wholly external form. 'That which Something is, it is wholly in its externality; its externality is its totality—it is equally its introreflected unity. Its Appearance is not only Reflection into other, but into self, and consequently its externality is the manifestation of that which it is in itself'.[14] In the upright stance of the body, humanity is like God. And our bodily likeness to God is the expression of our humanness. Thus it was in accord with the biblical understanding of humanity when the writers of the early church, in connection with a Platonic etymology,[15] indicated 'erect position' and 'elevated countenance' as a characteristic of humanity.[16]

This aspect of the 'image of God' statement in Gn 1.26 is recalled in a very pointed way in the charge of perverted worship which is formulated in the context of Paul's conception of the image of God in Rom 1.23: instead of honouring God and giving thanks to him (verse 21), humanity, appearing to be wise, exchanged the glory of the immortal God for a model, pictured not in the image of God but in the images of mortals or birds or animals or reptiles. In this charge it is crucial that when we cease to understand ourselves by reference to the image of God, we immediately range ourselves with the animals. Because we no longer understand ourselves according to the image of God and so give God glory ('the glory of God' in Paul is a technical term for the notion of the image of God), but instead understand ourselves and God in our own image, then the image of mortals is *eo ipso* ranged with the image of birds, animals or reptiles (as we can still observe today in museums, most impressively in the forms which, half human, half animal, show the correct order through the transition of forms into one another!). So we now seem to be ranged with the animals, from which we are nevertheless distinguished by our upright gait. This is grotesque. The note of parody in Rom 1.23 is not to be missed. Perverted worship is a parody of our humanness. Characterised by our upright stance as upright beings and understood through this characteristic as God's image, we forfeit our own human status when we forfeit

---
[14] G. W. F. Hegel, *Science of Logic* (ET London, 1929), vol II, p. 159.
[15] Cf. Plato, Cratylus 399c.
[16] Lactantius, *A Treatise on the Anger of God* VII.

God's glory. We deprive ourselves of our upright being when we deprive ourselves of our relation to God. We are nothing short of ruined.

The point of the charge which Paul sets out in parody form confirms that we ought not to undervalue our upright bodily stance as the expression of our likeness to God by regarding it as a 'merely external' phenomenon. Our external form is the form of our being. This is above all clearly confirmed where our behaviour calls into question the form of our being. To give one more example from the Old Testament, we may quote from the preacher—a particularly sound judge of human affairs: 'Behold, this alone I found, that God made man upright, but they have found out many devices' (Eccl 7.29).

In its externality, our erect body is our essential form. This becomes completely clear in the foundational Old Testament text for the doctrine of the *imago dei* when we observe the differentiation of humanity from the animals which immediately follows: 'Let us make man in our image, after our likeness; and let them have dominion ...'. Intrinsic to an upright stance is an upright gait. As those who are upright we *move* like only God besides. In this movement as upright beings, our determination to lordship is expressed. 'Being in the image of God is a call to lordship over life'.[17] Exercising lordship, as the Bible understands it, is a function of being a lord. The one who exercises lordship is a lord. Humanity as lord—this means *imago dei*.

But if in being lords we are in the image of *God*, then God himself is understood as a lord. Over against humanity, God is understood in the Bible to be humanity's lord. The fact that we have God as our lord does not, however, exclude but rather include the fact that we ourselves are lords. But we are not lords over our fellows. We are not God the Lord. Rather, we correspond to this Lord by being destined for a *common* lordship over the world with others. We are not destined to bow down before others, but rather to meet one another in an upright way, and so to advance together. Destined to a common lordship over the world and a common moving forward, we discover the world as *space* in which we are then allowed and enjoined *time* to

[17] W. Zimmerli, *Das Menschenbild des Alten Testaments* (Zürich, 1949), p. 20.

progress. As lords we are destined to progress and dependent upon progress.

It is not a matter of chance that we feel that those of our fellows who are prevented from walking or holding themselves upright are especially unfortunate and pitiable. They lack freedom for the future. In antiquity they were particularly ridiculed, evidently because their existence was a disturbing marginal comment on human lordship, with the result that since they seemed externally to lack the function of lordship, they were thought to be particularly domineering. The fact that today such ridicule of those prevented from walking upright is no longer a matter of course as it was in antiquity, has something to do with the fact that Jesus Christ, whom faith calls 'Lord,' was the *crucified*.

3. The sharpest expression of the idea that our being in the image of God means lordship as upright beings is found in the New Testament's designation of Jesus, crucified and risen from the dead, as Lord. 'Jesus is Lord' runs the basic confession of the Christian faith (1 Cor 12.3, Rom 10.9, 14.11, Phil 2.11). The predicate 'Lord', we should note, applies to the crucified Christ, who does not demonstrate, however, the power of death but rather its conquest. In him it is clearly shown that humanity in correspondence to God is not limited by death but by God. And so death no longer has dominion over him (Rom 6.9). Rather, the crucified and risen one rules over the dead and the living (Rom 14.9). In this way he is the one who corresponds to God (2 Cor 4.4).

Interpreting our upright gait and the lordship which it expresses through Jesus' resurrection from the dead has brought the human form into an eschatological dimension. That which was in the first instance expressed spatially is now clarified by the New Testament in its *temporal* structure. If the Jesus who was raised from the dead is the new humanity and therefore humanity in correspondence to God, then human being is understood as unreservedly related to the future. In this it is crucial that the risen one is not understood as a man who has left behind the life he has lived as an abandoned past. For the risen one is proclaimed precisely as the crucified (and not vice-versa). It is to the past that the future is given. Our unqualified relation to the future includes our past. Humanity in correspondence to God is humanity in its entire history.

The fact that the man Jesus existed among all and within the humanity of all was strongly affirmed by Barth as 'the central human factor':[18] 'The ontological determination of humanity is grounded in the fact that one man among all others is the man Jesus'.[19] In accordance with the self-understanding of the New Testament we have to conclude from this that when any person is addressed in his or her humanness, that person is addressed on the basis of being a fellow of Jesus Christ. Here existence in the image of God is defined most concretely. It is therefore appropriate that the basic Old Testament statement of humanity as the *imago dei* is specified and in a certain way also modified in the New Testament through language about Jesus Christ.

4. This specifying is present first of all in the fact that now—here we are following Paul—only one single man is called God's image. In 2 Cor 4.4, it is said of Jesus that he is 'the likeness of God' (this is pre-pauline tradition). For 'in the face of Christ' the glory of God is manifest. In that God's glory is characteristic of Jesus Christ alone, he is the image of God.[20] In a unique way he corresponds to God the Lord. And so he alone is eligible to be the archetype of human being. For—and here we reach the specifically Pauline point of this text—all will in their existence participate in what Jesus Christ *is*. It is not simply a matter of 'the glory of God in the face of Christ', but of that which has 'shone in our hearts to give the light of ... knowledge' (verse 6), which *gives a share* of this glory of God in the face of Christ. This happens linguistically, through *address*. Just as Jesus Christ *is* God's image, in that he has God's glory, so through proclamation he gives to those who believe a share in God's glory, by drawing us into his being in the image of God through the event of the word of the cross. The *imago dei*, which is Jesus Christ, here comes into consideration as a word-event happening to us.

In view of our 'participation' in Jesus Christ's being in the image of God, however, it is certainly very surprising that in this context

[18] *CD* III/2, p. 160.
[19] Ibid., p. 132.
[20] Δόξα (glory) in Paul is usually a parallel concept to εἰκών (in the polemic of Rom 1.23; cf. 1 Cor 11.7). This is rabbinic tradition which interpreted the 'after our likeness' of Gn 1.26 as 'after the glory of the creator' (on this, see J. Jervell, *Imago Dei* (Göttingen, 1960)).

Paul expressly refers to himself as a slave. It is, however, important to bear in mind that here Paul wishes to talk about the Corinthians' 'participation' in Christ's being in the image of God. And so he writes that he is the slave of the Corinthians 'for the sake of Jesus' who as the image of God is himself the Lord. In obtaining a share in his being in the image of God, we also obtain a share in his lordship. But in order that this may happen, the apostle has to be a slave, although he himself, on the other hand, precisely because he has this Lord, is a free man (1 Cor 9.1). There is therefore a specific Christian dialectic of Lord and slave, which is indeed grounded in the being of Jesus Christ himself.

Obviously there can be no sharing in the crucified's being in the image of God unless we consider ourselves as lords and slaves. Here we come upon a further specification of the Old Testament's view of the *imago dei*. But we have to take account of this dialectic of lordship and servanthood in those who come to participate in Jesus Christ the *imago dei* only because this dialectic already defines the being of Jesus Christ himself. In this history we discover that the dialectic is neither a paradox nor a contradiction; rather, the lordship and the servanthood of the same man are congruous in the closest possible way.

5. The Bible calls the destruction of this unity 'sin'. This is the expression of the fact that we violate both God and ourselves, and thus our being in the image of God.

From Rom 1.21–4 we have already gathered that we understand ourselves in our own image (and therefore also according to the image of the animal creation), thereby perverting the glory of the immortal God. Verses 24ff interpret this as follows: in that we no longer honour God as our Lord, we deprive ourselves of the glory of being in the image of God, namely being a lord *in* the world. In this sense Rom 3.23 tells us that 'all have sinned and fall short of the glory of God'. By misusing our lordship, we have forfeited the image of God.

We have to explain this in a way which shows that we do not match up to the fundamental anthropological definition 'Humanity is a lord as God is our Lord' if we seek to be lords without honouring God as our Lord. The point of our lordship plainly consists in our letting God be the Lord of humanity. Negatively formulated, this positive definition means that one who sets him or herself up as a lord of others is laying claim to God's place. By contrast, we prove ourselves to be true lords when we serve our fellows in freedom in such a way that both the one who serves and the one who is served have their Lord in God alone.

Once again, this can be clarified by referring to our upright stance which expresses our being in the image of God. This stance implies the possibility of bowing down. We can bow *because* we are lords. It is not a matter of bowing *before* someone: no lord does that. Rather it is a matter of *bowing down to* someone. Only one who walks erect can bow down deeply. This capacity belongs to our constitution as upright beings. We do not thereby surrender our lordship, but rather in this very way most clearly actualize that lordship.

Over against this there is the contrary 'possibility' (we should only call it this with some reservations) of allowing ourselves to be led astray by our upright stance into the desire to *transcend our humanity* and thus to aspire 'to the heights', to the place where— with good reason—we are not (or 'are not yet', as we suppose). One who aspires 'for the heights' in this way, who wishes in this way to transcend self, does not on principle bow down to others. For such a person is a lord, wishing to be lord among others, but without serving. But to wish to be lord among others without serving is to wish to be lord *over others*. This is what the human lord wills: to be a lord without limits. Such a person is without relations. And thereby such a person forfeits being in the image of God, which we formulated with the statement 'Humanity is a lord as God is our Lord'. When we cease *to set ourselves limits* and to affirm the limits imposed upon us by our societary ontological structure, we deny our humanness *de facto*.[21] One who wishes to be a lord without limits is incapable of lordship over him or herself. As lord over our fellows, we assume the role of God: *homo homino deus* (man is god to man). And this always means: *homo homini lupus* (man is a wolf to man).

By contrast, in Phil 2.6ff Jesus is called a lord since he did not consider equality with God a thing to be grasped, but rather *gave*

[21] Cf. E. Jüngel, 'Grenzen des Menschseins' in *Entsprechungen. Gott— Wahrheit—Mensch* (Munich, 1980), pp. 355–61. By the same token, when we wish to be lord over others, we misuse the *dominium terrae* (dominion of the earth) entrusted to us and pervert it into ruthless *imperium* (tyranny).

himself up, abased himself. In order to reveal to us what it means to be a lord, the Lord of humanity appeared as a human person, in the form of a slave who was obedient to death, in order that in death he should be highly honored by his Father, exalted and revealed as Lord. Jesus' resurrection from the dead is nothing other than the honouring of him in his death by God the Father, and in this, the eschatological raising of humanity as God's image. Humanity is justified in the crucified and risen Christ as an upright being. Humanity is not created to lie in the grave and become part of the forgotten past. Through the death and resurrection of Jesus Christ, death as our limit is shown to be a limit which we can shift in a relative way without fundamentally transcending it. This limit is nevertheless revealed 'from the other side' by the God who limits us in death, as an event which integrates and saves the whole history of our humanity and which transforms our past into an eternal future.

Accordingly, those who come to share in Christ's being in the image of God are able to respond to the honouring of him which takes place in his death and to the self-revealing glory which is expressed in his lowliness. Paul quotes the hymn in Philippians precisely because those to whom he writes can be addressed with that which is 'in Christ Jesus', so that 'in humility' they are to 'count others better than yourselves. Let each of you look not only to his own interests but to the interests of others' (Phil 2.3b–4). These remarks are paralleled in Rom 12.16 where Paul beseeches all Christians in Rome: 'do not be haughty, but give yourselves to humble tasks (or: associate with the lowly)'. And the very same thing is said again from God's viewpoint in Rom 15.5f: 'May the God of steadfastness and encouragement grant you to live in such harmony, in accord with Christ Jesus, that together you may glorify the God and Father of our Lord Jesus Christ'. To glorify God together as the Father of our Lord Jesus Christ, and in mutual freedom to count others better than oneself—in their indissoluble unity these are the ways in which God's image in humanity is fulfilled.

6. This Christological understanding of humanity in correspondence to God also modifies previous understandings of God. If Jesus Christ is confessed as Lord, then God is believed to be the one who raised Jesus from the dead. And therefore Jesus'

exaltation from the abasement of death must mean that God abandons himself to this abasement, in order to show himself to be 'the God and Father of our Lord Jesus Christ' in altercation with this death.

The clear consequence of this, formulated as a thesis, is: the distinguishing feature of divine *majesty* is a ceaseless movement into the *depths*. This thesis contains a reference to humanity, too, as the image of God. For as a ceaseless movement into the depths, the distinguishing feature of divine majesty is a ceaseless movement towards humanity. And so we could also say: the ceaseless movement into the depths is the *human* movement of divine majesty.

In this context it is appropriate to make clear that this human movement of divine majesty is not primarily motivated by *sin* but by God's own *love*, and so not only by a constraint imposed upon God but by the freedom of his grace. That it is in fact God's movement towards the sinner, that in fact God's free love leads his being not only to humanity but to suffering, relationless, sinful humanity, and brings him not only into the depths which are proper to humanity but also into the indecent depths of suffering in humanity's sin, not only in the fellowship of human life but in the fellowship of death which breaks off all fellowship in life—all this is certainly the consequence of sin. But we have to say that sin abounded so that God's grace abounded all the more (Rom 5.20). This means that the love of God is more fundamental than human sin, and therefore that God's movement into the depths is not primarily motivated by sin. It is not some human lack but rather the primordial overflowing of divine love which is ontologically primary.

In fact, however, the movement into the depths of humanity which is the distinguishing feature of divine majesty is a movement into the abyss of human imperfection, in order to raise us to the lowliness which is proper to us and which awaits us 'in Christ' (2 Cor 5.17). The fact that God's turning to humanity and his turning to the sinner coincide in the being of Jesus Christ gives us every justification for seeing that the divine movement into the depths which is the distinguishing feature of divine majesty has as its real aim not sinful humanity but the being of humanity as such. Indeed, this movement of divine righteousness is concerned with the justification of the godless as the human image of God. And so

God's relation to the sinner which takes place in the being of Jesus Christ has not only soteriological relevance but also anthropological relevance. The humanity which God saves is humanity as God intended us to be. In giving up his Son, God loved not only believers gathered together as the church, but also loved the world in them, though certainly it is only faith which acknowledges the significance of God's love and God's lowliness. Justification by faith is therefore not only the theological definition of the Christian but also the theological definition of *humanity*. For since the justifying word of God's abasement, heard by faith alone, is a word about God's abasement and our exaltation which takes place in the being of Jesus Christ, *it concerns all*.

We are therefore capable of responding to God's movement into the depths. We are those who are capable of responding to God's lowliness, those who are as such determined for correspondence to the majesty of God which reveals itself in this lowliness (Rom 6.5, 8.29; 1 Cor 15.49). This capacity belongs in a fundamental sense to our being in the image of God. The being of humanity is constituted and organized by the word. We are ourselves as hearers. Only because we can hear are we able to speak, think, act, be human. As hearers we centre ourselves upon God's relation to us, in order to correspond to our God.

7. Because of this, theological anthropology has at least this in common with philosophical anthropology, that it regards language as constitutive for human being. Both agree that humanity is socialised through language and that it is this which makes us really human. But on the basis of its definition of humanity as justified through God's Word, theological anthropology identifies a problematic state of affairs in the linguistic being of humanity. Two basic characteristics define our linguistic being. We are both those who are *addressed* and those who *state*. We are both at one and the same time. However, theological anthropology makes an ontological distinction between these two basic characteristics in their very togetherness. It must be clarified anthropologically not only that one of these two characteristics is the condition of possibility of the other, but also that that characteristic makes it possible—despite the other characteristic with its actual, if not necessary, threatening consequences—for us to be or to become again *human* persons.

The first basic characteristic of humanity as ζῷον λόγον ἔχον (a being endowed with language) is our capacity to make statements, represented by affirmative propositions. (In treating this characteristic in isolation, we need to be aware of a certain onesidedness and distortion in our method.) This characteristic of language is in some ways similar to counting, in that it contains a tendency to manufacture the world through the representation of actuality in signs, so that language becomes the totality of signs for a corresponding totality of things signified. As linguistic beings we are then distinguished from all other beings as *signifiers*, as those who give names to things and name them by name. This function of language socialises us, because there has to be agreement about the designation or names of things, whether that agreement already exists or has to be reached anew, or whether it be thought that this linguistic agreement is ontologically prior to our speaking. This aspect of our linguistic being, marking us out as those who state, is concerned with the process in which information is received and assimilated and used. The abundance of information which we have to assimilate, however, means that we must not only make distinctions by enumeration but also to make specific choices. Only in this way can we come to grips with the world. To say x not only means also to say y; to say x also means to say *not-x*. Otherwise, no definition, no reduction of the world to concepts would be possible. Otherwise, we would not be able to have dominion in the world.

This 'portraying' or signifying function of language in no way leaves unaltered the world which is portrayed or signified. When things are transferred into concepts, they are acted upon. If I have grasped something, I can 'make something of it'—and in the same way, if I have not grasped something, I am right to say 'I can't make anything of this'. In language there occurs a certain use of the world, which makes it possible for us subsequently to use the world in a different way from before. And because we are part of the world, we are no exception to this rule. In dealing with the world we can change the way in which we deal with ourselves, and in certain respects we thereby change ourselves. Changes in the world and changes in ourselves are linguistically determined. They are determined by the fact that we are speakers, that we think in the interplay of information and the assimilation of what we have grasped through language. In this respect, language makes it possible for us to think. And so thinking, i.e. the process of differentiating things through enumeration and making specific choices, is something like a command. Language commends, but thinking commands. At least in a limited sense, language leaves open what thinking concludes. But since in concluding and commanding thinking manifests itself in language that is, in new conventions about how to deal with the world and ourselves, this aspect of language can, indeed must, be called the language of dominion. The coincidence of language and thinking in the process of defining and conceptualising is an act of dominion *par excellence*, as the ancient philosophers realised and as the modern era is coming to see. There is, moreover, no essential distinction between understanding this dominion as a *grasping* of the world (for example, in a central metaphor of the modern era, that of the producer who seeks to *grasp hold of* the world), and understanding it as a dominion of pure θεωρία, theory (as in the metaphor of having an 'overall picture' of the world, 'grasping' it in this sense). To have an overall picture of the world is no less a striving for domination than 'grasping hold of' the world. Both have the same consequence: the human *deed*. Dominion is essentially active. Whether it seeks to change or to preserve (and, we should note, preservation is only possible through change) dominion causes activity. Such activity, however, unlike any possible animal activity, is directed by language. Language provides, as it were, an initial draft of such activity, above all for work itself. The same holds true for *experimental* activity, especially popular today, which would be scarcely possible without the open space which the commending word leaves to commanding thought. Insofar, then, as language provides us with initial drafts of our rational and irrational activities (and outbreaks!), and more importantly insofar as it provides us with initial drafts of our work which can in retrospect be distinguished from our activity, language in its apophantic structure is the origin of *homo faber* (the human maker). As linguistic beings who state, we are 'artificers'.[22] And because we socialize ourselves through language, in every successful work we erect a monument to that process of socialization. (At base, every successful work is a monument of this kind, whether it remains or passes away.)

---

[22] Cf. G. W. F. Hegel, *The Phenomenology of Mind* (London, 1949), pp. 704–8.

We have explained the fundamental linguistic structure of human beings as those who state, by looking at the dominion which is realized in thinking, without which no human work in which the world is changed would be possible. This lordly aspect of humanity does not have to stand in contradiction to human freedom. Quite the opposite! For theological anthropology, this lordly aspect of humanity as linguistic beings presents itself as a consequence of that freedom which makes humanity into humanity. If language assimilates the world in such a way that by enumerating and making choices it makes recommendations to thinking, which thinking for its part has to process into commands which administer the world, such acts of dominion are in their most fundamental aspect demonstrations of human freedom, on the basis of which we may properly be called 'lords'. 'The language of lordship' and 'the language of freedom' in *this* context ought not to be set against one another. For it is constitutive of human freedom to lead thinking to command, through initial drafts of our activities in language, and thus to enable the creation of works.

8. However, we must now look explicitly at the anthropological dimensions of two dangers which in fact are always present when we make statements and assimilate the world through works.

Part of the reality of existence is that everything has two sides, that the possibility of justice goes along with the possiblity of injustice, and so on. But part of faith in God is that we are made more aware of the conflicts and tensions and dangers which every good gift in fact brings with it. It would be rather too unworldly not to notice that the real dangers of our world are as a rule the consequences of the positive aspects, of the richness of our being. This holds true for faith and piety also. It is the curse of the evil deed that it must continually create evil. But at the very least we would be betraying remarkable theological naivety if we ignored the conflicts which can arise from the fact that even a good act can be a curse in its consequences – that we can be ruined and ruin others through the richness of our faith, that we can become tyrants for the sake of freedom. The devil is 'Part of that power, not understood/Which always wills the Bad, and always works the Good'.[23] Humanity, on the other hand, is the origin of that power

---

[23] Goethe, *Faust* I.1335f.

which wills the good and yet which with the good creates evil. And so when we consider the good nature of humanity, of humanity as the creatures which God made 'very good', we must at the very same time fix our attention upon those possible threats and dangers which are always given with human existence. Faith in justification makes us especially aware of this need.

One of the dangers and threats intrinsic to our existence as linguistic beings is that of a tendency towards a *total* assimilation of the world, a tendency which is bound up with the stating function of language. The world itself as a whole then becomes a completely human work, in every respect a manufactured and artificial world; in many respects, we already live in a world which is moving in this direction. It is not difficult to diagnose this tendency as a modern form of gnostic flight from the world, a form of disdain for the world which threatens to surrender at one and the same time the naturalness of the world and our humanity, giving way to a 'superman' who is ashamed of the body and places himself above the world as his own work.

One reason why this 'superman' does not succeed lies in the human desire for pleasurable union with another person which was happily given to us by our creator. To this pleasant impediment, we may add the other basic and constitutive characteristic of language through which we exist only as those who are addressed. Part of human physical desire is the language of love, in which we realize that we are addressed, and in which we seek not simply to address each other (which would mean that we would want only ourselves to speak) but rather to have another listen to us and experience him or herself as one who is addressed. In the language of love we remain faithful to the earth.

The relation of language, world and work, which is rooted in our linguistic existence as those who state, is bound up with a second danger and threat which is quite contrary to the first and which concerns our existence as agents. As a consequence of the lordly character of language, we have to act. Only as individuals can we escape this compulsion to act. Humanity as a whole, socialized through language, cannot do this. If we do not wish to perish, we must produce. And yet it is just this compulsion to produce which threatens to make us perish. This problem, whose roots lie in the nineteenth century and which still forces itself upon us today, could be formulated theologically by saying that we can no longer release ourselves from connection with our works. The actuality of this connection imprisons us. The work judges the person; the person is dominated by the work.

Theological anthropology cannot simply reverse this connection between person and work (as Luther would have said) by offering practical advice. But it may remind us of the fact that we are primarily those who are *addressed by God*. It is as such that we are persons. To be a person means to be able to be addressed by something over against us, which, in the midst of the indissoluble connection of person and work or person and productivity, makes me distinguishable as a self, an 'I'. The word of justification, which constitutes us anew in an eschatological way, gives us something over against us which addresses us and which takes us seriously, recognizes us and values us as persons in spite of our works. In the same way that the compulsion to produce and the indissoluble connection of person and work is not ape-like but human, so also is the capacity to be addressed by a personal reality over against us which in the midst of a person's works distinguishes that person from his or her works. This capacity to be addressed by God is the ontological implication of our justification through the Word of God. Our capacity to be addressed by someone over against us who absolves us from our works, whilst it certainly does not lift us out of the connection of person and works but simply out of the lordship of the works over the person, constitutes us as *free partners of God*.

This means that as those who are addressed we are granted, over against the actuality of what we assimilate as those who state, possibilities which cannot be assimilated but only enjoyed. Possibilities, which cannot be assimilated or made actual as works, are like open spaces which are realized only by themselves. Possibilities, which cannot be assimilated but only enjoyed, do not grow old, will not be exhausted if they remain; and they are realized when they pass away. It is decisive that such possibilities—unlike actuality which seeks to remain—are *capable of passing away*. Possibilities, which we cannot use (*uti*) but only enjoy (*frui*) can pass away without being exhausted as a result of being used. Some basic existential expressions of such possibilities are joy and gratitude. Real joy knows its limits. It can pass away. And concrete gratitude always refers to this or that, but never to everything.

So as linguistic beings who are addressed, we are beings of

possibility, whereas as linguistic beings who state we are beings of actuality. For us as linguistic beings, possibility has ontological priority over actuality (*contra* Aristotle).

I wish to clarify this by referring to a phenomenon which is decisive for our humanness, and which we ought to value highly: the art of forgetting. As those who state, who tend towards works and seek through those works to erect monuments to ourselves, we have to rely on the ability not to forget. Hence we stuff our computers full. What is not forgotten is known. And knowledge is power. Hence it may be that the past as it were tyrannizes the present and the future. To store up knowledge is to store up the past. Without computers, we would be overburdened with the past for the sake of knowledge. Having computers is not as yet a guarantee of the opposite. The computer does not necessarily but may well lead us to a future in which we are still ruled by the past.

As those who are addressed, however, we are conscious of the interplay between remembering and forgetting. As we are addressed as persons, we can forget our works when considering our persons. We can put them behind us and so become free for the future. Even with respect to knowledge itself we have to affirm that only the art of forgetting can form a human mind in such a way that it can really understand the world. One who forgets *nothing* is an uneducated person who will understand but little. This should not lead us to conclude that someone who forgets *everything* is for that very reason an educated and intelligent person. But one thing is clear: one who cannot forget cannot be happy. To address someone could, certainly, be very unpleasant. But to address someone *in God's name* always means to absolve that person of his or her past, to grant new possibilities and thus to grant the power to forget. This is human. As we address each other in this way, we correspond to the God who has justified us as human beings and called us out of the nothingness which we ourselves have made. It is thanks to this creative word which grants new possibilities that we exist. And as we express our existence through thanksgiving to God, we distinguish amongst ourselves between that which is worthy of remembrance and that which can be consigned to oblivion, not carelessly but confidently. If it is said of God that 'he will remember their sin no more' (Jer 31.34), then we for our part ought to forget the sin which God has forgiven. Such forgetting cannot of course be *commanded*: we have to be able to do it. And we are able to do it if we are granted a new future so that we are able to assimilate the past and the present. To be able to forget is our most creative possibility as linguistic beings. In it we turn the love which we have experienced into our own freedom.

9. To summarise: our true being is our correspondence to God's condescension in Jesus Christ, which is made possible for us through a word which addresses us. This condescension of God to us prevents us from rising to divinity. In the same way that God was revealed as Lord in lowliness, so the image of God is destined for the 'glory of the children of God' (cf. Rom 8.21) only through participating in this lowliness.

The specific task of theological anthropology, whose functions we have tried to set out, can thus be defined as *denying the divinity of humanity*. Although it is certainly fundamental to us that we can wish to make ourselves divine, theological anthropology must deny every tendency towards such divinization.

The *necessity* of denying the divinity of humanity follows from the inclination in human existence (an inclination not unknown to the unbeliever also) to ground itself and so to caricature itself. 'Man is by nature unable to want God to be God. Indeed, he himself wants to be God, and does not want God to be God'.[24]

The *possibility* of denying the divinity of humanity follows from the humanity of God as it took place in Jesus Christ. To let God be human in Jesus Christ, and for this very reason not to let humanity become God: this is the anthropological task which the Christian faith demands of thinking. Denying the divinity of humanity on the basis of the humanity of God would be the most rigorous interpretation of our humanity.

Cur deus homo, why did God become man? The *anthropological* answer to this question is, negatively, the denial of the apparently antithetical principles *homo homini deus* (man is god to man) and *homo homini lupus* (man is a wolf to man). The positive answer, on the other hand, ought not to be *homo homini Christus* (man is Christ to man)—a formula which contemporary theology likes to assert as an anthropological principle by referring to Luther in a rather inexact way.[25] Humanity in correspondence to God—we are such

---

[24] M. Luther, *Disputation Against Scholastic Theology*, *LW* 31, p. 10, thesis 17.
[25] Cf. M. Luther, *The Freedom of a Christian*, *LW* 31, pp. 366f.

as we remain human among others, becoming ever more human through them and for them and so with them: *homo homini homo,* man is man to man.

INVOCATION OF GOD AS THE ETHICAL GROUND OF CHRISTIAN ACTION

Introductory remarks on the posthumous fragments of Karl Barth's ethics of the doctrine of reconciliation

I

1. Karl Barth's *Church Dogmatics* remained a fragment, lacking the doctrine of redemption and the final part of the doctrine of reconciliation. The ethical chapter which concludes the doctrine of reconciliation of the *Church Dogmatics* is itself unfinished. One part of this chapter, the doctrine of baptism, was prepared by Barth for publication, though he held back paragraph 74, 'Ethics as a Task of the Doctrine of Reconciliation' which introduces the whole ethical chapter. This material was made available as a posthumous volume in Barth's collected works, together with the exposition of the Lord's Prayer which was drawn up for the central part of the ethics of the doctrine of reconciliation, but which breaks off with the interpretation of the second petition.[1] This posthumous volume demands the reader's attention in two ways. First, in reading these texts we need constantly to keep in mind their decidedly fragmentary character, not simply because what would have followed is lacking, but also because we are not certain that what we are dealing with here is the final form of Barth's thinking which he considered ready for publication. This should be borne in mind when one asks, perhaps, why this account of ethics discusses almost no particular ethical problems.[2] Second, the reader has to give

---

[1] E. Jüngel, H.-A. Drewes, ed., Karl Barth, *Das christliche Leben. Die Kirkliche Dogmatik IV/4. Fragmente aus dem Nachlass. Vorlesungen 1959–61* (Zürich, 1976). Page references in the body of this article are to the ET of this volume, *The Christian Life* (Edinburgh, 1981).

[2] For example, the exposition of the second petition of the Lord's Prayer does not repeat the positive analogies between the Kingdom of God, the Christian community and the civil community which are well-known from

attention to these texts in the setting of the *Church Dogmatics*, in such a way that not only are they to be understood from their whole context but also they are to show themselves to be useful in understanding that context. Not least, these posthumous texts of the *Church Dogmatics* are particularly interesting for the insight which they offer into the far-reaching modification of the whole manner of conceiving the ethics of the doctrine of baptism; the preface and appendix to the edition in the collected works furnish more precise information on this matter. Because they are fragmentary, the texts should not be overvalued; but nor should their fragmentary character lead us to undervalue them. They are illuminating in many ways, reflecting an ancient light and yet allowing that which we supposed ourselves to know to appear again in a new light.

From a systematic point of view, the fragments of the ethics of the doctrine of reconciliation are especially important within the *Church Dogmatics*, since Barth wants to understand the special ethics of both the doctrine of creation and the (no longer to be realized) doctrine of redemption as grounded in the ethics of the doctrine of reconciliation. That doctrine has 'the material primacy' (p. 9) over the other two forms of special ethics. For in the same way that in the earlier Christological-soteriological parts of the doctrine of reconciliation theology stood before its dogmatic centre, so here theology stands 'ethically . . . before the centre, the source of all the reality and revelation of God and man—Jesus Christ, who is not only the ontic but also the noetic basis of the whole of Christian truth and the Christian message' (p. 9). We are to understand both the being, action and commanding of God creator and redeemer, and the being and action of the human person as creature and 'future heir' (p. 9) out of the event of the reconciliation of God and

earlier writings by Barth, but only reflects upon the 'lordless powers' of the state when it renders itself absolute. But this should not lead us to shortcircuiting the discussion and concluding that Barth now had a less positive theological evaluation of the state. Rather, prayer for the coming of the Kingdom of God aims at liberation from the 'lordless powers' (which are perverted from being fundamentally good to being decidedly evil forces by the fact that they *become* lordless), so that here the positive definition of the state is not in question. We would not go wrong if we accepted that in the exposition of the next petition, 'Thy will be done on earth as it is in heaven', Barth gave an expressly 'positive' account of political power along the lines of his earlier publications.

humankind in Jesus Christ and out of the reconciling command of God. 'The core of every statement in the first and third chapters of special ethics will thus consist of statements taken from the second, of specific Christological and soteriological statements' (pp. 9f). And so in this text in the special ethics of the doctrine of reconciliation we have to do with the foundation of theological ethics as a whole, whose fundamentals have already been anticipated in a rather formal way in *Church Dogmatics* II/2 but which is now explicitly executed. With the doctrine of the command of God the reconciler we are concerned 'with the centre, core and origin of the totality as such' (p. 10). According to Barth, the special form of the ethics of the doctrine of reconciliation brings to speech 'as it were . . . the model of all that takes place between God and man' (p. 12). For from here both the ethics of creation and the ethics of redemption (which should equally be an ethics of the last judgment) are identifiable as different forms of one and the same command of the one God, 'who is gracious to man in Jesus Christ' (p. 9). The ethics of the doctrine of reconciliation makes clear that the fact of God's commanding is already grace, that God's command is nothing other than the gospel's claim upon us and, to that extent, 'the law of the gospel' (p. 35). This has consequences for our understanding of what comes into question as ethics in theology as a whole.

2. The ethics of reconciliation is eminently an ethics of freedom, not only because it has freedom as its object but much more because through its self-understanding as an intellectual discipline and its self-limitation it shows itself to be an ethics of freedom. The commanding of the God who is gracious to us in Jesus Christ is the expression of God's commanding which makes possible and demands immediate intercourse between God and ourselves and therefore also between ourselves and God. In this ethics we are concerned with 'the God who commands in royal freedom' (p. 6), but precisely so also with 'the man who acts in free responsibility in his relationship to this God' (p. 6). This ethic has to respect the freedom of both. It can and will not 'infringe upon . . . either the free disposing of God regarding the concrete meaning and content of his commanding or the free responsibility of the action of man. It has to respect the directness of the dealings between God and the man who obeys or disobeys' (p. 4). In terms of its ethical self-understanding this means that it can be set up neither as a 'legalistic

or casuistic ethics' nor as an 'obscure ethics of the *kairos*' (p. 5). One of the most impressive achievements of Barth's theology is the way in which his ethics, working from its Christological foundations and without lapsing into arbitrariness, does not seize in advance or ideologically anticipate concrete human action but rather sets it free as concrete action which in its concreteness is obedient through and through.

This holds true with regard to the being of the human person. Barth does not construct that person Christologically and then go on to construct his or her action. Rather he declares, in view of the person's existence as social and individual, historical and natural, rational and sensuous, what it is that makes this person human. And he does this by speaking of the man Jesus and his being as the truth of real humanity. Thus no one is violated by a theory, not even by a Christological construction. And the same is true of the action which is to be called good. It is not ethically constructed. It is not ethically deduced. Much more is it set out as something provoked from free responsibility, with the greatest definiteness called forth in the most profound freedom through God's gracious command.[3]

For Barth, then, ethics can only refer to 'the event—the many events—of the encounter between the commanding God and the man who acts' (p. 6); in this it must be 'a formed and contoured reference . . . which at least approximates to the concretion of that event' (p. 6). So ethics cannot 'anticipate' (p. 34) the event of concrete action and thus immediate intercourse between God and the human person. 'It cannot try to answer the question, "What shall I do?" ' (p. 34), but can only direct the human agent, who must act as a human being, to the *mandatum concretissimum* (most concrete command) of God. Ethics 'cannot itself give direction. It can only give instruction, teaching us how to put that question relevantly and how to look forward openly, attentively, and willingly to the answer that God alone can and does give' (p. 34).

But as ethics of reconciliation, theological ethics is already in its self-understanding as an intellectual discipline and in the self-limitation which springs from that, an ethics of freedom, since the demands of God which lay claim to the human person are 'no other than the sharply contoured imperatives of the love that is freely

---

[3] Cf. W. Krötke's remarks with particular regard to Barth's ethical fragments in 'Karl Barth und das Anliegen der "natürlichen Theologie" ', *Zeichen der Zeit* 30 (1976), pp. 177–183.

addressed to him, that freely affirms him, and that freely wills and accomplishes his salvation' (p. 36). The human person has for his or her part to correspond to these imperatives through love for God and through action which is in conformity to that love. The freedom in which God and the human person encounter each other directly is the freedom to love one another. 'Ethics has to adopt this criterion and apply it here and now to that event ... of God's commanding and man's response' (p. 35). The human person is claimed by the love of God and by that alone: this is the fundamental insight of Christian ethics, which equally makes human action thematic from the point of view of free decision and material determination.

3. In an ethics which is grounded in this way, we are not concerned with the purely formal structure of a categorical imperative of Christian provenance. One could, of course, advance such an imperative along the lines of *Dilige, et quod vis fac* (love, and do what you like),[4] in the sense that love, as a precept of the human will, sufficiently determines that will for every good work in such a way that it requires no further orientation. But the 'imperatives of the love of God' which demand human love transcend a purely formal ethics, as their plurality shows, without thereby grounding a material ethics of value. Barth's ethics moves beyond these alternatives. For on the one hand, what it considers as 'value' exists only in and through the act of divine commanding: 'God alone is good, and he decides what human action may be called good or not good' (p. 4). And on the other hand, it is intrinsic to God's goodness that it expresses itself not in a purely formal imperative but in a plurality of 'sharply contoured imperatives of the love that ... freely wills and accomplishes ... salvation' (p. 36), so that ethics as a whole is possible as instruction in the art of asking in a relevant way the question of what is to be done.

More precisely, this instruction is possible because the love of God which wills and accomplishes salvation demands a human action which is analogous to itself. It is this analogy, both supporting freedom and grounding attachment, which makes Barth's ethics— between the Scylla of 'a legalistic and casuistic ethics' (p. 5) and the

---

[4] Cf. Augustine, *Commentaire de la première épître de S. Jean*, Sources Chrétiennes 75 (Paris, 1984), p. 828.

INVOCATION OF GOD 159

Charybdis of 'an obscure ethics of the *kairos*' (ibid.)—into an ethics of liberty for material determination. For it understands the human act which is called good as a 'clear analogue' (p. 294) to God's act, which for its part is the act of the God who loves in freedom, and thus the act of the God who creates good in the overflowing of his own goodness. Analogy guards the difference between God and humanity, in that it emphasises as strongly as possible their partnership. In a human way, the human person has to act humanly and in no way divinely. But the goodness of such human action consists in the fact that 'even in its humanity (it) is similar, parallel and analogous to the act of God himself' (p.175). Barth desired to indicate the fact that in such analogous action we are concerned with the immediacy of the intercourse of the human person with God, by his decision to place the entire ethics of the doctrine of reconciliation under the term 'invocation of God', outlining it as an ethics of prayer.

4. The motif of analogy which dominates the ethics of the *Church Dogmatics* is already expressed within the systematic structure of the doctrine of reconciliation. The three parts assigned to the ethical chapter which was to form the fourth part-volume were evidently intended to correspond very closely to the three 'dogmatic' (in the narrower sense) chapters of the three part-volumes IV/1, IV/2 and IV/3. To the Christological movement of the Son of God into the far country in the first chapter, which considers the Lord as Servant and sets forth the judge as the one judged in our place, there corresponds the soteriological movement (which overcomes the counter-movement of sin as pride and fall) as it is portrayed in the justification of the sinner, in the gathering of the community and in the faith of the individual. In close analogy to this, the Christian life (understood as invocation of God) is brought to speech in the ethical context from the point of view of its foundation through an interpretation of baptism as prayer for the Holy Spirit. To the Christological movement of the homecoming of the Son of Man in the second chapter, which considers the Servant as Lord and sets him forth as royal man, there corresponds the soteriological movement (which opposes the counter-movement of sin as sloth and misery) as it is portrayed in the sanctification of humanity, the upbuilding of the community and in the love of the individual. In close analogy to this, the Christian life (understood as invocation of

God) is brought to speech in the ethical context from the point of view of its accomplishment in the act in which we lift up our hearts—*sursum corda!*—to invoke God as 'Our Father', by an exposition of the Lord's Prayer. To the Christological unity of both these movements in the third chapter, which considers Jesus Christ as the light of life and sets him forth as the true witness in the glory of his being as mediator, there corresponds the soteriological movement (which conquers the counter-movement of sin as falsehood and condemnation) as it is portrayed in the vocation of humanity, in the sending of the community and in the hope of the individual. In even closer analogy to this, the Christian life (understood as invocation of God) would, if the point had been reached, have been brought to speech finally in the ethical context from the point of view of its renewal through an interpretation of the Lord's Supper as thanksgiving (eucharist).

Moreover, the exposition of the individual petitions of the Lord's Prayer is laid out in manifest analogy to the architecture of the dogmatic parts of the doctrine of reconciliation which are constructed in parallel to each other. In the same way that there first Christology, then hamartiology and finally soteriology is brought to speech, so the ethics of the Lord's Prayer first speaks of the positive Christological grounding of the prayer (§77.1: The Great Passion; §78.1: The Revolt Against Disorder), then speaks of the negation to be overcome (§77.2: the ambivalence of the known and unknown God; §78.2: the disorder of the lordless powers); from here it goes on to speak of the divine act against this negation which is solicited in prayer (§77.3: Hallowed be Thy name!; §78.3: Thy Kingdom come!); and finally in analogy to this it speaks of the corresponding human action with a view to the world (§77.4: The Precedence of the Word of God; §78.4: *Fiat iustitia*).

5. The exposition of the Lord's Prayer also sets out in material terms the analogy between divine and human action. The difference which this analogy presupposes, the distinction between God's action and ours, is not, however, defined in an abstract way as a relationless difference of pure dissimilarity, but rather defined concretely as a relation of invocation. Invocation of God as 'Our Father' is 'the basic act of the Christian ethos' (p. 102). This invocation expresses the fact that we ask God for that which God alone can give. And it also expresses in a concrete way the

distinction between God's act and our action. For we invoke God in order to ask him for that which he alone can bring about: 'Hallowed be Thy name! Thy Kingdom come!' And in that the distinction comes to expression in this concrete way. Its character as a positive relation is set forth. For in that we ask and 'directly from below' (p. 152) invoke the God who is distinct from us to accomplish a work distinct from our own work, we for our part are already doing that which corresponds to the divine act for which we make our plea. In the act of invoking God, the human person is already in the picture as an agent who corresponds to the God who acts, and this, indeed, in the societary structure of a 'we', incorporated into which every 'I' does not pray to 'my Father' but to '*our* Father'.[5] Accordingly the fundamental ethical question should not be (as with Kant) 'What should I do?' but 'What should we do?'. This 'we' has a fundamental existence: something hidden, insofar as according to Barth it was human nature (not 'a man') which was assumed enhypostatically in the mode of being of the Son of God; something manifest in the event of common invocation of God. The degree to which this 'we', which is not self-constituting but already constituted, can come to expression beyond the basic act of invocation in the 'horizontal behaviour' of the Christian is a problem which Barth does not explicitly treat here.

This, then, is the fundamental ethical analogy: that in our invocation of God commanded of us by the God whose 'being is in act',[6] we are exalted to a life in act which corresponds to God, so that in our very relation to God we 'may and should be truly active' (p. 102). In the same way that God is no *deus otiosus* (redundant God), so also the human person is no *homo otiosus* (redundant human person). This is Barth's 'synergism' whose note has already been heard in the doctrine of baptism. The notion of a *co-operatio* (co-operation) between God and the human person in their mutual dealings with one another has here found a genuine Protestant, 'evangelical' formulation. In that this *co-operatio* has its *Sitz im Leben*

[5] The societary structure of the 'Our Father' becomes particularly pointed when we bear in mind that to the usual lexical content of God's name as Father there also belongs 'the community of the father of the family in the midst of his sons and heirs who participate together with him in the family property': A. Schenker, 'Gott als Vater—Söhne Gottes', *Freiburger Zeitschrift für Philosophie und Theologie* 25 (1978), p. 53.

[6] Cf. *CD* II/1 §28.1.

in prayer, that is, at the point where the distinction between divine and human action is experienced most clearly and sharply, then the Pauline notion that we are συνεργοί Θεοῦ (God's fellow-workers, 1 Cor 3.9) is given a new turn, which is able to help both Catholic teaching (properly understood) and the reformed understanding make some common progress. 'The grace of God is the liberation of these specific people for free, spontaneous, and responsible co-operation in this history' of the dealings between God and ourselves. In that God graciously commands us to invoke him as our Father, he 'purges himself from the base suspicion that he is (a) deity whose divine nature condemns him to be the only one at work' (p. 102).

6. If invocation of God, as the 'basic act of the Christian ethos' is the fundamental analogy which constitutes the human person as an agent and therefore as a co-worker in a manner which corresponds to God, then it has the function of a material analogue with regard to that which the Christian has to do in life in the future, whose material analogates are the structures of his or her 'worldly' action, which Barth defines in analogy to the action which Christians ask God to perform. Nevertheless, because all that the Christian does is determined and accompanied by the invocation of God, one may speak of 'worldly' action only in the sense that, just as in prayer the hearts of the agents are 'lifted up to God' and the whole world brought before him, so also each individual act keeps faith with the world precisely by resisting in an uncompromising way its tendency to absolutise itself, to make itself into a principle—what we might call its 'religious interpretation'. The action of Christians is 'worldly' insofar as 'they can say to all principles only a relative Yes or No' and thus 'think and speak in terms of theses and not principles' (p. 268) and act accordingly. Christians 'must resolutely refuse to swallow some of the strengthenings they are offered in order that they may go through world history with a stiffened backbone. In doing so, they will show that they have real backbone' (p. 268). In this sense those who invoke the heavenly Father seek the best for world and city. In this sense, defined by the thoroughly spiritual 'basic act of the Christian ethos', they act in a thoroughly worldly manner. They do so by analogy to their prayer, zealously striving for the hallowing of God's name by God himself; and thus for the putting to an end of the ambivalence in which God is known and unknown, to which the revelation of God stands opposed and of

which they themselves are guilty; and finally for 'the precedence of the Word of God' (p. 168). In this way they rise up and break out against the 'vacillation between the humanity and inhumanity of' their own 'thoughts and words and works' (p. 203) which mirrors this ambivalence, but also against all thoughts, words and works within and without the church which make both it and they incur 'some personal guilt for the regime of the balance of light and darkness' (p. 184). In their action they are loyal to the world by testifying through this action to the ontological impossibility of 'atheism' and all its variations. Just as Jesus Christ has taken them 'up into the movement of his own prayer' (p. 64) and so has become the origin of their action as Christians, so they for their part in their activity take the world into the vocative 'Father!' with which they invoke God and which 'as a vocative, whether expressed or not, is the primal form of thinking, the primal sound of speaking and the primal act of obedience demanded of Christians. In other words, it is the primal act of the freedom Christians are given, the primal form of the faithfulness with which they may correspond to his faithfulness' (p. 51).

7. By interpreting the word 'Father' as a word of invocation and correspondingly the Christian life as a life in the act which lifts itself up in invocation, Barth brought to speech the 'basic act of the Christian ethos'. Further, by interpreting prayer for the hallowing of God's name as the Christian's passion and so—in sharp contrast to the traditional ethics with its ideal of μεσότης (the mean)[7]— setting forth passion as a condition of what may be called good action, Barth recalled our attention to zeal for the precedence of the Word of God as the spiritual sting in and spur to all worldly action by the Christian. In the exposition of the petition for the coming of the Kingdom of God, at which point the ethics breaks off, Barth's ethical instruction becomes more defined with respect to the 'worldliness' of Christian behaviour. In analogy to the establishment of the Kingdom which will be effected eschatologically by God alone, Christians struggle on earth for *human* righteousness by hurrying towards that future. And in doing this they testify to all who hunger and thirst for righteousness that they shall be satisfied. That the promise of the beatitude can even now become concrete

---

[7] Cf., for example, Aristotle, Eth. Nic. 1106 b 27f.

in the parabolic form of human acts for human righteousness is part of the dignity of those good works through which the Christian is a human being to others, and sees the other person, in all the compulsions of that person's circumstances and roles, as distinguishable from those compulsions, and so has a human being, a self. By drawing alongside the other person for his or her own sake, the Christian testifies that that person has 'God on (his) side' (p. 270). *Homo homini homo* (man a man to man)—this fundamental worldly relation testifies to the one who 'however mistakenly or strangely or impotently, ask(s) after and seek(s) the right and dignity of man' (p. 270) that Jesus' beatitude is both materially and linguistically justified, as for its part it promises, in a fundamentally worldly metaphor, 'that he will be satisfied' (p. 270).

II

1. Ethics as instruction in prayer—this is the main thrust of the doctrine of the command of God the reconciler with which the fourth volume of the *Church Dogmatics* would have concluded. Even in the fragmentary form in which the ethics of the doctrine of reconciliation exists, Barth's intentions can be clearly perceived: to set forth 'the basic meaning of every divine command' (p. 44) as '*invocation* of the gracious God in gratitude, praise and above all petition' (p. 43). 'The question of what may be called *good* human action' (p. 3) finds its answer in an ethics of prayer.

This way of handling the ethical problem is not only remarkable because it is so startling. Of course, there is something startling about it. The fact that the ethics of the doctrine of reconciliation in the *Church Dogmatics* takes this form is hardly foreseen, to such an extent that Barth himself was in some measure startled to discover that it is possible to understand 'the command "Call upon me" (Ps 50.15) to be the basic meaning of every divine command' (p. 44). But to answer the question 'What should we do?' with the command to pray is, however, also startling in the context of modern formulations of the ethical question. Immanuel Kant, who defined religion from a subjective point of view as the 'recognition of all duties as divine commands',[8] expressly cautioned against

---

[8] I. Kant, *Religion Within the Limits of Reason Alone* (New York, 1960), p. 142.

'praying, thought of as inner formal service of God'; it is 'a superstitious illusion . . .; for it is no more than a *stated wish* directed to a Being who needs no such information regarding the inner disposition of the wisher' so that 'nothing is accomplished by it, and it discharges none of the duties to which, as commands of God, we are obligated; hence God is not really served'.[9]

By contrast, Barth outlines an understanding of invocation as action demanded of us, as action in the strongest sense, as that which may be called good human action. Once we become aware of this contrast, Barth's handling of the ethical problem is no longer as startling as it appears on first acquaintance. In his understanding of the ethics of the doctrine of reconciliation we are dealing with the sharpest expression of the fundamental decision in Barth's theology, a decision which makes the *Church Dogmatics* so provocative, both inside and outside the area of theology. The systematic power of the *Church Dogmatics* and its sheer ability as scholarly communication are once again brought into the discussion when we answer the question 'What shall we do?' (not 'What shall we pray?') with 'You should pray: "Our Father, who art . . ." '. In this understanding of ethics as instruction in prayer, both the real starting-point of the whole *Church Dogmatics* and the full range of its problems are present in the most acute way. Here I draw attention only to the most significant of these.

2. Barth's decision to discuss theological ethics as part of dogmatics means positively that even the question of what may be called good human action is thematic as a question posed by the highly particular event of the revelation of the triune God. Not only the answer, we note, but even the very question itself owes its origin to that unique event, which Barth customarily indicates in formal terms as the event of the Word of God. 'Theological ethics . . . finds both this question and its answer in God's Word' (p. 3). Along with this there goes a negative decision that for theology there can be no ethical problematic which precedes its dogmatic questioning and is independent of it, which could then be a possible horizon within which theology's dogmatic assertions might be verified. Consider a thesis such as that of Gerhard Ebeling: 'The ethical sets before us the problem of general obligation . . . But precisely this

[9] Ibid., pp. 182f.

makes ... the phenomenon of the ethical so significant for the dogmatic task. Here we are confronted with the problems of being human, which obtrude themselves independent of attitude towards the Christian faith'.[10] Such a thesis can only regard Barth as to be contradicted. For he plainly designates 'the problem of ethics ... the great theological problem',[11] and similarly designates 'the ethical question ... the existential problem of man' which 'theology recognises and treats ... as its most characteristic problem'.[12] For according to Barth it is 'not as if man first exists and then acts. He exists in that he acts. The question whether and how far he acts rightly is the question whether and how far he exists rightly'.[13] This insight is evidently for Barth a dogmatic judgment, firmly anchored in his definition of the relationship of gospel and law, so that he expressly sees himself as obliged 'to be on ... guard against an imminent possibility of aberration ... as though somewhere ... there is a problem of existence which, among other things, theology with its special presuppositions and methods has also to tackle'.[14] Over against this, it is only 'by the Word of God' that the problem of the ethical or the ethical question first 'acquires theological relevance'. The asking of the ethical question already has its 'origin' in the Word of God. As a question 'which is not first answered in the Word of God but already grounded in it', as a question 'which in the first instance is put by the Word of God itself',[15] the ethical question is a matter for theology.

How can an ethics drawn up in this way, one whose question can be treated 'only in this subordination and dependence',[16] make a claim to be generally obligatory? Does it not abandon its universal relevance? Barth can formulate the ethical problematic as the question of 'the Christian life'[17]—and not, note, in the context of the doctrine of reconciliation but already at this early stage, in the context of his fundamental discussion of the relation of dogmatics

[10] G. Ebeling, 'Die Krise des Ethischen und die Theologie. Erwiderung auf W. Pannenbergs Kritik' in idem., *Wort und Glaube* II (Tübingen, 1969), pp. 47f.
[11] *CD* I/2, p. 790.
[12] Ibid., p. 793.
[13] Ibid.
[14] Ibid.
[15] Ibid.
[16] Ibid., p. 794.
[17] Ibid.

and ethics. How can a theological ethics which understands itself as a specialised inquiry into the Christian life do justice to the—at the very least—peculiar contemporary form of the ethical problem 'which not only has to do with what is bound up with the Christian faith', since in dealing with the ethical a 'common human problem' appears, in the light of whose 'manifestness' and 'crisis' everyone can be addressed?[18] 'It would be a serious matter if a theological ethics knew only how to talk of that which concerns Christians alone,' remarks Ebeling rightly.[19] Does not Barth's basic decision lead to just this grave consequence? Is that consequence not very definitely present if ethics is set out as exposition of the prayer which Jesus taught his *disciples* to pray? What kind of understanding of morality is at the root of an ethics which, conceived as the doctrine of the command of God, discerns in 'the command "Call upon me" (Ps 50.15) ... the basic meaning of every divine command' and in 'invocation according to this command ... the basic meaning of all human obedience'? Indeed, can such a theory claim at all to be an *ethical* theory? Can it in any way have morality as its object?

3. To indicate the acuteness of this problem, I contrast Barth's view of ethics with a text from his teacher Wilhelm Herrmann, which connects with the views of Kant which we have already cited and which Ebeling[20] cites as testimony for his view of the 'manifestness of the ethical': 'Morality is contaminated in its root as soon as one notion, however holy to every pious person, is made the *ground* (italics Ebeling's) of moral certainty, namely the notion that the moral command is the command of God. Without this notion we certainly cannot live as Christians. But if we see in it the ground of our moral certainty, we have no moral certainty at all'.[21]

Barth can hardly have come to the decision to conceive of ethics as the doctrine of God's command, with its centre as the doctrine of the command of God the reconciler, in ignorance of the objections which his teacher Herrmann time and time again (almost,

[18] G. Ebeling, 'Die Krise des Ethischen', p. 47.
[19] Ibid.
[20] G. Ebeling, 'Die Evidenz des Ethischen und die Theologie' in *Wort und Glaube* II, p. 21, n. 18.
[21] W. Herrmann, 'Religion und Sittlichkeit' in idem., *Schriften zur Grundlegung der Theologie* I (ed. P. Fischer-Appelt, Munich, 1966), p. 265.

we might say anachronistically, as a precaution against his pupil) hammered into his hearers and readers. Barth clearly intended to give in his way even more radical significance to Herrmann's view that 'real morality . . . is the genuine dependence of the free'.[22] But of course the starting-point in the one case is as antithetical as it could be to that in the other case. For Herrmann, genuine obedience of the free is only humanly possible when the person 'produces the notion of the good from him or herself' instead of 'simply taking it upon him or herself as something given'.[23] For Barth we are only confronted with the question of what may be called *good* human action when we are told what is good and what God requires of us (cf. Mic 6.8). But precisely on the basis of such a question of what deserves to be called good at all, oriented in this way to the Word of God, we reach the dimension in which the genuine obedience of the free is seriously considered. Barth would agree with Herrmann that 'we are not dealing with morality but with an expression of the deepest immorality' if we make it a condition of right behaviour 'that we must bow down to an almighty will', and if we are then as a consequence expressly 'told what this will commands us to do'.[24] Barth's ethics knows no such almighty will before which we must bow down solely by virtue of its omnipotence. Within the terms of his ethics, such an abstractly conceived almighty will has nothing to say. For Barth's ethics, the commanding God is always the God who has already turned to us in the gospel, and therefore the gracious God. For all their relative independence, in each of the three forms of special ethics, that is, the command of the creator, the reconciler and the redeemer, there comes to speech 'the one command of the one God "who is gracious to man in Jesus Christ" ' (p. 9). The 'material primacy' (p. 9) of the second article, which Barth maintains with great emphasis—even with respect to the general problem—leads to the fact that the condition for moral behaviour is virtually the opposite of submission to an almighty will. If the God who is gracious to us in Jesus Christ is the divine will which commands and lays a claim upon us, then the view which Herrmann combatted, 'that in the regions high above human affairs we are to seek the highest'[25] which tells us what may be

[22] ibid., p. 267.
[23] Ibid., p. 266.
[24] Ibid., p. 265.
[25] Ibid., p. 269.

called good human action, is replaced by a view of ethics which, like Herrmann,[26] bases the genuine obedience of the free in the trust which 'through the self-revealing goodness' of the—not, as Herrmann says, 'other'[27] but rather 'wholly other'—God is made a pressing possibility and therefore an urgent demand. What Herrmann formulates in a general anthropological way as a condition for understanding 'the moral', Barth set forth in Christological singularity as an ontological and noetic condition for the 'ethical question'. Through this Christological singularity Barth gave unequivocal definition to the concept of the self-revealing good, and identified the trust which corresponds to that good as faith in the God who is gracious to us in Jesus Christ.

4. Against this concrete identification of the trust without which moral behaviour is not possible with faith in the gracious God, one could object that it renders problematic the universality of the ethical problem. But what use is the universality of the question of what may be called good human action if the concept of goodness is itself equivocal? Barth's proposal, on the other hand, profoundly related to reality, is just this: it is an error to hold that the goodness of human conduct 'can be directly perceived and therefore demonstrated, described, and set up as a norm'.[28] This is not only true of the goodness or holiness of the Christian life. Barth is making a dogmatic judgement as much as he is giving expression to experience of life when he disputes the view 'that the goodness' both of human conduct in general and of specifically Christian conduct and thus 'the holiness of the Christian character . . . is not hidden with God in Christ (in spite of Col 3.3), but can be directly perceived and therefore demonstrated, described and set up as a norm'. Barth's assertion that 'the holiness of the Christian character is not less visible in Jesus Christ, but also not less hidden in the life of Christians, than the remaining content of Christian proclamation'[29] is a plea for the unequivocalness of the concept of the goodness of good conduct, and for consent to the real ambiguity of that which is called good *extra Christum* (outside Christ). It is not possible to think of anything within or even outside of the world

[26] Ibid.
[27] Ibid.
[28] *CD* I/2, p. 782.
[29] Ibid.

that can be held to be unreservedly good, other than that human action which corresponds to the gracious will of God, which is revealed as such in Jesus Christ alone. The 'theoretical' exclusivity with which this univocity of the good is 'purchased' is surpassed by 'practical' universality. For Jesus Christ—and, we should note, he himself, and 'no a priori theology, anthropology, or even Christology'—grounds the 'assurance' that the gracious God and the person who he claims 'belong together' as necessarily as 'father and child'. 'This accounts for the astonishingly natural way in which the New Testament always speaks of God in practical relation to man and of man as claimed in practice for God. In his whole nature and its perversion man belongs from the very first to God' (p. 43).

5. Barth does not regard this self-evidence as rendered problematical by the modern era. And so he unfolds his ethics of the *Christian* life as the ethics of *human* life rightly understood. When God is invoked as 'our Father', we represent human life as such. For 'man is empowered for this (invocation), and obligated to it, by God's grace. In it man in his whole humanity takes his proper place over against God' (p. 43). And in his zeal for the precedence of the Word of God, in his prayer 'for the hallowing of God's name by God himself', there arises from the Christian a way of behaving which is for 'people as such, and concretely the people with whom he has dealings in his place and time' (p. 203). The exclusive nonconformism of the Christian, who is claimed by the God who is gracious in Jesus Christ and of whom zeal for God's honour is categorically demanded, is 'most striking' in the fact that he offers 'to other men of the world ... the image of a strangely human person' (p. 204). The 'astonishingly natural way in which the New Testament always speaks of God in practical relation to man and of man as claimed in practice for God' (p. 43) also shows that Barth, too, holds it to be decidedly 'bad if a theological ethics is able to speak of what only concerns Christians'.[30]

To close, I wish to allude a little further to the problem of the relevance for truth of this ethic whose foundational value consists in invocation of God.

6. If invocation of God, and therefore prayer, and above all

[30] G. Ebeling, 'Die Krise des Ethichen', p. 47.

INVOCATION OF GOD

petitionary prayer, is that which may be called good human action, then ethics is in a way faced with the question of truth in a form more radical than any other in which it is usually asked. The grounding of moral action in the categorical imperative is a possible parallel. For imperative and petitionary prayer, command and invocation, are all far removed from what can traditionally be held to be in any way true. If truth is understood as *adaequatio intellectus et rei* (correspondence of mind and thing), then only propositions which count as expressions of the intellect, only the λόγος ἀποφαντικός can make a claim to be true, and accordingly be either verified or falsified. Only a proposition which brings a state of affairs to truth can be true or indeed false. A petitionary prayer is as little a proposition as is a demand. The statement of Mt 4.17, 'the Kingdom of Heaven is at hand', can be true or false. But the statement of Mt 6.10, 'Thy Kingdom come', can be neither true nor false. Apophantic language is always language which should exhibit 'what is the case',[31] and thus is either true or false. However, 'a prayer is a sentence but is neither true nor false'.[32] Consequently, an ethics oriented to prayer, like a morality oriented to a categorical imperative, seems to be irrelevant to truth. This irrelevance to truth becomes as it were even more potent if invocation is for its part grounded in a 'word of command'. If neither a prayer nor a command can be true or false, then even less can a prayer which is commanded be true or false. The triumphant centre of this ethic of commanded prayer appears to be Hobbes' amoral statement (which so deeply concerned Carl Schmitt): '*authoritas, non veritas, facit legem*' (authority, not truth, makes law).[33]

The alternative to the understanding of truth as correspondence between statement and state of affairs is to understand it much more primordially as that interruption of the ontological cohesion of the (created) world (the cohesion of its actuality), through which we attain to the position of being over against our world so that something like *adaequatio intellectus et rei* becomes possible. For this elemental interruption of the cohesion of our actuality ought to contain within itself an even more primordial correspondence and unconditional trustworthiness. Is invocation of God this kind of elemental interruption of our life and so of the world?

[31] L. Wittgenstein, *Tractatus logico-philosophicus* (London, 1961) 4.024.
[32] Aristotle, De int. 17 a 4.
[33] T. Hobbes, *Leviathan*, XXVI.

7. It is indeed such, in that it is by no means arbitrary but rather that interruption which occurs indispensably when God reveals himself, the God who is absolutely trustworthy and who in the midst of ever greater contradictions is yet more congruent with himself. For then invocation comes from truth which is occurring (in something of the same way in which Kant's categorical imperative comes from the legislative reason). And it bears within itself the certainty of being answered. As the interruption of the cohesion of the world, it brings that world into a light which does not issue from itself, a light which makes everything appear in a new light. In this sense, an ethics of invocation gives an eschatological perspective to human conduct. It is in no way a legal ethics of mere obligation but rather an ethic of the certainty of the Coming One and thus of the obligation which has already been made possible, and made possible for all. For since when it is understood in this way invocation of God as the Father who wills to have all as his children is an interruption of the cohesion of the whole of actuality, those who pray after this manner incorporate all people into their invocation of God as our Father. They pray like the watchmen 'on the walls of sleeping Jerusalem . . . to the glory of God and the salvation of all who dwell within the walls . . . Their prayer when they cry "Our Father" is a prophetic prayer' (p. 102); as such, their prayer is the basic action by which they fashion the world in a new light. In the manner in which they deal with the world and those who belong to it, there is reflected the light which, coming into the world, enlightens all. Precisely because the action demanded of Christians reflects this eschatological light, φῶς ἐρχόμενον (Jn 1.9), Christians show themselves to be those 'strangely human persons' (p. 346). They behave in such a way that the precept of their will may in every case be equally the principle of a general giving of the law, in which it is clearly true that *veritas, non authoritas, facit legem* (truth, not authority, makes law).[34]

[34] Accordingly the Christian is not irritated but rather pleasantly surprised, when from a quite different foundation value, others know themselves to be obliged to act in the same way. For the same truth is at work in the *regnum gratiae* (kingdom of grace) and the *regnum potentiae* (kingdom of power).

EXTRA CHRISTUM NULLA SALUS—A PRINCIPLE OF NATURAL THEOLOGY?

Protestant reflections on the 'anonymity' of the Christian

I

By its very nature, Christianity is not only not anonymous but explicitly hostile to anonymity. Not only is Christian faith recognised by the name of the one to whom it owes its existence and to whom it refers, but it also wants to be recognised by and burdened with this name. For this reason, confessing with one's lips is part of believing with one's heart (Rom 10. 9f.). And for the same reason, Christianity entered its religious environment as an extremely polemical 'religion'. This hostility towards its religious environment is the polemical expression of the Christian faith's hostility towards anonymity. Both historically and systematically, the expressions 'anonymous Christianity' or 'anonymous Christians' seem paradoxical. And there are the gravest hermeneutical objections about its theological use.

But there are also practical, or, if you will, moral reservations. Here we may only hint at them by asking whether it would not amount to a gross violation of respect for others if they had to find themselves addressed as anonymous Christians, only because they strive to live out the mystery of being human in their own, non-Christian (in the usual sense that the word would have for them) way. Talk of anonymous Christians could unintentionally overstep the limits and become offensive. Moreover, logically it implies the assertion that 'non-Christian' is a pseudonym, which could easily be interpreted as a reproach. In short, the language of anonymous Christianity is anything but felicitous.

Having stated in advance these reservations and recommended that a better name be found for the matter under consideration, we attempt in what follows to discuss from a genuinely reformed Protestant starting-point the dogmatic problem indicated by the infelicitous expression—though, of course, 'the name itself is unimportant'.[1] For the problem which Rahner indicates by speaking of anonymous Christians touches upon the central questions of Christian theology, and to this extent is important for controversial theology.

First of all, then, I venture to cast some doubt upon Rahner's supposition that 'from a dogmatic point of view, this doctrine is perhaps even a *peripheral* phenomenon whose necessity, lawfulness and correctness derive from many other individual data of ecclesiastical teaching'.[2] This is contradicted by the Christological grounding which Rahner gives to this doctrine and without which it would, indeed, be without foundation.[3] The following reflections concern the extent to which faith in Jesus Christ as the Son of God become man necessarily implies that which is indicated by the infelicitous expression 'anonymous Christian.' As we look, at this, however, we will have to bring out the importance of that hostility towards anonymity which we have already reminded ourselves to be a basic characteristic of Christian faith, and we will have to show that it is intrinsic to correct theological thinking in this matter—as Rahner himself does, though critics easily overlook the fact. If we were successful in bringing both together, the result would be a new approach to solving the old problem of natural theology.

---

[1] K. Rahner, 'Anonymous Christians' in *Theological Investigations* VI (New York, 1974), p. 398.

[2] Ibid., p. 396.

[3] Cf. ibid., pp. 393f. Heinrich Ott confuses occasion and foundation when he asserts that 'Rahner's line of argument can certainly call upon many universalistic concepts in the Bible' ('Existentiale Interpretation und anonyme Christlichkeit' in E. Dinkler, ed., *Zeit und Geschichte* (Tübingen, 1964), pp. 374f.). But in the essay quoted ('Dogmatic Notes on "Ecclesiological Piety"'), *Theological Investigations* V (London, 1966), pp. 336–65), Rahner does not ground his thesis biblically but rather—to put the matter somewhat superficially—'sociologically'. The essay quoted by Ott argues from the doctrine of grace. The real grounding of the thesis that the human person is an anonymous Christian can be found in the essay 'Christianity and the Non-Christian Religions' (ibid., pp. 115–34) and above all in the essay 'On the Theology of the Incarnation' (*Theological Investigations* IV (London, 1966), pp. 105–20). Rahner certainly only later referred explicitly to the Christological grounding of his thesis: cf. 'Anonymous Christians' (*Theological Investigations* VI (London, 1969), pp. 390–98).

II

One important way of understanding 'natural theology' in the sense of the assertion that 'God, the beginning and end of all things, can be known with certitude by the light of natural reason from created things'[4]—would be to say that it enables us to identify every person as an 'anonymous theist' or at least as in essence a *potential* 'anonymous theist'. Rahner has given this function of natural theology a Christological-soteriological turn by supplementing the possibility of natural knowledge of God, which according to Catholic teaching is indisputable, with the doctrine 'that every human being is really and truly exposed to the influence of divine, supernatural grace which offers an interior union with God and by means of which God communicates himself whether the individual takes up an attitude of acceptance or of refusal towards this grace'.[5] (It remains an open question whether this supplementary idea could not equally serve as a basis of the extended doctrine.) He says unmistakably that this grace 'is given to men as a gratuitous gift on account of Christ',[6] that the salvation which this gift effects is and must be 'the salvation won by Christ',[7] since 'there is no salvation apart from Christ'.[8] This proposal could be seen as the starting-point for a 'natural Christology'. But it seems to me more correct to understand it in the sense of a new Christological basis for 'natural theology'. This would be supported by the main point of the proposal, that 'it must be possible to be not only an anonymous theist but also an anonymous Christian'.[9]

The truth on which this proposal rests is formulated in the insight which Rahner has expounded more than once, namely that the salvation which comes to us is 'Christ's salvation, since there is no other salvation'.[10] *Extra Christum nulla salus* (outside Christ there is no salvation)—without losing its exclusiveness but rather as the furthest reach of that exclusiveness, this exclusive truth claim becomes an inclusive granting of a truth that concerns every human

---

[4] Vatican I, Session III: *Dogmatic Constitution concerning the Catholic Faith*, II, in R. J. Deferrari, ed., *The Sources of Catholic Dogma* (London, 1957), p. 443.
[5] K. Rahner, 'Christianity and the Non-Christian Religions', p. 123.
[6] Ibid., p. 121.
[7] Ibid., p. 122.
[8] Ibid., p. 123.
[9] Ibid., p. 132.
[10] Ibid.

being as such. For its part, the claim expresses the identity of the soteriological uniqueness of Jesus Christ with the anthropological universality of the God-man. Rahner offered a more specific basis to this unity of soteriological exclusivity and anthropological universality in the being of Jesus Christ in the course of his remarks 'On the Theology of the Incarnation'.[11] Later Rahner explicitly noted that this already prepared and grounded the proposal about anonymous Christians: 'If one takes it seriously, that God has become man, then—it must be said—man is that which happens when God expresses and divests himself. Man is accordingly in the most basic definition that which God becomes if he sets out to show himself in the region of the extra-divine. And conversely, formulating it from the point of view of man: man is he who realizes himself when he gives himself away into the incomprehensible mystery of God. Seen in this way, the incarnation of God is the uniquely supreme case of the actualization of man's nature in general'.[12]

On this Christological basis, an entirely new construction of natural theology presents itself, one of whose basic principles would be the thesis: since *extra Christum nulla salus*, then every human being must—*per propter Christum datam* (by Christ's own gift)—be capable of being an anonymous Christian.

It ought to be noted, however, that although according to this doctrine the being of Jesus Christ, the salvation which does not exist without him, and the grace which offers this salvation all constitute an *ontological* link to the rest of humanity, nevertheless the 'anonymity' of being a Christian is not asserted of every human being in actuality. In this respect Rahner's proposal remains within the limits to natural knowledge of *God* drawn by Vatican I, according to which we may not assert more than the possibility of certain knowledge. By analogy, the Christological basis of being an anonymous Christian shows no more than that 'it must be *possible* to be ... an anonymous Christian'. Rahner specifies particular conditions for the realization of this possibility which we will not consider here. In the present context we are only interested in the fact that Rahner explicitly refuses 'to declare every man, whether he accepts the grace or not, an "anonymous Christian"'[13] as also

---

[11] In *Theological Investigations* 4 (New York, 1966), pp. 105–20.
[12] K. Rahner, 'Anonymous Christians', p. 393.
[13] Ibid., p. 394.

EXTRA CHRISTUM NULLA SALUS

one 'who in his basic decision were really to deny and to reject his being ordered to God, who were to place himself decisively in opposition to his own concrete being, should not be designated ... an anonymous theist'.[14] The limitation of the ontological relation between the being of Jesus Christ and the being of all to the ontological mode of possibility is indispensable, if one does not wish to be identified with the condemned teaching of Baius.[15] The limitation is also necessary in order not to let the truth *extra Christum nulla salus* annul what 'is just as valid today as it was in the days of the Fathers', that '"outside" the Church there is no salvation'.[16] If no distinction were made between the ontological possibility of every person being an 'anonymous Christian' and the ontic realization of that possibility by particular persons, then it would be impossible to see why a distinction still needs to be drawn between 'anonymous Christians' and confessing Christians. For a person's anonymous Christianity has to be understood precisely as a 'stage of development' of this Christianity, which realises itself in and as the church, so that 'this explicit self-realization of his previously anonymous Christianity is itself part of the development of this Christianity itself—a higher stage of development of the Christianity demanded by his being'.[17] And so at least unconsciously 'anonymous Christianity bears within itself the urge (ὄρεξις) to abandon its anonymity—in the same way that already the possibility of a person being an 'anonymous Christian' implies not only the capacity of 'hearing a possible word from his hidden God',[18] but also that that person positively expects such a word from the 'revelation of grace which man always experiences implicitly in the depths of his being'.[19]

---

[14] Ibid., pp. 394f. This does not, however, exclude the possibility of 'an inculpable atheism'. Rahner believes that Vatican II's *Dogmatic Constitution on the Church* §16 (*DV*, pp. 366f.) hints that under such atheism may well lie 'an unreflected, merely existentially actualized theism (precisely by a radical obedience to the dictates of conscience)' ('Anonymous Christians', p. 397).

[15] Cf. H. U. von Balthasar, *Karl Barth. Darstellung und Deutung seiner Theologie* (Cologne, 1962), pp. 280f.

[16] K. Rahner, 'Dogmatic Notes on "Ecclesiological Piety"', p. 353.

[17] K. Rahner, 'Christianity and the Non-Christian Religions', p. 132.

[18] K. Rahner, 'Anonymous Christians', p. 392.

[19] Ibid., p. 394. On the entire problem, see Rahner's book *Hearers of the Word* (New York, 1969).

III

The theory just outlined is an impressive attempt to interpret our humanity within the horizon of the gospel. As such, it offers a positive challenge to Protestant theology. It would be tempting indeed to confront Rahner's new Christological basis for natural theology, especially as it is presented in his proposal about anonymous Christianity, with Barth's roughly contemporary teaching about the 'ontological connection between the man Jesus on the one side and all other men on the other, and between active Christians on the one side and merely virtual and prospective Christians on the other'.[20] Striking parallels as well as far-reaching differences in the argument would need to be worked out. Thus for example, Rahner's view that the incarnation of God is 'the uniquely supreme case of the actualization of man's nature in general' and that the human person is 'that which happens when God expresses and divests himself' immediately connects with Barth's interpretation of the *assumptio humanae naturae* (assumption of human nature) which occurs in the event of God's becoming man as the exaltation of humanity as such and in general. It is precisely at these points of contact, however, that we are able to discern how fundamentally contrary are the movements of thought which lead both theologians to expound the theologoumenon of the 'anonymous' or 'virtual and prospective' Christian. These two movements of thought, which, however contrary, lead to two doctrines which seem almost identical, may perhaps help us to discern the degree to which in all their differences Catholics and Protestants are dealing with the same issue—and the degree to which in all their agreement, it really is the same issue with which they are dealing. But to pursue this would take us back to the beginning; instead of this, I limit myself to some reflections which take their rise from a thesis of Luther. In these reflections, we will consider the fact that every person is or could be a virtual (anonymous) Christian from the particular or, if you wish, sharper,

---

[20] *CD* IV/2, p. 275. On this problem, see my study 'Karl Barths Lehre von der Taufe' in *Barth-Studien* (Gütersloh, 1982), pp. 246–90, esp. pp. 270–3, and '"...keine Menschenlosigkeit Gottes...". Zur Theologie Karl Barths zwischen Theismus und Atheismus' in ibid., pp. 332–47.

aspect of the doctrine of justification. I begin, then, with a biblical observation.

The prologue to the Gospel of John emphasises in the strongest possible way that a fundamental division was brought about within humanity by the Word's becoming flesh. Over against those who did not receive the Logos who came to his own (Jn 1.12), those who did receive him are said to be—indeed, initiated into their existence as—the children of God. The criterion for this existence is their faith in the name of the one whom they have received, in the name of Jesus Christ, which we are to think of as inscribed over the entire prologue. Thus humanity is *divided* as faith or unbelief are realized in it. We would be wise, however, not to speak too hastily of dualism here, for according to the Gospel of John, the opposition of faith and unbelief is only possible because of the Logos, who came into the world as the true light which enlightens *everyone* (Jn 1.9). If there is such a thing as 'Johannine dualism', then it is an 'historical' dualism.[21] It is, in other words, highly relative, a dualism only made possible by a unity which unifies that which is contradictory. The fundamental tension of the prologue consists in the relation between the unity which unifies and the separation of humanity which is actually made possible by this unity. The 'Johannine dualism' of faith and unbelief is an opposition made possible by the possibility of faith, a separation only realized by the shining of the light. But for this very reason, this dualism must remain a *problem* for faith. For the believer who perceives, recognizes, and lets him or herself be enlightened by the true light will not be able to obscure the fact that this φῶς ἀληθινόν (true light) enlightens *everyone*.

In this connection, it can hardly be overemphasized that the light which is here spoken of is the true, real, authentic light insofar as it brings the truth with it. The truth of humanity comes to light as the light falls upon humanity. It is true light because it makes true that which it enlightens. It is a light which changes us and our world, for which the sun which changes night into day can be but an innocuous parable. It is for this reason that it is said of those who did not attempt to obscure this light but rather consented to its illuminating power by receiving the Logos who came to his own: he gave them power to become children of God. Their faith

[21] R. Bultmann, *The Gospel of John* (Oxford, 1971), p. 55 with n. 1.

allows the truth, and the existential truth, of that which has been made true by the transforming power of the light which enlightens everyone, and which encounters everyone in his or her humanity.

These exegetical reflections could be extended through looking at other biblical texts, such as Rom 5.12ff. On the Christological basis which such exegesis offers, it is in my judgment not only theologically possible but theologically indispensable to affirm what is meant by talking of anonymous Christians. For the sake of the light of the gospel (to use Paul's formula), true theology must view *all* in this light which makes things true—even those who, blinded by the god of this world, do not see 'the light of the gospel of the glory of Christ' (2 Cor 4.4). Those who are blinded are (in 2 Cor 4.3) said to be those who are perishing (ἀπολλύμενοι); we can only make sense of the sharpness of this expression if we grasp that the gospel which is 'veiled' in them does indeed define everyone in a fundamental way. Luther expressed this in his thesis that justification by faith is the theological definition of the human person.[22] This theological definition concerns the *whole* of the person and therefore *all* persons. Clearly, however, such a claim raises a number of objections.

It could be objected that this definition of humanity is governed by a presupposition in that it defines humanity by reference to God, whereas it is in fact through analysis of humanity that the possibility or necessity of something like God has first of all to be demonstrated, in order that the word 'God' can be used meaningfully at all.

At first sight, the objection is compelling. Certainly we must agree that language about God is meaningful only if 'God' is understood to be a word which is 'aimed at the whole', a word whose particular claim contains universal validity. But this function of the word 'God' cannot be shown to be necessary *without God*. In the end, it is not simple obduracy or intellectual confusion which leads honest philosophers to a *non liquet* ('verdict deferred') in this respect. The thesis that we are theologically defined through justification *sola fide* (through faith alone) takes this into account. We are, indeed, working with a presupposition here. Nevertheless, this carries the advantage of being able to emphasize that God is a hypothesis which must verify itself. And it carries the further

---

[22] M. Luther, *The Disputation Concerning Man*, thesis 32, *LW* 34, p. 139.

advantage that from the very outset God is defined concretely, namely as the *deus iustificans* (God who justifies), and thereby as the one who communicates himself, whose self-communication takes place *sola gratia* (by grace alone) and therefore in freedom, but which at the same time promises the 'freedom of the children of God.' God defines himself materially as the one who justifies in his grace; the formal implication of this is that the word 'God' is a 'word of offer'. The freedom which liberates can only establish itself in freedom. The compelling aspect of this freedom cannot in any way consist in a proof of its own necessity, for this could only be accomplished apart from freedom. Rather, it can only consist in the setting forth of its own dignity, which cannot take place apart from our situation as those who are to be liberated and who are in desperate need of justification. The compelling aspect of the freedom which liberates, only setting itself forth within our situation, is not the compulsion of mere force; it is the compulsion of wooing, of appeal—both the Old and New Testaments contain many examples of this.[23] Understood in this way, 'God' is a word which courts us for itself, and which is fundamentally hostile to the idea that that which it names should be proved to be necessary. Nevertheless, it must have a universal claim if it is to fulfill the function of defining humanity. Such a claim is included within the thesis that the human person is theologically defined through justification by faith. In this respect, that thesis also includes a claim in the area of natural theology. Consequently, we must ask how this claim can be made good in a more satisfactory way than in traditional natural theology.

IV

In answering that question, it is helpful to begin by laying out the condition which we must meet if we are to do justice to the concern of natural theology. The desire to prove that all persons always exist in relation to God independent of the saving revelation which occurs in Jesus Christ shows that natural theology has been guided by the concern to make clear that *God is self-evident*. The self-evidentness of God is the real claim of natural theology. Thereby it

[23] Cf. my essay 'Die Autorität des bittenden Christus' in *Unterwegs zur Sache* (Munich, 1972), pp. 179–88.

wishes to prevent God from appearing in the drama of being in world history and in the drama of human life merely as a *deus ex machina*, to prevent the name of God from abuse as 'a mental short circuit' because of our 'inability to master intellectually contradictory arguments or objections'.[24] This concern has also to be met, though in a different way, by a Protestant theology which seeks to avoid what it regards as the false trails of natural theology. But how can this be done?

The best approach is to attempt a positive interpretation of the basic problem in the undertaking of natural theology. This basic problem is that natural theology attempts to *demonstrate* that which ought to be *self-evident*. But to try and demonstrate that which ought to be self-evident is to render problematical this very self-evidence. Intrinsic to the concept of 'self-evidence', it seems, is the identity of being and knowing, of *ratio essendi* and *ratio cognoscendi*. That which is self-evident can be brought to mind; but as the self-evident, it cannot be proved, without its self-evidence being thereby called fundamentally into question. If God is self-evident, then the concern of natural theology ought to be satisfied immediately. Clearly, however, this is not the case. For either the claim that God is self-evident is false, or the dimension of the self-evident (not the least in view of this claim) is shown to be determined by a highly differentiated logic. This logic would, for example, allow that something self-evident could be surpassed by something else self-evident, or that alongside that which *has always been* self-evident something else *becomes* self-evident.

If we try to take account of the concern of natural theology from within a theology which seeks to expound God's revelation in Jesus Christ, it becomes essential to work out these differentiations within the concept of the self-evident.[25] God in his revelation is experienced in a way which calls into question that which has been hitherto self-evident. Revelation is not simply a highly particular repetition of that which is the case in general; rather, it is a unique event which must establish itself historically in the horizon of the world and which must often, though not always, do this over against the prevailing *sensus communis*, and over against that which

[24] Cf. C. Schmitt, *Political Theology. Four Chapters in the Concept of Sovereignty* (Cambridge, Mass., 1985), p. 39.

[25] Such differentiations, obviously, ought to be valid not only in the theological realm but generally.

is (not without justification) held to be self-evident and which of itself could hardly be called into question. On the other hand, however, this unique event of revelation is bound up with a claim—a highly particular claim—to self-evidence, a claim which can be made good only within the horizon of that which is already held to be self-evident. How can both these things be held together?

V

The problem we have posed can be solved if we think of God's revelation as that which is *more self-evident* than the self-evident. Some biblical considerations support this possibility. In the present context, I refer simply to the task set by the gospels, namely that of interpreting the wisdom which calls 'beside the way' (Prov 8.2) and which is understood by all, as the horizon of the particular mystery of the Kingdom of God. In the horizon of wisdom, the gospel of the Kingdom of God comes to speech in the particular event of parabolic discourse which, over against the self-evidence of the world, sets free a surplus of self-evidence. In terms of the logic of the self-evident, this increase means that the self-evident has to be thought of as *historical*. The historicality of the self-evident allows for an increase in self-evidence. It occurs as a constitutive moment in the formation and history of tradition. It is significant, however, that the comparative cannot be neatly deduced from the positive. At all events it is true that revelation does not take its rise as an increase of the self-evident, but rather establishes itself from itself, in an absolutely underivative way, as that which over against the self-evident is more self-evident. In this case, the comparative makes the positive into the positive of a comparative. Indeed, the comparative, that which is more self-evident, can deprive that which is hitherto self-evident of its self-evidence, so that henceforth it is anything but self-evident. It can also, of course, preserve it as the positive, or show it to be only too self-evident. At all events, we have to do with a *critical comparative*, which brings that which is hitherto self-evident into a new light, in which it is shown to be *either* all too self-evident *or* anything but self-evident, *or* self-evident in the future also. The comparative could also be called eschatological, calling to mind Luther's hymn: 'Das ewig Licht geht da herein/gibt der Welt ein neuen Schein: In him the eternal light breaks through/Gives the world a glory new'.[26]

[26] M. Luther, 'All praise to Thee, O Jesus Christ', *LW* 53, p. 241.

In connection with the thesis that the human person is defined theologically by justification by faith, our results have anthropological consequences. The first of these is that we are defined in our humanity by that which is over against us, which presents itself in freedom, whose presence we may in no way compel. We are dependent upon the *freedom of another*,[27] without which we would not be human—as little as we would be if we could deduce that others were necessary for us.[28] Intrinsic to our humanity is freedom to encounter as an encounter with freedom. God is neither superfluous nor a necessary function of humanity. God is more than necessary for us.

If we are defined in encounter with God who freely presents himself, then our humanity can only be understood dialectically in a way which corresponds to the logic of the self-evident. That humanity cannot really be human without God is the somewhat fatal maxim by which the enterprise of natural theology stands or falls. This thesis is to be rejected, since it does not respect what we have already said about humanity's dependence upon the *freedom of another*. Nevertheless, there is a grain of truth in the thesis which we need to bring out. This is the insight that God is one who concerns our humanity in such an unconditional way that the revelation of God makes us thematic in our humanity. This happens in such a way, however, that for our part we are revealed as those whose humanity consists in becoming *ever more human*. Over against our humanity which, certainly, already establishes itself in the midst of and despite our inhumanity, the incarnation of God and the justification of humanity which it accomplishes show that our humanity is able to be increased. And so the theological conception of humanity implies the comparative 'ever more human'.

This comparative 'ever more human', like the 'more self-evident' of revelation, is an eschatological comparative, bringing that which has been held to be human into a new light in which it is displayed *either* as all too human *or* as not human at all *or* as having been opened up by that comparative and therefore remaining human. In

---

[27] And therefore not only morally engaged for the freedom of another!

[28] This is valid for our relation to God, but has an exact analogy in our relations to our fellow human beings. We are dependent upon others in order to be human, but upon others as they give themselves in freedom. Free, mutual self-giving is constitutive of humanity.

view of this third possibility, it cannot be stressed too strongly that the justification of the sinner which takes place at the cross of Christ has *ontological* significance for our humanity; it has the power to give a future to that which has been, by qualifying it anew. Although it might be objected that such an eschatological comparative devalues what has gone before, it ought to be pointed out that not every increase means a devaluation of that which is surpassed. That which is *better* than the good does not make the good *worse*, but lets it remain good. It would be inappropriate for the sake of the better to read the increase 'good ... better' in reverse, as 'better ... worse'.[29] At any rate, the eschatological 'better' returns to the good, taking the good with it.

Mention should also be made of another consequence of the discussion so far. Given with the eschatological comparative is a claim that the particular event of justification is universally binding, and that, accordingly, language about God has anthropological relevance. But this claim can only be made good if theological statements about humanity yield an anthropological gain for the unbeliever also. Consequently, it is essential that anthropological statements made with the presupposition of the concept of God drawn from revelation must be meaningful and able to be used even if the word 'God' is misunderstood and used as a mere blank. To someone who can make no sense of the expression 'the truth of God,' for example, to say that our true being is *hidden* in the truth of God means that we exist in a certain withdrawal from ourselves. But nothing is said of the nature of this withdrawal, which is in itself *gracious*. It remains ambivalent. Or again, to someone who can make no sense of the idea of a divine call, to say that we are ourselves as those who are addressed, acknowledged and called out of ourselves by God means that we are dependent upon being addressed and acknowledged and that we are called ceaselessly to go beyond ourselves. How and where we are to go beyond ourselves remains an open question. We can be coaxed beyond ourselves, or we can be ordered out. And if we do go beyond ourselves, we can be infinitely blessed or we can make complete fools of ourselves. *Deo remoto* (apart from God), all this remains ambivalent. And so every statement in theological anthropology

---

[29] A comparison which leads to devaluation is not a necessary part of an increase.

must be formulated in such a way that, without 'God' being mentioned, that statement is understandable, meaningful and profitable. But every such statement thereby changes from a statement of the gospel to a statement of the law, from an unequivocally beneficial statement to one which is ambivalent. The *specific* 'plus', in which faith is above all interested, cannot be said in a different way. The highly particular gain which faith rejoices to have found in God is suspended in statements of law. For this gain is enclosed in the name of Jesus Christ and not to be had under any other name. And hence to offer this eschatological surplus is equally to mediate the insight that *anonymous* Christianity is an existential impossibility.

VI

This aspect of the problem to which we have just referred takes seriously that—according to Luther's thesis—it is justification *by faith* which defines humanity. But to assert that in Rom 3.28 Paul gave a concise definition not simply of the being of the Christian but of humanity provokes the objection that, whilst it is appropriate for faith to define the church and its members as a particular community of quite specific people, it may not define humanity as such. However, this objection fails to take into account the fact that faith is that human act in which we allow what God has accomplished in our regard to be and to occur for ourselves. The justification which takes place in Jesus Christ stands under the rubric of Jn 19.20: τετέλεσται (it is finished). In no way is it first brought about by faith. In view of the justification of all which has already taken place, faith is that human attitude in which we affirm that we are justified and thereby also affirm that we need add nothing to our salvation and have nothing to add apart from this affirmation.

Thus our human being is defined by a tension, which we might characterize as a tension between a fundamental passivity in which we are, as it were, endowed with ourselves, and an activity which corresponds to this passivity. In this activity, we ourselves affirm the significance of our passivity and, as a consequence, make it fruitful as the creative power for the emergence, accomplishment and responsibility of all further human activities. This tension means that, whilst we can deny that our being is determined by a fundamental passivity, we cannot annul the fact. When we do not affirm that we are passively affirmed by God, the result is not the destruction of human nature but a self-contradiction in the *acting out* of what we are: we come to think we have to replace our passive affirmation by God with our own activities, with self-affirmation and self-justification. If we ignore and contradict our affirmation by God, and because of that negation struggle violently to create acknowledgement on our own, we do not destroy ourselves; and if this is so, it is because of the particular character of justification. For as the forgiveness of sins, justification is a divine attack upon our sin which, without rendering it insignificant, condemns it to ruination. Sin remains an attempt which cannot be brought to completion.

All the more, then, is faith an integrating component of the theological definition of humanity. This is for the simple reason that faith restricts itself to making nothing more of humanity than it already is through divine justification.[30] Unbelief, because it does not restrict itself in this way, is the already doomed attempt to make more of humanity than humanity is. But even such inhuman attempts cannot make us inhuman. The inhuman is itself an inhuman category. The meaning of this category ought to be restricted to the inhumanity of human action. Because humanity is defined by justification, inhumanity is relegated to the dimension of works, for which, nevertheless, the human person is to be made responsible.

Finally, what has been set out here throws light on the dark category of godlessness. For if humanity is defined by justification by faith, then subjective godlessness is made objectively impossible by the humanity of God. Faith is the human admission that this most magnificent enterprise of human activity has foundered, though its magnificence will never be disavowed *coram mundo* (before the world). And yet it is for this very reason that faith is demanded of us. As the admission of the failure of human godlessness, faith is our *existential* consent to the truth that there is no salvation *extra Christum*, but that Christ is the salvation of all and thus the guarantor of the humanity of all. Faith disavows the human *ambitio divinitatis* (aspiration to divinity) by holding to the distinction

---

[30] We may again remind ourselves that the process of becoming ever more human is ontologically constitutive.

between God and humanity, definitively accomplished in the incarnation of God, as the proper human condition: 'In summary: we are to be men and not God; it will not be otherwise . . .'.[31]

[31] M. Luther, Letter to George Spalatin, 30.6.1530, *LW* 49, p. 337.

THE CHURCH AS SACRAMENT?[1]

I

1. The evident stagnation of the process of ecumenical understanding between the Roman Catholic church and the churches of the reformation is rooted in a different understanding of the church which has not so far been overcome, and which, indeed, a good number of commentators do not think can be overcome. The notion that both churches could agree on the doctrine of justification received wide notice and approval; and since, at least in the understanding of Lutherans, this doctrine is the *articulus stantis et cadentis ecclesiae* (the article by which the church stands or falls),[2] if it no longer divided the churches, then agreement in *ecclesiology* would follow. This, however, seems to have been a brief flame, quickly extinguished. On the Protestant side, there is an increase of critical voices declaring that 'as things stand, a union with the Roman church is impossible', precisely because of the Roman Catholic understanding of the church and the sacraments.[3] According to Gottfried Maron,[4] the self-understanding of the Roman Catholic church as a *sacrament*, which

[1] A paper given at the Lutheran-Roman Catholic congress on questions of the ecclesiology and theology of Martin Luther, at the Pontifical University of Salamanca, 27 September, 1983.
[2] Cf. in the Lutheran confessional writings, *Apology of the Augsburg Confession* IV: justification is 'the main doctrine of Christianity' (*BC*, p. 107); *Smalcald Articles* I: 'Nothing in this article can be given up or compromised, even if heaven and earth and things temporal should be destroyed... On this article rests all that we teach and practice against the pope, the devil, and the world. Therefore we must be quite certain and have no doubts about it. Otherwise all is lost, and the pope, the devil and all our adversaries will gain the victory' (*BC*, p. 292). On the history of the formula, see F. Loofs, 'Der articulus stantis et cadentis ecclesiae' *Theologische Studien und Kritiken* 90 (1917), pp. 323–420. On the issue, see E. Wolf, 'Die Rechtfertigungslehre als Mitte und Grenze reformatorischer Theologie' in *Peregrinatio* II (Munich, 1965), pp. 11–21.
[3] G. Ebeling, *Dogmatik des christlichen Glaubens* III (Tübingen, 1979), p. 315.
[4] G. Maron, *Kirche und Rechtfertigung. Eine kontroverstheologische Untersuchung* (Göttingen, 1969). Cf. J. Dantine, 'Sakrament als Gabe und Feier', *Theologische Zeitschrift* 38 (1982), pp. 3–27, esp. p. 20.

was accepted at Vatican II,[5] is one of the most important reasons why the 'ugly, broad ditch' between the Protestant doctrine of justification and Roman Catholic ecclesiology has once again become impossible to overlook and, indeed, impossible to cross.

There are, however, other voices. As recently as 1982, Otto Hermann Pesch still maintained that the doctrine of justification does not necessarily divide the church and so ought not to be allowed to divide the church.[6] For strategic reasons, he wants to treat the question of the unity of the churches separately, 'since the existence of certain forms of church life which—on both sides!—hardly, if at all, correspond to belief in justification by faith, does not annul consensus about the doctrine of justification, but merely indicates that the churches are still living in contradiction to the core of their own teaching'.[7] In the Luther jubilee year, Heinrich Fries and Karl Rahner declared agreement between the churches to be a 'real possibility'.[8] And a number of Roman Catholic and Protestant theologians[9] intended to settle all misunderstandings

---

[5] Cf. *The Constitution on the Sacred Liturgy* §5: 'For it was from the side of Christ as he slept the sleep of death upon the Cross that there came forth "the wondrous sacrament of the Church"' (*DV*, p. 3); ibid., §26: 'Liturgical services . . . are celebrations of the Church which is "the sacrament of unity"' (*DV*, p. 10); *Dogmatic Constitution on the Church* §1: 'the Church, in Christ, is in the nature of a sacrament—a sign and instrument, that is, of communion with God and of unity among all men' (*DV*, p. 350); ibid., §9: 'All those, who in faith look towards Jesus, the author of salvation and the principle of unity and peace, God has gathered together and established as the Church, that it may be for each and everyone the visible sacrament of this saving unity' (*DV* p. 360); ibid., §48: 'Christ . . . sent his life-giving Spirit upon his disciples and through him set up his Body which is the Church as the universal sacrament of salvation' (*DV*, p. 407). Cf. also the *Pastoral Constitution on the Church in the Modern World* §45 (*DV*, p. 947), and the *Decree on the Church's Missionary Activity* §1 (*DV*, p. 813) and §5: 'the Lord . . . founded his Church as the sacrament of salvation' (*DV*, p. 817).

[6] O. H. Pesch, *Gerechtfertigt aus Glauben. Luthers Frage an die Kirche* (Freiburg, 1982), pp. 53–5.

[7] Ibid., p. 42.

[8] H. Fries, K. Rahner, *Einigung der Kirchen—reale Möglichkeit* (Freiburg, 1983). Cf. E. Jüngel, 'Einheit der Kirche—konkret', *Süddeutsche Zeitung* 1–2 October, 1983.

[9] Cf. K. Lehmann, E. Schlink, ed., *Das Opfer Jesu Christi und seine Gegenwart in der Kirche* (Göttingen, 1983). This consensus was prepared by, amongst other things, the discovery of a number of misunderstandings in

THE CHURCH AS SACRAMENT?

about the sacrifice of the mass, finally rendering obsolete Luther's notorious statement in the Smalcald Articles: '(B)y God's help I will suffer myself to be burned to ashes before I will allow a celebrant of the Mass and what he does to be considered equal or superior to my Saviour, Jesus Christ. Accordingly, we are and remain eternally divided and opposed the one to the other. The papists are well aware that if the Mass falls, the papacy will fall with it. Before they would permit this to happen, they would put us all to death.'[10]

2. In what follows I want to put the case to the test in my own way. Putting a large question mark against my title—the church as sacrament?—I want to make some proposals about how we might correctly define the relation between church and sacrament. Following some basic reformation insights, I will make full use of the freedom of a Lutheran theologian (even—especially—in respect of Luther himself). My intention is to return to genuine Protestant doctrine in order to pave the way for the future—towards the 'sacrament of unity' which is not the church but Christ himself. It is unnecessary to note that Pesch's remark about my earlier treatment of the notion of sacrament is still valid for the present attempt: 'Jüngel is not representative'.[11] It is sufficient to be felt as the thorn in the flesh of Protestant theology in this matter. And this is going to be the case anyway since I am dissatisfied with the neglect of the question of the correct notion of sacrament in recent Protestant theology. Any attention to that notion must start with the fact that in the New Testament, *sacramentum* is nothing other than the eschatological mystery of the saving divine decree in favour of sinners which was enacted in the history of Jesus Christ. In what follows I presuppose this basic meaning of the notion of sacrament as the criterion, from which alone we orient our handling of the question of the sacramental character of the being and activity of the church.

---

sacramental theology. Cf. W. Schwab, *Entwicklung und Gestalt der Sakramententheologie bei Martin Luther* (Frankfurt, 1977), pp. 170–226, 365–89.

[10] *Smalcald Articles* I (*BC*, p. 294).

[11] O. H. Pesch, 'Das katholische Sakramentsverständnis im Urteil gegenwärtiger evangelische Theologie' in E. Jüngel et al., ed., *Verifikationen. Festschrift für G. Ebeling zum 70. Geburtstag* (Tübingen, 1982), p. 332.

II

1. To talk of the church as sacrament immediately poses a number of terminological problems which seem to make it advisable to put a question mark against my title. This does not mean that terminology alone would cause ecumenical agreement about the nature of the church to fail. If both churches were found to disagree for terminological reasons alone, then it certainly ought to be possible—indeed, in view of the importance of the issue, *necessary*—to say the same thing in different words, in the knowledge that such a translation could put the same position into a new context within which old confrontations could well prove to be obsolete. But if this is the aim, it is all the more necessary to be first of all conscious of the problems which were bound up with the old terminology, lest the problems return to haunt us.

2. Language about the church as sacrament seems to have become important only in the more recent Roman Catholic theology. In terms of official ecclesiology, it was newly introduced by Vatican II,[12] though in reliance upon Cyprian.[13] Scheeben had already spoken of the church as 'one great sacrament', and Oswald had asserted that the church was to be called 'not so much *a* sacrament as *the* Christian sacrament', although both affirmations had little consequence. From around 1940, however, the language has become familiar first amongst Romance language speakers and then in the German-speaking Catholic world.[14] In his book of the title, Semmelroth spoke of the church as the 'fundamental sacrament' (*Ursakrament*),[15] and wrote in the *Lexikon für Theologie und Kirche* under this heading.[16] Even Karl Rahner initially talked of the church as the 'fundamental sacrament': 'The Church is the abiding presence of that primal sacramental word of definitive grace, which Christ is in the world, effecting what is uttered by uttering it in sign. By the very fact of being in that way the enduring presence

---

[12] H. Mühlen, *Una persona mystica* (Munich, 1967), p. 363; G. Maron, op. cit., p. 18.

[13] Cyprian, Letter 69.6: *inseparabile est unitatis sacramentum*, inseparable is the sacrament of unity (*Letters 1–81* (Washington, 1964), p. 248.)

[14] Cf. Maron, op. cit., p. 19.

[15] O. Semmelroth, *Die Kirche als Ursakrament* (Freiburg, 1963).

[16] *Lexikon für Theologie und Kirche* X (Freiburg, 1965), p. 568.

THE CHURCH AS SACRAMENT? 193

of Christ in the world, the Church is truly the fundamental sacrament, the well-spring of the sacraments in the strict sense. From Christ the Church has an intrinsically sacramental structure'.[17] But if the church receives its sacramental character *from Christ*, since he himself is the 'fundamental sacramental word' in which God promises himself to humanity, and since Jesus Christ is the symbol which definitively signifies and effects the presence of the gracious will of God, then it ought rather to be Jesus Christ himself who is understood as the 'fundamental sacrament'. In this case, language about the church as the fundamental sacrament is a bold usurpation—an apparently typical Catholic identification of the church with its Lord. Pesch, however, wastes little time on this process: 'there is some irony in the fact that the Catholic side took so long to recognize that at the same time Christ is also described as the fundamental sacrament—and only then was it thought necessary to make a terminological distinction between Christ as the *fundamental* sacrament and the church as the *basic* sacrament'.[18] With this terminological distinction, the concept is 'firmly rooted in Catholic ecclesiology'.[19]

3. In *Protestant* ecclesiology, however, language about the church as the fundamental or basic sacrament can scarcely be found. This is all the more so because of the strong reservations against the very idea of sacrament from the very beginnings of Protestantism. As is well known, in his great polemical writing *The Babylonian Captivity of the Church* (1520) Luther pondered the possibility of following biblical usage by reserving the term 'sacrament' for Christ alone, whilst calling the sacramental actions of the church *signa sacramentalia*, 'sacramental signs'.[20] Melanchthon followed that path in the first version of the *Loci communes*, though he gave up the idea in his later years.[21] In 1523, Zwingli went so far as to criticize the use of the term 'sacrament' as giving away too much to the

[17] K. Rahner, *The Church and the Sacraments* (Montreal, 1963), p. 18.
[18] O. Pesch, op. cit., pp. 334f. Cf. K. Rahner, 'Was ist ein Sakrament?' in E. Jüngel, K. Rahner, *Was ist ein Sakrament?* (Freiburg, 1971), pp. 75f.; idem., *Foundations of Christian Faith* (New York, 1978), pp. 411–13.
[19] O. Pesch, op. cit., p. 334, n. 66.
[20] M. Luther, *The Babylonian Captivity of the Church*, *LW* 36 p. 18. Cf. *Disputatio de fide infusa et acquisita*, *WA* 6.86.7f.: 'the holy Scriptures have only one sacrament, which is Christ the Lord himself'.
[21] 'Those things which others call "sacraments" we call "signs", or, if

use of the term 'sacrament' as giving away too much to the papacy.[22] And in 1524, Karlstadt demanded a theological disclaimer concerning the term 'sacrament', and the Council of Ansbach proposed to make its use an offence. For centuries, Protestant theology has retained its basic mistrust of the term. Initially Luther's determined resistance against wholesale prohibition of the language of sacrament (on the grounds that Christian liberty even in the choice of words was to be respected)[23] was generally accepted. However, with Schleiermacher all the reservations against this unpopular term return. Consequently, he treats the doctrines of baptism and the eucharist without any reference to the term which, taken as a generic term, he holds to be meaningless and confusing. In this respect, Schleiermacher continues to influence even those twentieth century theologians who criticize him in other respects.[24] The late writings of Barth show a return to the exclusively Christological use of the term 'sacrament' in the tradition of Luther in 1520; in Barth's case this is bound up with polemic against 'the sacramental character of the Church and its action'.[25] The Catholic notion of the church as the basic sacrament is approximated to most nearly by Richard Rothe in his—apparently quite contradictory and certainly unique—proposal that the state is *'the complex* of all universal means to enact community between humanity and God, and thus *the* sacrament *par excellence'*.[26]

4. When we compare this limited selection of diverse critical statements by Protestant theologians about the use of sacramental terminology with Luther's statements, there can be in my view no doubt that it is the exclusively Christological use of the term 'sacrament' which comes closest to his ideas. This is precisely because

you please, "sacramental signs" ', P. Melanchthon, *Loci communes* in W. Pauck, ed., *Melanchthon and Bucer* (London, 1969), p. 135.

[22] H. Zwingli, *The Defense of the Reformed Faith* in E. J. Furcha, ed., *Writings* I (Allison Park, PA, 1984), p. 102.

[23] M. Luther, *Against the Heavenly Prophets in the Matter of Images and Sacraments, LW* 40, pp. 149–52.

[24] F. D. E. Schleiermacher, *The Christian Faith* (Edinburgh, 1928), pp. 657f. For the influence of Schleiermacher, see, for example, the separate treatment of the doctrine of the Lord's Supper and the doctrine of baptism in W. Elert, *Der christliche Glaube* (Berlin, 1956).

[25] *CD* IV/2, p. 55.

[26] R. Rothe, *Theologische Ethik* II (Berlin, 1867), p. 459.

THE CHURCH AS SACRAMENT?

Luther combines a desire to use the notion of 'sacrament' in an exclusively Christological way with a high regard for what ought to be called a sacrament. His high regard for the sacraments became increasingly evident. In a letter of 1524 to the Christians in Strassburg, the reformer confesses that five years previously he would have regarded it a great favour if someone had convinced him that 'only bread and wine were in the sacrament ... At that time I suffered such severe conflicts and inner strife and torment that I would gladly have been delivered from them. I realised that at this point I could best resist the papacy.'[27] It is clearly the *self-presentation of Jesus Christ* in bread and wine, enacted through the creative power of his word of promise which provokes and strengthens faith, which made Luther value the sacrament so highly that he thought it necessary to 'resist the papacy' not by devaluation of the sacrament to a mere sign but in a quite different way. For Luther, the decisive point is that in the sacrament, *the gracious God himself is the one who acts*. Hence the relation *solo verbo—sola fide* (Word alone—faith alone) is also, indeed especially, constitutive for the sacrament[28]—whether in the sense of the early Luther as a sign, given through the command of God and bound up with a word promising divine grace,[29] or in the sense of the later Luther as an element constituted by the word through the institution of Jesus Christ.[30] Rightly understood, the sign or element emphasises the spiritual or corporeal externality of the Word of God. But if this word is absent or if its constitutive function is neglected, the sacramental event comes to be dominated by the *signum* as *human action* (though of course under one aspect it has always to be

---

[27] M. Luther, *Letter to the Christians at Strassburg in Opposition to the Fanatic Spirits*, *LW* 40, p. 68.

[28] Cf. G. Ebeling, 'The Protestant View of the Sacraments' in *The Word of God and Tradition* (London, 1968), pp. 225f., 233.

[29] M. Luther, *The Babylonian Captivity of the Church*, *LW* 36, p. 124: 'Nevertheless, it has seemed proper to restrict the name of sacrament to those promises which have signs attached to them ... Hence there are, strictly speaking, but two sacraments in the church of God—baptism and the bread. For only in these two do we find both the divinely instituted sign and the promise of forgiveness of sins'.

[30] Cf. Luther's definition of baptism in a sermon of 1534 as 'water with the Word of God' (*WA* 37.262.18f). See also the *Confession Concerning Christ's Supper*, *LW* 37, p. 338: 'the words ... connect the bread and the cup to the sacrament'. Cf. also *WA* 30/I.24.11f.; 122.11f.

regarded as such). Thus already in 1520 Luther had protested against the representatives of a sacramental theology who in his opinion 'cling only to the sign and the use of the sign, and draw us away from faith to the work, away from the word to the sign'.[31] The relation of *solo verbo—sola fide* preserves the character of the sacrament as divine action and prevents it from being misunderstood and abused as a human action. Luther's thesis that 'The sacraments ... are not fulfilled when they are taking place, but when they are being believed',[32] and his polemic against the scholastic assertion that the sacraments are effective *ex opere operato*, by the work performed,[33] can only mean that Luther wishes to ensure that the sacrament is understood and celebrated as *God acting upon us*, and is not perverted into our *handling of God* in the form of a work of piety.[34] The dominance of the Word of God in the tight unity of Word and element (sign) ensures that the worldly element (sign) is properly understood as a piece of the world which testifies to the earthly, corporeal and external presence of the God who acts. It is in accordance with the dominance of the Word of God to link the efficacy of the sacrament to the faith of the recipient; by no means does this call into question from a subjective point of view the validity and certainty of the sacrament's efficacy. For Luther, the assertion that the sacrament is effective *ex opere operato, when rightly understood*, could not be offensive. 'Luther retains more energetically than ever before the validity and infallibility of the ... sacrament *ex opere operato* in the form *ex verbo dicto* (by the word spoken)'.[35] Corresponding in the sacrament to *solo verbo, sola fide* has no other function than confirming the nature of the sacrament from our side as God's action upon us, as the self-communication of the gracious God. For faith is trust in God's

[31] M. Luther, *The Babylonian Captivity of the Church*, LW 36, p. 67.
[32] Ibid., p. 66.
[33] Cf. ibid., pp. 47f.
[34] Cf. E. Grötzinger, *Luther und Zwingli. Die Kritik an der mittelalterlichen Lehre von der Messe—als Grund des Abendmahlstreites* (Gütersloh, 1980).
[35] O. Bayer, *Promissio. Geschichte der reformatorischen Wende in Luthers Theologie* (Göttingen, 1971), p. 186. Recently, Schwab, op. cit., pp. 196–205, has emphasised that Luther's polemic against the thesis the efficacy of the sacraments *ex opere operato* and against the idea of the sacrament as a good work are tightly bound up with the scholastic understanding of the mass as the (most important) work of supplication, and thus is problematic or even wrong in its orientation.

THE CHURCH AS SACRAMENT? 197

promise, and thus is the complete opposite of human activity. Even if faith is understood as noble human action, it is nothing other than a wholly passive action in which we experience ourselves as absolutely dependent upon the grace of God. According to Rom 4.5, the believer is 'one who does not work'.

If the relation *solo verbo*—*sola fide* is understood in this way as constitutive of the sacrament, it becomes clear why Luther can expect that the sacrament—in spite of the fact that it always remains a human (ecclesial) action—will be effectual only on the basis of a correspondence between the Word of God and our faith. 'The same rule, that our activity or work does not accomplish anything but solely God's command and ordinance ... applies here as far as the sacraments are concerned: We join the water to the word, as he commands us to do; however, not this action of ours, but Christ's command and ordinance make it a baptism. According to his command we join bread and wine to the Word of Christ; however, not this action of ours, but Christ's word and ordinance effect the change.'[36] The connection between the Word and faith is asserted most emphatically in this statement: 'The words teach you to give thought and attention to why Christ is present; they will cause you to forget your work and to wait only upon his. For a sacrament is a matter of faith, because in it only the works of God proceed and are effected—through his Word! ... Bread and wine, or the body and blood of Christ, regarded without the words, will teach you to give thought and attention to your own works. They will drive you away from pondering God's work and the reason why he is present, so that you will be quite anxious to do a lot for him, and will not let anything be done to you. Thus the sacrament becomes purely a matter of works.'[37]

5. From this perspective, it appears problematic to describe the church as a sacrament or the basic sacrament. This terminology shows a certain affinity to the misunderstanding of the church as an institution which handles both human persons and God. To conceive of the being and activity of the church as a sacrament or

[36] M. Luther, *The Private Mass and the Consecration of Priests*, *LW* 38, p. 202.
[37] M. Luther, *The Adoration of the Sacrament*, *LW* 36, pp. 295f. On this, see H. Hilgenfeld, *Mittelalterlich-traditionelle Elemente in Luthers Abendmahlsschriften* (Zürich, 1971), p. 312, and W. Schwab, op. cit., p. 191.

the basic sacrament is to rouse suspicion that the 'matter of faith' of the sacrament is changed into a 'matter of works'. Can this suspicion be overcome?

In what follows I will try to clarify the conditions for overcoming this suspicion, and thereby to come to responsible ecumenical agreement with the ultracatholic language of the church as basic sacrament. It is probably best to put oneself into the lions' den right at the beginning of any such attempt, to find out whether we have in fact arrived at the time of ecumenical peace in which the Roman Catholic lion and the Protestant lamb can exist peacefully with and alongside each other, if not for each other. For Protestant theology, this lions' den is the Roman Catholic understanding of sacramentality as symbolic representation. The Roman Catholic church is most truly itself in the act of *repraesentio Christi* (representation of Christ)—as it is focused most sharply in the sacrifice of the mass. According to the fathers of Trent, Christ himself bequeathed to the church the sacrifice of the mass as a visible sacrifice in order that his own priesthood should not be brought to an end through his death. In this sacrifice the bloody sacrifice of his death is to be represented (*repraesentaretur*).[38] We need to keep this formulation in mind when we read the following statement from a contemporary Roman Catholic theologian: 'Sacramentality means: symbolic *representation* . . . According to its self-understanding, the Catholic church is to represent God's salvation in the history of the world'.[39] It is just this, however, which has always raised the gravest misgivings from Protestant theology. Here I refer only to Barth who claims that the church of this world can only 'attest' the 'actuality' of Jesus 'in its proclamation and therefore in baptism and the Lord's Supper' but which may not 'represent or repeat in any other way' that actuality 'either in its preaching or in baptism and the Lord's Supper'.[40]

It is possible, however, to understand the notion of symbolic representation in a different way, not as if the church, by *representing* Christ himself, *repeats* or *renders effectual* his reality. Barth himself can speak of the church as the (provisional) *representation* of the sanctification of the whole of humankind which takes place in Jesus

[38] Council of Trent, *The Most Holy Sacrifice of the Mass*, DS 1740, CT 747.
[39] O. Pesch, op. cit., p. 334.
[40] *CD* IV/2, p. 55.

Christ. And no less a thinker than Schleiermacher distinguishes between the causative action of daily life and the liturgical action of the church, and calls the latter 'representative action' in which the rest of life is interrupted for its own sake.[41] This is certainly a possible way of translating *repraesentatio*. Accordingly, the Catholic church's self-understanding as a representation of the definitive realization of the saving will of God in Jesus Christ, and the corresponding description of the church as a sacramental event, do not necessarily have to be repudiated *a limine* as contrary to the gospel. Testimony and representation are not alternatives. On the other hand, Protestant reservations about an ecclesiological usurpation of the high priestly office of Jesus Christ have to be taken seriously, since they point to the centre of the controversy between Protestants and Catholics. And it is just this which makes an ecumenical examination advisable. Is it in accordance with the doctrine of the justification of the sinner by grace alone, accomplished in Jesus Christ alone, to be received only through the word and through faith? Agreement on this issue could lead to agreement in many other areas. Final and unbridgeable disagreement here, however, would mean that many, if not all, of the ecumenical links so far established would eventually prove fragile.

III

1. From these last remarks it is already evident that an ecumenically acceptable understanding of the church as a symbolic representation of Jesus Christ would have to clarify the character of that representation as *action*. The *fact* that in this context representation means action is indisputable. But who is the *subject* of that action? And how can God's work and human work be distinguished within it? How can the liturgical action of the συνεργοί θεοῦ, fellow-workers of God (cf. 1 Cor 3.9) be guarded from a 'synergistic' misunderstanding?

Starting from the visible, the symbolic representation of Jesus Christ through the church seems to be a matter of the church's actions. Protestant theology, too, cannot dispute the fact that the being of the church occurs and manifests itself in certain actions. As

---

[41] Cf. *CD* IV/2, p. 614; F. D. E. Schleiermacher, *Die praktische Theologie*, in *Sämtliche Werke* I (Berlin, 1840), pp. 69f.

both *ecclesia docens* (the teaching church) and *ecclesia audens* (the hearing church), the church in preaching, hearing, praying, confessing, singing and celebrating engages in action. Even, let it be emphasized, as the *hearing* church! Although the act of listening as a receptive activity is certainly characterized by passivity, we should not overlook the fact that *recipere* (to receive) also means action—as can be clearly seen in the decision not to listen. Hence it is all the more important to clarify the character of that action which, as the action of the church, at the same time 'represents' the action of God.

2. If we seek to gain some clarity here by starting from the authoritative texts of the Catholic church, we at once come upon a peculiar ambivalence. Here I concentrate on statements about *liturgical* action, presupposing that the essence of the church occurs in worship.

The Council of Trent explicitly anathematized the teaching that 'in the Mass a true and proper sacrifice is not offered to God',[42] and that 'the sacrifice of the Mass is merely an offering of praise and thanksgiving ... and not propitiatory'.[43] This is to be understood in the sense that the bloody sacrifice of Jesus' giving up of his life on the cross is represented by the unbloody action of the priest in such a way that Jesus Christ himself is the one who acts in the mass: 'For it is one and the same victim: he who now makes the offering through the ministry of priests and he who then offered himself on the cross; the only difference is in the manner of the offering'.[44] The representation of Jesus Christ through the sacrificial action of the priest is clearly understood in terms of an *identity of action*: as the *primary acting subject* Jesus Christ identifies himself with the priestly action. However, in this way the priest becomes another—even if only *secondary—acting subject* who cannot be replaced by other Christians (who for their part belong to the priesthood of *all* believers). Only the priest, set apart by the sacrament of ordination, can join in this identity of action as a secondary acting subject. As Vatican II puts it, in line with Pius

---

[42] Council of Trent, *Canons on the Most Holy Sacrifice of the Mass*, DS 1751; CT 756.
[43] Ibid., DS 1753; CT 758.
[44] Council of Trent, *The Most Holy Sacrifice of the Mass*, DS 1743, CT 749.

THE CHURCH AS SACRAMENT?

XII, the ordained priesthood differs 'essentially and not only in degree' from the common priesthood of all the faithful.[45] Pius XII had also called the priest '*superiorem* ... *populo* (superior to the people)'.[46] This can only mean, however, that the sovereignty of Jesus Christ as the primary acting subject is limited by the priest as secondary acting subject in the sacrifice of the mass. And thereby much more is ascribed to the priest's action than simply *testimony*. Like the apostles, the priest must 'set in train through the sacrifice and sacraments' the 'work of salvation which they preached'.[47]

Accordingly, the liturgical action of the whole church is held to be a *perficere* (completing) of the work of Christ. Certainly it is Christ himself who accomplishes his work in the liturgy. But his work of salvation is an *opus perficiendum* (a work to be completed).[48] The liturgical action is 'an action of Christ the Priest and of his Body, which is the Church'.[49] This is evidently because the axiom of classical sacramental doctrine is equally true for the church's action: they effect what they signify and they signify what they effect. Since they effect what they represent, the liturgical actions of the church must be, according to Catholic understanding of the matter, the action and work of Christ.

In view of this emphasis on the active being of the church, it is expecially surprising to read the fine declaration in the prologue to Vatican II's *Constitution on the Sacred Liturgy*, which states that the church is 'zealous in action and dedicated to contemplation' with action 'directed toward and subordinated ... to contemplation'.[50] This introductory statement makes the official statements about the action of the church notably ambivalent, and a Protestant definition of the church's action should aim to avoid such ambivalence.

3. It was Luther above all who protested against the idea that the liturgical *action* of the church could be anything other than a *receiving*, a receiving of divine benefits. It is necessary to make a

---

[45] *Dogmatic Constitution on the Church* §10 (*DV*, p. 361). It ought to be noted that Vatican II does speak of the faithful's participation 'in the offering of the Eucharist' (ibid.).
[46] Pius XII, *Mediator Dei, DS* 3850; *CT* 768.
[47] *The Constitution on the Sacred Liturgy* §10 (*DV*, p. 4).
[48] Cf. ibid., §7 (*DV*, p. 5).
[49] Ibid.
[50] Ibid. §2 (*DV*, p. 1.).

soteriological distinction within the concept of action. The difference between the creator and his creation, and the saving work of God which defines this difference, means that every human action is characterized by a fundamentally *receptive* action, by a creative *passivity*, that is, by faith rather than by good works in which we seek to do something to God in direct correspondence to his benefits. Christians do good works *on the basis of* faith, for the benefit of their fellow humans, but not for the benefit of God. According to Luther, Christians can and should be even another Christ to their fellow humans,[51] whilst according to the Catholic view it is the priest in his liturgical action who is marked out as an *alter Christus*, another Christ.[52]

For Luther, liturgical action is to be radically distinguished from God's action primarily because the *meritorious work of Jesus Christ* in his suffering and death is definitively *accomplished*. It is not an *opus perficiendum* but, one might say, an *opus operatum* (a work performed). It has once for all won the forgiveness of sins. The passion and the cross are the sacrificial event in which Christ *has* suffered the godforsakenness of sinners, and thereby definitively acquired salvation for them: *extra nos, illic et tunc* (outside us, there and then).

All this is to be distinguished from the *promise* and *appropriation* of the saving work of God accomplished *extra nos* which takes place in the sphere of the church. This promise and appropriation is again the work of Jesus Christ in the power of the Holy Spirit, not to accomplish his meritorious work or sacrifice, but to carry out the *distributio meriti* (distribution of merits). To understand the matter correctly, we need to attend to the fact that 'the *merit of Christ* and the *distribution of merit* are two different things ... Christ has once for all merited and won the forgiveness of sins on the cross; but this forgiveness he distributes wherever he *is*, at all times and in all places'.[53] This takes place as the work of Christ is represented and presented through his word. 'If the work were presented without

[51] M. Luther, *The Freedom of a Christian*, LW 31, pp. 366f.: 'I will therefore give myself as a Christ to my neighbor, just as Christ offered himself to me ... (W)e believe in him and are Christs one to another and do to our neighbor as Christ does to us'.

[52] Cf. Pius X, *Exhortatio ad Clerum catholicum* in *Acta Apostolicae Sedis* 41 (1908), p. 569.

[53] M. Luther, *Confession Concerning Christ's Supper*, LW 37, p. 192.

the Word, it would help no one'.[54] And this word generates faith: 'For where there is the Word of the promising God, there must necessarily be the faith of the accepting man'.[55] This is why according to Luther every action of the church is fundamentally characterized by the receptivity of faith, for 'no one is God's servant unless he lets him be his God and perform his work in him'.[56]

To let God perform his work—this and this alone is the function of the church's action. Since 'in all ... sacraments and in the sermon' no one 'gives God anything or does him any service, but instead takes something', the activity of Christian worship is 'not a work but only an exercise of faith'.[57] In the action of the church, there occurs an elemental *interruption* by God himself of all the achievements which are essential for us to live as creatures of the world, of all those actions through which we can and must put something into effect or make something, and which for that reason constantly threaten to degenerate into acts of human self-realization. And so the liturgical action of the church is the very opposite of religious self-realization.

4. In order to ensure that in that liturgical action of the church God himself is experienced as the real acting subject, with whom neither the priest nor the congregation in their activities can be brought into union, the reformers strongly opposed any understanding of the church's action as an *opus* (work) and of the mass as a *sacrificium* (sacrifice) which of itself acts upon God, setting against it an interpretation of the liturgical action of the church as a *word-event*: 'the chief worship of God is the preaching of the gospel'.[58] The same is true for the sacraments, which should be 'administered according to the Gospel, and only then really *are* sacraments'.[59] Thus Luther can even call the mass 'the sum and

---

[54] M. Luther, *That these words of Christ, 'This is My Body,' etc., Still Stand Firm Against the Fanatics*, LW 37, p. 92.
[55] M. Luther, *The Babylonian Captivity of the Church*, LW 36, p. 39.
[56] M. Luther, *The Magnificat*, LW 21, p. 350.
[57] M. Luther, *A Treatise on the New Testament, that is, the Holy Mass*, LW 35, p. 93. Only on the basis of this soteriological *passivity* can liturgical works in Luther's judgement 'be *rightly* taken to be good works in that they correspond to the work of Christ': E. Grötzinger, op. cit., p. 37; cf. WA 6.364f.
[58] P. Melanchthon, *Apology of the Augsburg Confession* XV (*BC*, p. 221).
[59] P. Melanchthon, *The Augsburg Confession* VII (*BC*, p. 32).

substance of the gospel'.[60] In the liturgical action of the church, 'nothing else ... should happen than that our dear Lord himself should speak his holy Word to us and we in turn speak to him in prayer and hymns of praise'.[61]

The constitutive significance of the word for the church's action points in several ways to the fact that in the worship and hence the sacramental existence of the church it is a matter of God's action alone. This is primarily because the gospel proclaims the work of salvation, accomplished in the death of Christ and revealed in his resurrection, as the *opus operatum et perfectum* (work performed and completed), and so excludes any understanding of it as an *opus perficiendum*. 'It is finished' (Jn 19.30). Hence it is impossible for the action of the church, as a human work, to equate itself with the divine work which it represents. The fundamental distinction between the action of God and the action of the church is preserved by the fact that the word as it were makes use of a divine work which has already been accomplished, and so does not need to be completed. The sacramental action, in which a *verbum* is joined by a *signum* (that is, in which an element is comprised by a word), is not a completion but rather the visible, concrete form of that representation and presentation of the sacrifice of Christ accomplished *illic et tunc* and already brought to speech in the gospel.

The word, however, does not only bring to speech what has already taken place. It not only *represents* but also *presents* the represented event in such a way that it can be received in faith. Forgiveness of sins, life and blessedness—'all this the words of the Supper offer and give us, and we embrace it by faith'.[62] The word of the gospel is in a strict sense a *signum efficax gratiae* (effectual sign of grace). As *representation* of Christ's work it is at the same time the *presentation* of that work, and as such a manifestation of the presence of Christ in the power of the Holy Spirit. The gospel effects what it signifies. Through the event of the proclamation of the gospel, the action of the church generates on the human side that creative receptivity and passivity which allows God alone to be the benefactor and to work his work in us.

[60] M. Luther, *The Babylonian Captivity of the Church*, LW 36, p. 56.
[61] M. Luther, *Sermon for the Seventeenth Sunday after Trinity, 1544*, WA 49.558.16–18.
[62] M. Luther, *Confession Concerning Christ's Supper*, LW 37, p. 338.

5. The speech-event of the proclamation of the gospel, however, once again raises the question of the relation between the action of God and the action of the church. For it is God himself who wishes to come to speech through this act of human speaking. God is himself the one who speaks; and so once again an equating or even identity of divine and human action seems to emerge, this time at the level of the word. 'Thus says the Lord' becomes something the preacher may say about his or her proclamation, for which as a consequence the preacher does not need to ask for forgiveness.[63]

Nevertheless, to describe the action of the church as a word-event rather than as an *opus* allows us to make a more appropriate distinction between the divine acting subject and the human acting subject. For in accordance with its very *raison d'être*, the church is primordially defined as the *hearing* church. Only as the *hearing* church is it also a *speaking* church. As the *ecclesia audens* it preserves the place of God as the primary acting subject. As the *ecclesia audens* it makes it possible to conceive of God's Word *secundum dicentem deum* (according to God's speaking) even when spoken by the *ecclesia docens*.[64] Since the church comes into being as the hearing church and only by hearing becomes what it is, an appropriate representation of the work and word of God becomes possible. In its—very lively—passivity, the church represents in a fundamental way the activity of God. Thereby the church's speaking which comes from its hearing, and the church's celebration of the sacraments, are guarded from being misunderstood as in some way *effecting* our

---

[63] Cf. M. Luther, *Against Hanswurst*, *LW* 41, p. 216: 'A preacher should neither pray the Lord's Prayer nor ask for forgiveness of sins when he has preached (if he is a true preacher), but should say and boast with Jeremiah, "Lord, thou knowest that which came out of my lips is true and pleasing to thee" (Jer 17.16); indeed, with St Paul and all the apostles and prophets, he should say firmly, *Haec dixit dominus*, "God himself has said this" (1 Cor 1.10). And again, "In this sermon I have been an apostle and prophet of Jesus Christ" (1 Thess 4.15). Here it is unnecessary, even bad, to pray for forgiveness of sins, as if one had not taught truly, for it is God's word and not my word, and God ought not and cannot forgive it, but only confirm, praise, and crown it, saying, "You have taught truly, for I have spoken through you and the word is mine." Whoever cannot boast like that about his preaching, let him give up preaching, for he truly lies and slanders God.'

[64] In his table talk, Luther remarked against the fanatics that 'They define the word not as it was spoken by God but as it was received by men', *WA. Tischreden* 3.670.18f.

salvation. Rather, the church which speaks and celebrates the sacraments represents God himself and God alone as the one who acts for our salvation. This it does because even in its speaking and sacramental celebrations it does not cease to be the hearing church, a gathering of believers who receive God's grace.

Representation of Christ occurs in a fundamental way in the form of the hearing church and in the form of the gathering of believers who receive the grace of God. The church represents Christ by renouncing any self-representation. Hence it is hardly possible to say that the divine mystery of salvation is 'continued in the Church', as Vatican II thought it appropriate to state.[65] By living from Jesus Christ as the one and really unique sacrament, the church celebrates the sacramentality of *his* being. And only insofar as it celebrates his sacramentality, that is, the history of Jesus Christ as the declaration and impartation of God's gracious presence, can the church be called, not a basic sacrament but rather the great *sacramental sign* which represents Jesus Christ. The church is the analogate which points to Jesus Christ as the analogue. As analogate, the church reveals that Jesus Christ himself is the one who brings men and women into correspondence with himself as the church. And so we may—with Schleiermacher—speak of a *self-representation of Jesus Christ* occurring in the actions of the church.

IV

1. It is advisable, finally, to look for a criterion by which to test the relation between the church which represents Jesus Christ and the church's Lord which it represents. In my view, the fifth petition of the Lord's Prayer serves as such a criterion. How can and must the church pray for the forgiveness of sins?

To speak of the church as *mater ecclesia* (mother church) seems to contradict the idea that the petition for forgiveness is made in the church's own name. If we would not willingly have our natural mother spoken of as a sinner, we will be even less willing in the case of our spiritual mother. Thus Pius XII in the encyclical *Mystici Corporis* (1943) explained unmistakably: 'if at times there appears in the Church something that indicates the weakness of our human nature, it should not be attributed to her juridical constitution' (i.e.

---

[65] *Dogmatic Constitution on the Church* §52 (*DV*, p. 413).

THE CHURCH AS SACRAMENT?

to her mystical essence) 'but rather to that regrettable inclination to evil found in each individual'. The church itself is not really touched by that weakness. Rather: 'the loving Mother is spotless in the Sacraments, by which she gives birth to, and nourishes, her children; in the faith which she has always preserved inviolate; in her sacred laws imposed on all; in the evangelical counsels which she recommends; in those heavenly gifts and extraordinary graces through which, with inexhaustible fecundity, she generates hosts of martyrs, virgins and confessors. But it cannot be laid to her charge if some members fall, weak or wounded. In their name she prays to God daily: "Forgive us our trespasses"; and with the brave heart of a mother she applies herself at once to the work of nursing them back to spiritual health'.[66] *Roma locuta, haec autem causa non finita,* Rome has spoken, but that is not the end of the matter. It is worth asking whether the theologians of the early church were wise to place the designation of the church as *mater* alongside the biblical designation of God as Father, and even to assert 'You cannot have God for your Father if you no longer have the Church for your Mother'.[67] But the idea of 'mother church' is deeply rooted. If it is impossible to expunge it, it ought at least to be possible to guard it from misunderstanding. I will attempt to do this by going back to Luther.

2. The reformers took up the traditional expression *mater ecclesiae* in a positive sense. Calvin, for example, writes in his letter to Cardinal Sadolet: 'The Church ... cultivates and observes unity of faith and brotherly concord ... (A)s we revere her as our mother, so we desire to remain in her bosom'.[68] And even Luther can call the church the mother of us all. In expounding Gal 4.26ff., he called the church (identified with Sarah) 'our free mother'.[69] And the fact that he takes seriously the expression 'mother church' is proved by his definition of the church as 'the bride of Christ who gives birth to all'.[70] In another place, he talks of mother church who 'begets

---

[66] Pius XII, *Mystici Corporis* §66, in *Foundations of Renewal. Four Great Encyclicals of Pope Pius XII* (Glen Rock, NJ, 1961), pp. 31f.
[67] Cyprian, *The Unity of the Catholic Church*, ed. M. Bévenot (Oxford, 1971), p. 67.
[68] J. Calvin, 'Reply to Sadolet' in *Theological Treatises*, ed. J. K. S. Reid (London, 1954), p. 231.
[69] M. Luther, *Lectures on Galatians 1535, LW* 26, p. 441.
[70] Ibid.

and bears every Christian'.⁷¹ Along these lines, it may seem appropriate to bring the church nearer to the bridegroom in his sacramental character, by talking of the church as a sacrament or basic sacrament.

At this point, however, the reformers' counterarguments enter. In the first place, Luther's assertion that 'mother church' only begets and bears every Christian 'through the Word of God' exerts a critical influence.⁷² In his exposition of Gal 4.26ff., he says of our free mother: 'She goes on giving birth to children without interruption until the end of the world, as long as she exercises the ministry of the Word, that is, as long as she preaches and propagates the Gospel'.⁷³ Hence it is the *ministerium verbi* (ministry of the Word) that generates Christians. More precisely, it is not the *ministry* of the word but the Word of God itself by which Christians are begotten and born. 'Mother church' does not stand over the individual Christian; rather 'mother church' *is* Christians as they belong together through the Word of God and derive from the Word of God. In the same context in which Luther speaks of 'mother church' he declares unmistakably: 'In this way we are all fathers and children, for we are born one of another. I was born of others through the Gospel, and now I am a father to still others, who will be fathers to still others; and so this giving birth will endure to the end of the world'.⁷⁴ Christians are generated by other human beings only by the proclamation of the gospel, which is the real generative power. Even the church possesses that generative power only because and insofar as it proclaims the gospel. As 'our dear mother' in whose lap Christ lays those who become Christians 'by means of Baptism and the Word of God'⁷⁵, the church is nothing other than the congregation of believers which always precedes the individual Christian, in which the gospel is taught purely and the sacraments are administered rightly.⁷⁶ If we are here to speak of an opposition, it is not between 'mother church' and the Christians but between the Word of God and the church. Over against the Word of God, the church is *filia* (daughter) and not

---

⁷¹ M. Luther, *The Large Catechism* (*BC*, p. 416).
⁷² Ibid.
⁷³ M. Luther, *Lectures on Galatians 1535*, *LW* 26, p. 441.
⁷⁴ Ibid.
⁷⁵ M. Luther, *Sermons on the Gospel of John*, *LW* 22, p. 291.
⁷⁶ Cf. *The Augsburg Confession* VII (*BC*, p. 32).

mater. Luther expresses the point sharply in his assertion that the church 'is the daughter who is born from the Word; she is not the mother of the Word'.[77] Even the church 'is conceived, formed, nourished, begotten and brought up by the gospel alone'.[78] In his great polemical work *The Babylonian Captivity of the Church*, Luther made the distinction sharper still by calling the church not even *filia verbi* (daughter of the Word) but rather 'a creature'.[79]

Hence reformed use and meaning of language about the church as mother offers no support to the idea of the church as a sacrament or the basic sacrament. The fact that for Luther such an idea must be rejected will become perfectly clear if we look more exactly at the idea of the church as the *bride of Christ*, which is inseparable from that of 'mother church'.

3. On the basis of the biblical tradition, Luther was fond of referring to the church as the bride of Christ. This picture seems immediately to blend into the idea of the church as a fertile mother who, because of her union with Christ, brings the individual Christian into the world. As we have already seen, Luther himself made some statements of this kind. But the point of his language about the church as the bride of Christ is totally different. This is already apparent when we consider that Luther uses the very same image of the bridegroom and the bride to talk of the relation between Christ and the soul of the sinner. His account of this relation in *On the Freedom of a Christian* is especially well known. There we read: 'Christ and the soul become one flesh and there is between them a true marriage . . . (I)t follows that everything they have they hold in common, the good as well as the evil. Accordingly the believing soul can boast of and glory in whatever Christ has as though it were its own, and whatever the soul has Christ claims as his own. Let us compare these and we shall see inestimable benefits . . . Who can understand the riches of the glory of this grace? Here this rich and divine bridegroom Christ marries this poor wicked harlot, redeems her from all her evil, and adorns her with all his goodness.'[80]

[77] M. Luther, *Lectures on Genesis*, LW 2, p. 101.
[78] M. Luther, *Ad librum eximii Magistri Nostri Ambrosii Catharini . . . responsio*, WA 7.721.10f.
[79] M. Luther, *The Babylonian Captivity of the Church*, LW 36, p. 107.
[80] M. Luther, *The Freedom of a Christian*, LW 31, pp. 351f.

If we are to interpret correctly the Reformation's language about the church as the bride of Christ, we need to keep these sentences in mind. For Luther, the church is distinctive because 'There is no greater sinner than the Christian Church'.[81] This idea of the church as *peccatrix* (sinner) can claim a considerable theological tradition, of which Hans Urs von Balthasar reminds us in his fine article 'Casta Meretrix'.[82] Recent Catholic theology and the Second Vatican Council have taken up that tradition. However, already at the Council itself some reservations were voiced: there was willingness to speak of the church of sinners but not of the sinful church. The church is bound up with sin only 'in its members', we are told in the *Decree on Ecumenism* (which as a whole is full of papal injunctions), whilst the *Dogmatic Constitution on the Church* contains the remarkable statement that 'The Church ... clasping sinners to her bosom, (is) at once holy and always in need of purification'.[83]

This distinction between the immaculate holiness of 'mother church' and the sin of its fallible members completely misses the point which Luther was making when he said that there is no greater sinner than the Christian church. Vatican II was probably attempting to reconcile its own statements with those of Pius XII. The holiness of 'mother church' seems to be incompatible with sin. Yet Luther found in the church's recognition of its own sinfulness a proof of its true holiness.

In a sermon on Mt 28, preached on 9 April, 1531, Luther says 'There is no greater sinner than the Christian church'.[84] We should note carefully that he does not consider the church's existence as the 'greatest sinner' to stand in contradiction to its existence as the one, *holy*, catholic and apostolic church; rather, it is a proof of the church's holiness. Luther is speaking of the church which *knows* that it exists as the 'greatest sinner' and which *recognizes* itself to be

---

[81] M. Luther, *Sermon for Easter Day, 1531*, WA 34/I.276.7f.

[82] H. U. von Balthasar, 'Casta Meretrix' in *Sponsa Verbi. Skizzen zur Theologie II* (Einsiedeln, 1961), pp. 203–305.

[83] *Decree on Ecumenism* §3 (*DV*, p. 456); *Dogmatic Constitution on the Church* §9 (*DV*, p. 358). Cf. ibid., §40, where following Jas 3.2 we are told that 'since we all offend in many ways, ... we constantly need God's mercy and must pray every day: "And forgive us our debts"' (*DV*, p. 454). For an exposition of this, see K. Rahner, 'The Sinful Church in the Decrees of Vatican II' in *Theological Investigations* 6 (London, 1969), pp. 270–94.

[84] WA 34/I.276.7f.

such. On his view, the church could never express its holiness by regarding itself as the mother without blemish, asking forgiveness of sins not for itself but only for its fallible members. Luther does not simply take over the early church's language of *casta meretrix* (pure harlot). For although this tradition had stated that 'the Church is made up of sinners' whose 'great prayers are the prayers of sinners: "Forgive us our trespasses" ... Sin is in the Church, contagious and ineradicable, like the weeds in the field that are forever obstinately encroaching',[85] nevertheless it saw itself as 'a continuation of Christ and so as a source of holiness and therefore as faultless'.[86] According to the insights of the reformers, on the other hand, the union of the church and its Lord, understood by analogy from the soul's marriage to Christ, and the holiness which flows from that union, must lead the church to understand itself as *peccatrix maxima* (the greatest sinner), and thus—to put the matter with Luther's phrase summing up the intention of the Epistle to the Romans—to 'magnify' sin.[87] It is precisely through the church's understanding of itself as *peccatrix maxima* that the intimate relation between the church and Jesus Christ is expressed. And thereby Jesus Christ is taken seriously as the Son of God who in his holiness is not simply concerned with 'his own person' but with 'all sinners' so that in the power of his holiness he became 'a sinner of sinners'.[88] His holiness, because it is a holiness which takes pity on sinners, makes him into the *peccator peccatorum* (sinner of sinners) *in their place*; the holiness of the church, on the other hand, leads it to recognize itself as *peccatrix maxima*. As the *peccator peccatorum*, Christ is holy because he wipes away our sins, whereas as the *peccatrix maxima* the holy church remains ever dependent upon the fact that its sins have been wiped away. He is the sacrament which the church receives, to which the church can only testify and which the church must hand on as a recipient. And so prayer for the forgiveness of its *own* sins is the criterion by which we decide whether, in representing and presenting the sacramental event, 'mother church' understands itself *secundum dicentem deum* or whether it misunderstands itself as self-representation.

[85] E. Mersch, *Theology of the Mystical Body* (London, 1951), p. 308, as cited by von Balthasar, op. cit., p. 304.
[86] Von Balthasar, op. cit., p. 304.
[87] M. Luther, *Lectures on Romans, LW* 25, p. 3.
[88] M. Luther, *Lectures on Galatians, LW* 26, pp. 277f.

4. *Sacramentum*, we recall, is the Latin translation for μυστήριον. And μυστήριον means the mystery of God's gracious primal decision in favour of sinners, which, in the life, death and resurrection of Jesus Christ was enacted, revealed and, as revealed, made effectual. The church recognises itself as *peccatrix maxima* as it comes into being through the revelation and effectual character of that mystery, the mystery of God's gracious primal decision in favour of sinners. In the power of the Holy Spirit, the church celebrates Jesus Christ as the one and only sacrament, by praying in the certainty of being heard: forgive us our sins. In this very way, the church entrusts itself to the mercy of God and confesses the life, death and resurrection of Jesus Christ as guaranteeing the victory of the love of God.

Theses

1. According to New Testament usage, 'sacrament' means the mystery of God's gracious primal decision in favour of sinners, which was historically enacted in the life, death and resurrection of Jesus Christ, was revealed, made effectual in that revelation, and which in the power of his Holy Spirit becomes ever newly effectual.

2. As the sacrament of God, Jesus Christ acts in the power of his Holy Spirit, revealing his saving work as definitively completed, and representing and presenting himself in human words and actions (preaching, baptism, the Lord's Supper) as the Word of God which awakens and strengthens faith.

3. In that Jesus Christ represents and presents himself in human words and in the celebration of baptism and the Lord's Supper, he unites us to his body, which as the gathering of believers testifies to the self-representation and self-offering of Jesus Christ, and which to this extent may be called the sacramental sign corresponding to the sacramental being of Jesus Christ: one holy, catholic and apostolic church.

4. The church testifies to the sacramental being of Jesus Christ by listening to him as God's Word through which the sinner is justified (*ecclesia audens*, the hearing church), and by bringing to speech and celebrating him as that Word in human words and actions (*ecclesia docens et celebrans*, the teaching and celebrating church).

5. In testifying to the self-representation and self-presentation of

Jesus Christ, and in its own way representing him, the church understands Jesus Christ as the analogue and itself as the analogate.

6. The church remains fundamentally distinguished from the saving work of God as it was enacted in the life, death and resurrection of Jesus Christ. As a sacramental sign, the church refers to Jesus Christ as the *opus operatum dei* (the divine work performed), by testifying to, celebrating and living from that *opus*, without representing itself as its continuation or equating itself with it.

7. The church testifies to and celebrates Jesus Christ as the one and only sacrament most clearly in confessing its own sins and in confessing Jesus Christ as the Holy One of God who has made himself the *peccator peccatorum*, and through whom sinners have been made into saints.

8. The church testifies to and celebrates Jesus Christ as sacrament in baptism, by confessing that through his death and resurrection Jesus Christ has condemned to destruction the sins of this world and thus the sins of every individual person, and has once for all broken their power so that we might be free.

9. The church testifies to and celebrates Jesus Christ as sacrament in the Lord's Supper by confessing that Jesus Christ died for us, that through his death sinners are sanctified for communion with God and with one another, and that through his own presence he renews that communion until he comes to reveal in an irresistible way before the whole world the victory of the love of God which is already guaranteed in him.

THE EFFECTIVENESS OF CHRIST WITHDRAWN

On the process of historical understanding as an introduction to Christology[1]

I

'In Swabia people say of something that took place long ago that it is so long since it happened that it can hardly be true any more. So Christ died for our sins so long ago that it can hardly be true any more'. It was the Swabian Hegel who laid down this premise and drew out its larger consequences in his Jena diary.[2] Later on Hegel was to think very differently about the death of Jesus, but this is not our concern at present. Here we need to focus on the hermeneutical peculiarity which the saying reflects, namely that *the length of time* 'in between', the time between a past occurrence and a present which in itself has already passed, *seems to rob the past of its truth*. 'It can hardly be true any more', we say. What do we mean? What do we mean by saying also of the life, activity, and death of Jesus Christ 'it happened so long ago that it can hardly be true any more'?

We take Hegel's Jena diary entry as a starting point to reflect on the meaning of the question which every Christology has to answer: *Who is Jesus Christ*? It is important to note the way in which the question is asked. We do not ask: *Who was Jesus*?, but rather *Who is Jesus Christ*? We need to give some account of the difference between these two questions. We need to consider whether it would make sense to ask who Jesus *was* without also asking the question of who Jesus Christ *is*. But equally, we have to consider whether it would be possible to ask who Jesus Christ *is* without exposing ourselves to the question of who Jesus *was*. What is the meaning of

---

[1] The following reflections form part of the introductory section of a Tübingen lecture series on Christology, discussing the formulation of the question 'Who is Jesus Christ?'

[2] *Dokumente zu Hegels Entwicklung* II, ed. J. Hoffmeister (Stuttgart, 1936), p. 258.

the distinction between 'is' and 'was', between 'being' and 'having been', in the case of a person born nearly 2000 years ago, whose time is quite clearly not our own? And what is the meaning of the distinction between asking about a *Jesus* who once existed and asking about the *being* of Jesus *Christ*? From where does this additional name come? How can we explain this state of affairs?

II

Hegel's thought-provoking comment that the death of Jesus took place so long ago that it can hardly be true any more points us to two problems. The first is a general hermeneutical problem concerning our own relation to the past, the possibility we have of letting ourselves still be addressed by something from the distant past. There something was—here I am. What does this something have to do with me? What does this piece of the past, this 'once upon a time', have to do with my existence here and now? This general question of historical existence has to be considered even when we ask about *Jesus Christ*. Certainly the question about this person may be a quite unique one, but it nevertheless implies the general question of the relation between our historical existence and that which took place long before we existed.

For the present, this will suffice as a sketch of the first problem. It is a much more complex affair to characterize the second problem which Hegel's diary entry poses—as is always the case with theological problems. For here we are concerned with a particular theological problem, one which is certainly closely connected to the general problem but which nevertheless has to be distinguished from it. At a purely logical level, it is striking that in Hegel's diary the general saying 'it happened so long ago that it can hardly be true any more' when applied to the case of Jesus does not subsume within it—as we might expect—the statement 'his *life* took place so long ago that it can hardly be true any more'. Instead, Hegel speaks of the *death* of Jesus Christ. It is his death which happened so long ago. For Hegel, the person of Jesus Christ is represented more by the death of Jesus than by his life. Here we come across another peculiarity. On the basis of the general saying, we would most naturally expect the statement: 'So Jesus died so long ago that it can hardly be true any more'. But what would be the sense of doubting the death of a human being—for the sole reason that that death happened nearly *2000* years ago? If we know that the person had lived around 2000 years ago, it would be entirely logical to conclude from the intervening length of that time that the person must be dead by now. But the point is not the fact of being dead. The point is rather the *meaning* of the death of a person for others. Thus Hegel writes 'So *Christ* died *for our sins* so long ago that it can hardly be true any more'. The diary entry betrays skepticism or concern (we need not at present decide which) about the unique meaning of the death of this person. From the New Testament and the theological tradition of the church, as well as from his own piety, Hegel is familiar with the idea that the man Jesus who was put to death on the cross did not die only 'for himself' but rather died 'for all', 'for us', or, more precisely, 'for our sins'. Whatever this may mean, it should at least be clear that *if* this is *true*, then the death of this man, and hence this dying man, must have been something 'very special'. To him we have to attribute a special, if not unique, meaning. If it is true that one particular man has died for all, this truth must be a unique truth. This is the theological problem to which Hegel's diary entry draws our attention. Or, more exactly, it is the *presupposition* of a theological problem.

Hegel expresses this presupposition by speaking of 'Christ'. Christ is originally not a personal name but a title, a sovereign title. The sovereign title 'Christ' identifies the bearer as one who acts *in the name of another*. The other in whose name Christ acts is God. Without God, there is no Christ. If Jesus rightly bears the title 'Christ', then, accordingly, it means that as a human being he is not himself without God. And thus without introducing language about God it would be meaningless to say that Christ died for our sins. Yet in Hegel's diary entry, the most notable fact is that he subsumes this very special thing, this unique truth, under the general rule: it is so long since it happened that it can hardly be true any more. Only now can we come to see the theological problem which this diary entry draws to our attention. The problem consists in the fact that a truth which is considered *divine*, a so-called *eternal truth*, could be grasped in the form of an *historical event*, and thus must be understood wholly within the temporality of history. If we are to evaluate Hegel's note rightly, we need to have in mind Lessing's famous distinction between the 'accidental truths of history' and the 'necessary truths of reason', and the corresponding (and often misunderstood) statement that 'accidental truths of history can never become the proof of necessary truths of reason'.[3] Lessing had explicitly refused to accept—indisputable—historical events as proof of eternal truths. Against the neo-orthodox theologians of his time (as those who introduced 'novelties'), he objected: 'when will we cease to wish to hang nothing less than the whole of eternity on a spider's thread? Scholastic dogmatics never hit upon such profound wonders of religion as historical exegesis now does daily'.[4] Compared to the eternal truth with which religion ought properly to deal, accidental truths of history are said to have no more weight than a spider's thread. In a different context, Fichte in 1806 expressed the same thing in this way: 'the metaphysical only, and not the historical, can give us blessedness; the latter can only give us understanding'.[5] Fichte's statement, like Lessing's, refers to the meaning of the life and death of Jesus Christ within the limits of space and time, which has to be distinguished from the eternal truth—metaphysics. Hegel, on the other hand, can no longer make that kind of distinction. The fact that Christ died for us turns out to be a problem for him precisely because it took place 'so long ago that it can hardly be true any more'. The eternal truth is *as such* historical, and therefore it is problematic. The theological problem posed by Hegel's note could, therefore, be expressed in the form of a question: can eternal truth become obsolete?

Who is Jesus Christ, if this question arises about his person? Is it not the most natural thing in the world that people and their works become obsolete? Why is Hegel so concerned that this may be true of Christ? What gives rise to the concern that the truth of the life and death of Jesus could become obsolete, to the extent that it would hardly be true any more?

Having roughed out both problems in this preliminary way, we turn to deal with them in greater detail.

III

Hegel's remarkable diary entry points to the particular character of historical existence. Historical existence is exposed to *time* in a

---

[3] G. E. Lessing, 'On the Proof of the Spirit and of Power' in *Lessing's Theological Writings*, ed. H. Chadwick (London, 1956), p. 53.
[4] G. E. Lessing, 'Ein Duplik' in *Sämtliche Schriften* XIII (Leipzig, 1897), pp. 31f.
[5] J. G. Fichte, *The Way Towards the Blessed Life, or the Doctrine of Religion* in *The Popular Works of J. G. Fichte* II (London, 1889), p. 392.

particular way. The truth that the sum of the angles of a triangle is 180 degrees is valid *at any time*. Time does not make it any more or less true. Time is indifferent to this truth; this truth is indifferent to time. Historical existence, by contrast, appears to relate to time in a different way. For time can apparently make it more true, and equally can make it less and less true until 'it hardly seems to be true any more'. Why is this so? Why are there so many things that to former times seemed to be indisputable truths but which today are no longer true? To give one's life for 'God, King and Country' was once a self-evident duty stemming from the indubitable truth that life is not the highest good. Today, however, much of this truth has been exposed as a lie, and the trinity of God, King and Country has vanished. Why is this so?

Instead of simply duplicating examples arbitrarily, we want here to attempt a fundamental answer. We start from the superficial fact that historical existence is located in *time*. Already, however, this superficial state of affairs is a multi-layered phenomenon. The superficial fact that historical existence has its place in time leads us deep into the hermeneutical problems of historical existence. We want to analyze these problems by distinguishing their different elements.

We must first of all acknowledge that we ourselves are under examination when we look into the particular character of historical existence. We ourselves are located within time, we exist historically. Our *existence within time* connects us fundamentally with all historical existence.

Admittedly, this may sound trivial at first. In the end, it is our *existence in space* which connects us with everything which exists spatially (materially, corporeally). But this state of affairs, too, can lose its apparent triviality very easily—if it is linked, for example, to the experience that my existence in space always refers me to a certain place, in the same way that everything which exists spatially exists only in this or that location. But a location in space can obviously be changed. A location in space is itself exposed to time. I experience space only in a limited way; but those limits can change. Space can become narrow, alarmingly narrow. Or it can become alarmingly broad. There are, of course, positive experiences of such changes in space. But always time is at work if changes in location or experience of space occur. Existence in space is temporally mediated.

The same is all the more true for existence within time. And so the fact that we ourselves exist within time and are therefore fundamentally related to all other historical existents is anything but trivial. We exist *within* time; and time itself is the medium *through* which we are related to everything else which also exists within time. This is obviously the case in the relation of our present to our immediate future. We cannot live today without being aware that tomorrow there will again be for us a common 'today'. We may certainly differ in our opinion of how things will look tomorrow; we may, indeed, disagree in a sharp—but nevertheless responsible—way about these matters. But what cannot be disputed is the fact that tomorrow there will again be for us a common 'today'—unless we put an end to the dispute by putting our disputants to death. Yet if I alone survive, there will be no longer a *common* future. As long as I do not exist alone in time, however, I am linked through time with all my contemporaries in such a way that we have to face together the nearest, most immediate future. To examine the validity of this for the furthest, most distant future would demand a further investigation. Does time link me with historical existents which exist at a time when I have ceased to do so?

I take up that question in terms of the relation of past and present. In some future 'today' in which I have ceased to exist, I will be past. Consequently, the same problem can be discussed in terms of the relation of the past to our own present. But in looking at the matter in this way, we will need to distinguish between *the relation of the past to our own present* on the one hand, and *our relation to the past* on the other. To what extent are we ourselves at issue in a discussion of the relation of past and present in this double sense?

IV

There something was—here I am: how does that concern me? In this way we described the general hermeneutical problem posed by Hegel's statement. Is there a necessary connection between that which once was and our present? Is there a necessary relation between a distant 'there and then' and our own 'here and now'? How does a certain *illic et tunc* (there and then) affect our own *hic et nunc* (here and now)? As we ask this question, we begin with our own relation to the past.

Our relation to the past can happen as a conscious act through, for example, historical research or through historical falsification. From the hermeneutical point of view, the latter is more interesting, for historical falsification betrays something of the necessary character of the connection between our present and the past. How?

Though it need not be, historical research can be pursued as a kind of respectable *curiosity*. It is always open to the charge of arbitrariness, if for no other reason than that it has to make choices. We can never study the whole of the past. Because this encyclopedic ideal of historical research can never be attained, there is a real question as to whether dependence on choices does not surrender all historical research to the arbitrariness of mere curiosity. Is mere curiosity a sufficient guide to knowledge? In what way is historical interest more than mere curiosity? What makes the past of interest to the present, so that one might somehow want to participate in the past or have the past participate in our present? Could historical interest be *necessary* for the present? What is historical interest? And what is the present if the past ought to be necessary and interesting for it?

As a rule historical interest is interest in something particular—a particular person, situation, event, social structure. But this immediately raises the question of why we should be interested in *this* person, situation, event, rather than some other. Why Gabriel Biel or Cleopatra? Why not Spartacus or Lucullus? And why do we choose these particulars, rather than all? The mere existence of these persons, situations, events, and structures does not of itself make them of *necessary* historical interest to us; and so the pursuit of historical scholarship, when it is not motivated by other reasons, seems comparable to a love of antiques or curiosities fit only for a museum.[6] Those strange flowerings of historical research which we call dissertations certainly make it easy for us to be properly suspicious of the *necessity* of historical research. And it would not be wholly unjust to argue that this kind of historical fixation upon the past unnerves and weakens attention to the relation of the present to the *future*. Interest in the future is, however, indisputably necessary. The future constantly presses upon us, approaches us

---

[6] On the positive cognitive value of curiosity, cf. above all H. Blumenberg, *The Legitimacy of the Modern Age* (Cambridge, Mass., 1983), pp. 229–453; H. O. Oberman, *Contra vanam curiositatem* (Zürich, 1974).

ceaselessly. If it is the essence of the future constantly to present itself, we could define the *present* as the self-presentation of the future. The present would then be wholly defined by the future, so that interest in things future would be indisputably necessary. The past, on the other hand, would seem to be a present which has receded from view. And not only that: over against a future constantly presenting itself, the past would be receding further and further all the time. The past is intrinsically increasing its 'pastness'; it can be defined as a constant, ever-increasing self-distancing from the present. It is precisely this which makes the past noticeable in the present. In this way, it is 'here'. Thereby it shows that the present lacks things which once belonged to it. By its passing away, the past lays claim upon the present.

But if this is so, can the present have any interest in the past other than wanting to separate itself from that past? Could we say, then, that the proper function of historical research is to pin down past acts of historical life as facts, to file away the living acts of the past and thus to lay them to rest? Historical research would in that case serve to relieve the present of the past. And the need to do this would even prove the necessary character of the connection between present and past—the connection being the fact that the present is *burdened* by the past. The necessity of historical interest would then consist in the fact that through the strenuous labour of historical research and political assimilation we would free our present from the burden of the past. *Per aspera ad acta*: this would be the ethos of historical research.

V

The files of history themselves, however, speak against the idea that the past could as it were be buried in them. Those files are constantly being altered, sometimes, indeed, consciously falsified. Why has the history of the Communist Party of the Soviet Union been rewritten so often? Why does the past undergo a later revision? The obvious reason is that we cannot simply cut the present off from the past—though quite often this is what is desired, as is revealed with painful clarity in the skilful cuttings in the files of German theological faculties after 1945. It is just this kind of falsification of history which reveals especially clearly the necessary connection between our present and the past. The connection evidently consists in the fact that every present has to work through its past.

Thus it is not enough to say that the present is defined by the self-presentation of the future. The present is equally and just as fundamentally a working through of the past, whether this is undertaken consciously or unconsciously. This is the necessary connection between any particular 'here and now' and that which once was: here and now, we have to work through what once existed. The compulsion to work through the past in the present is a constitutive moment of historical existence. From the very beginning, time, in which being existed, demanded that this be done. As long as this working through occurs unconsciously, it is relatively harmless. History would be worked through as it were naturally—as, for example, it has always been done in ritualization, and as it has taken place in the animal world. Without some such unconscious, natural working through of the past, there would be no present for historical existence. However, historical existence is particularly characterised by *conscious* working through of the past, by an *historical* working through of the past corresponding to a *natural* working through of the past. Human nature has a tendency to work through the past historically, though not in a way which displaces a natural working through of the past. Only in this way can we have some influence over the future which constantly presents itself. This, indeed, is the reason why the past is falsified: by working through the past in *this* way, we believe ourselves to be able to make a better future. To work through the past in some way or other means to work on the future. And so we may define the *present* as *working on the future by working through the past*. The continuity of time demands that we be interested in the past, and in a way which goes beyond mere arbitrary curiosity. Scholarly historical research is justified if it enables us to work on the future by working through the past. It helps us acquaint ourselves with what needs to be worked through. The better acquainted we are with our past, the more accurately we can understand and shape our future—whether for good or ill.

But in doing this we need to be on our guard against the naive illusion that working through the past can ever be finished business. This would be to anticipate the last judgment. World history can never be the judgment of the world—quite the contrary! Not even a particular item of the past could be worked through completely so that it could be safely filed away. For, as we have seen, part of the character of things past is that they grow ever more distant.

This means, however, that their 'post-history' (*Nachgeschichte*) is constantly being supplemented. They are as it were being enriched by their own consequences. This being the case, the relation between things past and any particular present moment must change. And hence historical research about the same subject never reaches a terminus. Each present must work through the *entire* past of a particular event afresh, in full knowledge that it can only be partially successful. Any sort of 'mastering of the past' is fundamentally impossible. Things past continue to pass away from hour to hour, moment to moment, and yet do not cease to exist as things which have once been; and so the past, in its very transience, continues ever to affect the present. The more something which has happened recedes from the present into the past, the more insistent its presence can become. There is—if we may make use of a frequently misused category of Gadamer's—not only a *positive* effective history, in the sense that we feel the effects of a past event long afterwards. There is also a *private* effective history, in the sense that sometimes a piece of the past (a person, situation, event) is effective only as it recedes further and further into the distance, whether for good or ill. In such a case, it is the *withdrawal* that has effects: as it recedes from us, we come to realise what something has meant to us, or how it has made us suffer. At all events, it is characteristic of the past as a mode of time to recede further and further from us; but this is no reason to separate the past from the present. Rather, the ever increasing distance of the past also increases the need always to work through the past in order to work on the future.

Working through the past, however, is only possible if the present itself participates in the matter to which the past referred. Working through the past is not just a matter of restoring relics: it is a *present* dispute about a matter which concerns the present. Thus Barth rightly says that 'no one can understand the theology of the nineteenth century or any other century unless in some way he has himself taken upon himself the burden of theological work'.[7] And Bultmann says the same: 'We do not stand outside historical forces as neutral observers; we are ourselves moved by them; and only when we are ready to listen to the *demand* which history makes on

---

[7] K. Barth, *Protestant Theology in the Nineteenth Century* (London, 1972), p. 16.

us do we understand at all what history is about'.[8] If the matter which concerned the past is not in some way also an issue which concerns the present, there can be no working through of the past or even a falsification of the past. In that case, the matter would be a matter from so long ago that it could hardly be true any more. But as long as we are concerned that a matter may soon be no longer true, because it is a matter from so long ago, we still retain a relation to this issue, and are still capable of working through this past.

With these last reflections, however, we have already begun to incorporate into the relation of our present to the past the relation of things past to any particular present. It is incumbent upon us to reflect on the relation of the past to the present in order to clarify how the necessary relation of the present to the past (our working through of the past) is possible. What makes it possible to work on the future by working through the past?

VI

If Hegel's quoting of the Swabian proverb expresses the opinion that truth can go out of date, he implies that historical existence is not *true* by virtue of its mere facticity. It is not the fact that Christ died that can hardly be true any more because it happened so long ago, but rather his having died *for our sins*. The truth of historical existence exceeds the actuality of a 'brute fact'. An assertion of a brute fact can either be correct or false: *tertium non daretur* (there is no third possibility). If the assertion is false, the asserted actuality simply does not exist. Here it would be true to say *verum et factum convertuntur* (truth and fact are interchangeable). Either Napoleon is dead or he is not dead. And if he is not dead, he must still be alive: *tertium non daretur*. But to say of something that it may soon no longer be true is to move beyond the alternatives of correct or false, to refer to something which, although it happened with the actuality of a fact, is nevertheless more than that which can be observed. But what is this 'more'? What is it in actuality that is more than actual, so that it can be meaningful beyond its actuality?

The answer is the *potency* of actuality, its *potentiality*. The potentiality of actuality—of an actual person, for example—belongs

[8] R. Bultmann, *Jesus and the Word* (New York, 1958), p. 4.

THE EFFECTIVENESS OF CHRIST WITHDRAWN 225

to actuality without always being already actualized or being exhausted in such actualization. The actual is more than simply actual, more than naked facticity. A brute fact would be meaningless for the present if its actuality did not imply certain possibilities which do not pass away with the actuality of the brute fact. It is the possibilities which actuality brings with it and leaves behind which make a fact occurring in time into something like an event of historical truth. In this sense, Hölderlin formulated a counterpart to Hegel's Jena diary entry in his statement 'Long is the time, but the true occurs'.[9] The event of truth involves more than a brute fact in the long chain of events which we habitually think of as time. The event of truth involves the opening up of possibilities which do not necessarily disappear into the past. Kierkegaard elaborated on this hermeneutical insight: 'The possibility from which emerged the possible that became the actual always accompanies that which came into existence and remains with the past, even though centuries lie between. As soon as one who comes later repeats that it has come into existence ... he repeats its possibility'.[10] The actuality of the past cannot be repeated: what is done is done. But the possibility from which it arose, like the possibilities which it opened up, remain. And as long as they remain, the past can be worked through and so the future can be worked on. Discovering the possibilities of present existence is a matter for conscious, historical working through of the past which, even if it recedes from us further and further, does not take its potential with it but rather leaves it to our safekeeping.

Walter Benjamin spoke in this sense of the 'revolutionary energies that appear in the "outmoded"'.[11] We could describe the proper task of dealing with the past as bring these 'revolutionary energies' to light. We do not work at the past to reach new insights about the old; rather, the past demands that we work through it so that in our own present we may become new. This is the respect which we owe to history: nothing other than responsibility for *our own possibilities*.

We now go a step further and ask about the character of the effect which an historical event has, not least through its passing

[9] F. Hölderlin, 'Mnemosyne', *Sämtliche Werke* II (Stuttgart, 1953), p. 202.
[10] S. Kierkegaard, *Philosophical Fragments* (Princeton, 1985), p. 86.
[11] W. Benjamin, 'Surrealism' in *Reflections. Essays, Aphorisms, Autobiographical Writings* (New York, 1978), p. 181.

away. This general hermeneutical question will at the same time lead us back to the specific Christological problem.

VII

The hermeneutical problem of historical being is in large part the problem of its effectiveness. We can see this immediately if we begin to try to understand past events in order to understand ourselves and our possibilities. Every understanding of history is itself influenced by the effects of the history which it seeks to understand. Gadamer has undertaken a special analysis of this problem in *Truth and Method*, using the catch phrase 'effective history'[12] to call for a hermeneutic of historical understanding. He has combined the insight that we are always subject to the effects of what we seek to understand with the methodological demand that we must reflect on the historicality of historical understanding in order to be able to make the historical object an object of understanding in a hermeneutically appropriate way. Intrinsic to all true knowledge is the need to find and define the object appropriately: true knowledge consists in *appropriate objectification*. According to Gadamer, a hermeneutically appropriate objectification in the process of historical understanding would have to take place in such a way that we would 'learn to see in the object the counterpart of itself and hence understand both'.[13] Thereby he presupposes that that which is historically alien (past) always belongs to our own present (or vice versa) in the same way that something 'other' is related to that which is our own (ἕτερον, the other, is a correlate of 'this'). If the historical past is recognised as the 'other' of our 'own' (as a new possibility, as potential for our present), the relation of effectiveness between 'then' and 'now' has been taken into account. In making this demand for a method of understanding taking effective history into account, however, Godamer is clearly aware of the factual limitations of any such enterprise. He is conscious that it is impossible that 'we should become completely aware of effective history'.[14] To assert the possibility of this kind of complete knowledge of effective history would be 'just as hybrid a statement

[12] I have removed the awkward hyphen used in this catch phrase in the standard English translation of Gadamer's work (TR).
[13] H.-G. Gadamer, *Truth and Method* (London, 1979), p. 167.
[14] Ibid., p. 268.

as when Hegel speaks of absolute knowledge, in which history would become completely transparent to itself'.[15]

We have to endorse the modesty of an effective historical hermeneutic because of the simple fact that far too much is lost to any conscious grasp of history for any complete knowledge to be possible. Our historical knowledge covers only what remains. The past as a totality is always being lost—to us, though not to God the reconciler. And many particulars within the totality are also lost. But what is lost is as much part of the effective history as what is preserved in the archives of historical consciousness. Indeed, it often happens that those things which could not and cannot be worked through because they have been lost are far more fundamental than those things of which we are historically conscious. Historical understanding must therefore always admit its losses, and that those losses nevertheless determine the consciousness of those who live after to which they are lost.

This is particularly true in the case of Jesus. In considering his historical existence we have to admit that only a scanty remainder of his life has been handed down to us as an historical certainty. Our historical knowledge of him refers to only the few years of his public activity which preceded his death, and we cannot even be sure of the length of this brief period. Yet it would not be right to trace the effectiveness of Jesus simply to what we know of him historically. We are prevented from doing this by an unprecedented occurrence in early Christianity, an occurrence which can only be understood as an attempt to portray the whole of Jesus' historical existence, though without intending to say everything or present all the details. It is noteworthy that Jesus' factual effectiveness is also demonstrated by the fact that, despite the scanty tradition of what can be known about him there arises a new literary genre about him alone which sees its role to be that of portraying the whole of his historical existence: the gospels.

These portrayals of the whole of Jesus' historical existence consciously refrain from constructing an uninterrupted life story, an unbroken chain of details. Rather, it was much more important that Jesus' existence had produced a quite particular effect: he assured those whom he addressed—even after his death—of their 'salvation' (whatever that may mean—we shall return to that later).

[15] Ibid.

But for this very reason, the 'whole Jesus' had to be portrayed, not in order to say everything about him but in order to understand him as a unity. The rather scant knowledge available about him was enough to answer the question of who he was, or rather, of who he is, namely one who makes possible salvation or fellowship with God. The whole of his historical existence is portrayed from the perspective of this particular aspect, without adding together all the individual details of his life. For the gospels, that kind of adding together would be less than the whole of what they intend. The important point was to show that the whole of his existence, by which certainty of salvation was effected, is a saving event. Every pericope of the gospels seeks to do more than simply report one event out of a sequence of events. Rather, it seeks through one particular event to bring out something that is characteristic of the whole of Jesus' being. And so, for example, in Mk. 2.5 the sins of the paralytic are forgiven; but even though Mark records no other healing which is combined with forgiveness of sins, this does not mean that Mark 2.5 is about a unique event. Rather in this one particular story, Mark seeks to bring out something which is characteristic of all Jesus' healings. Jesus' healing activity is in itself that which forgives sins. The same holds true for his table-fellowship with tax-collectors and sinners in Mk 2.15; what we have here is not a description of a single occurrence, but a portrayal of behaviour which characterized the whole of Jesus' existence: he ate and drank with tax-collectors and sinners, and as such was himself. We might call this kind of portayal, which instead of giving an unbroken series of events makes a single event stand for the whole, *synecdoche*. The gospels talk about Jesus by means of synecdoche.

In order to show that it is a matter of the whole of Jesus' existence as a saving event, the gospels had to frame his existence with a beginning and an end. The (twofold) end was already given: death and resurrection. The beginning, however, was still relatively unfixed. If Jesus' history was to be portrayed as a whole, as a unity and as effective in that unity, a beginning had to be described to integrate or constitute Jesus' saving acts as a whole—hence a beginning with *God*. And so it was necessary to work back from the end of Jesus' life to a beginning, an ἀρχή, whilst the portrayal of what had been framed by the beginning and the (twofold) end could itself well remain fragmentary. It is, accordingly, not by chance that the gospels talk about the beginning of this saving event in very different ways. Mark, the oldest gospel, begins forthrightly with the statement 'The beginning of the gospel of Jesus Christ', and goes on to quote a 'word of Scripture' from the prophet Isaiah ('As it is written in Isaiah the prophet . . .'). The quotation (Isa 40.3) is interpreted as referring to John the Baptist whose appearance introduces the history of Jesus which for its part begins with his baptism by John. The frame which defines the whole is thus a prophetic 'word of Holy Scripture' and its historical fulfilment through the appearance of John the Baptist whose baptizing opens up and initiates the effectiveness of Jesus through this word of Scripture. This prophetic word of Scripture, however, refers the historical activity of Jesus back to God himself.

Matthew and Luke, on the other hand, go about the matter in a very different way. Matthew begins with a family tree, with a 'book of the genealogy of Jesus Christ, the son of David, the son of Abraham'. Hence the *birth* of Jesus (rather than his public appearance) is presented as initiated in the sacred *history* of the Old Testament (rather than by a sacred *word*). Matthew continues with the story of the miraculous generation of Jesus and its preceding history. This is also Luke's starting point, after he has made an initial declaration of his literary intentions. Through the miraculous generation of Jesus, Matthew and Luke trace the whole of Jesus' existence back to an immediate origin in God, although they combine this with the story of an earthly family. The gospel of John goes further by setting out God's eternity as the ἀρχή of Jesus' historical existence, at the same time exposing that eternity to a relation to earthly history: 'In the beginning was the Word, and the Word was with God, and the Word was God'.

'He' (that is, the one defined in Jn 1.14 as the one who became flesh) 'was in the beginning with God'. Everything that follows these very different statements in the gospels about the 'beginning' is fragmentary, and only through the end (through death and resurrection) are they made into a whole once more. This process shows that the whole of Jesus' existence had to be expressed, since Jesus' effect referred back to his whole existence, his entire history— and that whole had by no means to be equated with the sum of what can be known historically about him. Our insight that we are affected by more than we can know historically is confirmed by the concrete example of what we might call the soteriological effect of the history of Jesus. Total effective historical consciousness is impossible.

We can summarise in three points what according to Gadamer is not only necessary but also possible in his effective historical hermeneutic:

(a) It is necessary, but also possible, consciously to elaborate the historical horizon belonging to the situation of the one who seeks to understand.

(b) It is necessary, but also possible, to sketch out the historical horizon of the object which we seek to understand and its tradition.

(c) It is necessary, but also possible, to incorporate the historical horizon of the object into the historical horizon of the existence of the person who seeks to understand, so that 'in the process of understanding there takes place a real fusing of horizons, which means that as the historical horizon is projected, it is simultaneously removed'.[16]

We must refrain from critical discussion of the very unhappy category of 'fusing of horizons.' But we have to point out that one constitutive part of effective history is the passing of time, the process of becoming ever older, which makes it possible to say that something happened so long ago that it can hardly be true any more, or to say, on the other hand, that something has become all the more true now. It is part of the hermeneutical character of historical existence to recede into the distance, and as that which once was, to recede ever further and further. And it is also part of its character to have an effect upon the present through this passing away, even to have such an effect only by passing away, since during its existence it prevented its own effect, as it were standing in its own way.

Historical existence has an effect not only by handing itself down intact to the future. Nor does it have an effect only by handing down its effective consequences, its immediate effects, to the future in constantly new historical mediations. Effective history does not simply consist in the process of history handing down things past (through historical mediations) and of future times receiving what is presented to them out of the past in manifold historical mediations. Effective history also consists in the maelstrom left behind by something that passes away, in the withdrawal of what

[16] H. -G. Gadamer, op. cit., p. 273.

THE EFFECTIVENESS OF CHRIST WITHDRAWN 231

once existed and in the abandonment of future generations who can at best gaze after what once existed, who, even if they widen their horizons as far as possible, can only watch it disappear—but who in spite of this are very much affected by the disappearing and passing away of what once was. This state of affairs we called the 'privative effective history'.

When we ask after the historical existence of Jesus, we are faced with this privative effective history in a particularly intense and special way. For Jesus' effectiveness consists in his *death*, in his *withdrawal*, which faith in his resurrection does not reverse but rather confirm. Perhaps there is no abandonment more creative than that experienced by those whom Jesus had addressed and from whom he was then withdrawn. This fact can be formulated with the thesis that the *death* of Jesus evoked *faith* in Jesus Christ, and that the *absence* of Jesus gave rise to the *New Testament* as a testimony to his presence. What kind of creative absence are we dealing with here? What kind of death full of consequences, what kind of positive withdrawal? To answer these questions would mean getting involved in the dogmatic question of God in the midst of the process of historical understanding. For only if the death of Jesus and God belong together would it make sense not only to ask who Jesus *was* but to move on to the question of who Jesus Christ *is*.

BIBLIOGRAPHY

Jüngel's main works to date are:

Paulus and Jesus (Tübingen, 1962)
Gottes Sein ist im Werden (Tübingen, 1964)—ET *The Doctrine of the Trinity* (Edinburgh, 1976)
Tod (Stuttgart, 1971)—ET *Death* (Edinburgh, 1975)
Unterwegs zur Sache (Munich, 1972)
Gott als Geheimnis der Welt (Tübingen, 1977)—ET *God as the Mystery of the World* (Edinburgh, 1983)
Entsprechungen (Munich, 1980)
Barth-Studien (Gütersloh, 1982)—partial ET *Karl Barth, A Theological Legacy* (Philadelphia, 1986)

For a near-complete bibliography to 1984, and a study of Jüngel's work, see J. B. Webster, *Eberhard Jüngel: An Introduction to his Theology* (Cambridge, 1986), and the same author's 'Eberhard Jüngel: Annotated Bibliography', *The Modern Churchman* 28 (1986), pp. 41–5.

INDEX

act, agency 9, 10, 11, 105f, 147, 187
actuality 5f, 13, 16f, 41, 66f
   and act 100 (s.v. act, agency)
   and possibility 8f, 16f, 92, 95–123
   ontological priority of 97–100, 150f
Allemann, B. 22, 26 n. 11
analogy 5, 11f, 24, 37, 58, 89f
Anaximander 96
'anonymous Christianity' s.v. Rahner, K.
anthropomorphism 7f, 72–94
Apel, K.-O. 51 n. 87
Aristotle 4, 7, 84, 163, 171
   on metaphor 33–45, 57, 60
   on actuality and possibility 97–101, 102
authority 118
Augustine 158

Bacon, F. 78f
Barth, K. 3, 10, 11f, 87, 102, 111 n. 51, 178, 194, 198f, 223
   on analogy 159–63
   on baptism 161
   dogmatics and ethics 155f, 165f
   on divine commands 167f
   ethics 154–72
Bayer, O. 196
becoming 6, 9
Benjamin, W. 225
Bible, biblical interpretation 72–94
Biser, E. 22, 52 n. 87
Bloch, E. 102
Blumenberg, H. 22, 22 n. 7, 25, 25 n. 10, 220 n. 6
Brentano, F. 27f n. 16
Bühler, K. 22
Bultmann, R. 118, 121, 179, 223f

Calvin, J. 207
church
   as sacrament 13f, 189–213
   as bride of Christ 209

   as mother 206–11
   sinful 206–11
Conzelmann, H. 104
covenant 113
creation 109–16
cross 64–7, 94, 108f, 110f, 112, 142f, 202 (s.v. Jesus Christ, death of)
Cyprian 207

Descartes, R. 2, 84

Ebeling, G. 102, 165–7, 189
Eichholz, G. 22
epistemology 1f
eschatology 103
   and anthropology 10f, 124f, 184f
   and language 23
ethics 154–72
eucharistic sacrifice 200f
experience with experience 13

faith 186f
Fichte, J. G. 217
forgetting 151f
freedom 120, 156f
Fries, H. 190
Fuchs, E. 4, 22, 65, 67, 102, 118

Gadamer, H.-G. 91 n. 82, 226, 230
Gese, H. 88f
God
   being in becoming 112
   comes to the world 5, 59, 88f, 91, 94
   creator 110f
   distinction from the world 5, 14, 58f, 62f, 110–16
   first mover 100
   freedom of 8
   humanity of 94
   identity with Jesus Christ 59, 132
   language about 5–7, 58–67
   love of 157f
   movement into depths 144

mystery 67
self-evident 181f
godlessness 187
Goethe, J. W. 148
Gogarten, F. 102, 109 n. 49
grace 1, 14
Güttgemans, E. 22

Hartmann, N. 97, 98, 101, 110
Hegel, G. W. F. 4, 123 n. 68, 137, 147, 214, 215, 216, 217
Heidegger, M. 4, 16, 56 n. 101, 92, 102
Heraclitus 28, 42, 96
Herrmann, W. 12, 167–9
Hesiod 73 n. 1
historical-critical method 85–7 (s.v. Spinoza, B. de)
history 214–31
Hobbes, T. 171
Hölderlin, F. 225
Holy Spirit 202
Homer 36, 44, 73 n. 1
hope 114f
humanity
  co-humanity 136, 142, 161
  correspondence to God 11, 124–53, 158
  defined by Christology 132, 140f, 143, 152
  defined by justification 127, 133f, 143–5, 150, 178–81, 186–8
  hearer 11, 125f, 145
  image of God 135–43
  indefinability 127–32
  limited 142
  linguistic being 145–8
  lordship 138–43
  passivity 11, 186f
  self-transcending 11, 126
  subject 1
  (s.v. act, agency; eschatology)
Hume, D. 90

Jesus Christ 159f
  death of 215f, 226–31
  and God 59, 64, 94, 132, 229
  history of 214–31

resurrection of 67
sacrament 192–7
Son of God 66 n. 115, 67
justification 3, 9, 95–123
  articulus stantis et cadentis ecclesiae 104, 189
  ontology of 104–23
  (s.v. humanity)
Kant, I. 4, 49 n. 85, 89–91, 115, 161, 164f, 172
Käsemann, E. 103
Kierkegaard, S. 88, 120 n. 64, 225
knowledge 42
Köhler, L. 136
Krötke, W. 13, 157 n. 3

Lessing, G. E. 74, 128, 216f
Link, Chr. 13
Lohmeyer, E. 22
Löwith, K. 22, 49 n. 85
Luther, M. 3f, 9, 23, 50f n. 86, 59, 75, 82 n. 53, 102, 109, 114, 115f, 119, 119 n. 63, 127, 152, 178f, 186, 188,191, 194–7, 201–3, 207–11

Magass, W. 22
Mann, T. 122f
Maron, G. 189f
Melanchthon, P. 203
Mersch, E. 211
metaphor 5–7, 16–71
  as address 43–5, 46–8, 51–3
  and concept 57
  and definition 45
  as discovery 51f, 53, 60–3
  and faith 58–67
  linguistic history 48f, 61f
  linguistic innovation 43f
  and narrative 61–3
  necessity of 47
  and ontology 6, 41
  and parable 20
  and rhetoric 21, 24–6
  and truth 6, 25, 56f
Metz, J. B. 61 n. 105, 66 n. 115
miracle 111f
Moltmann, J. 102, 114

INDEX

Musil, R. 123 n. 68

natural theology 12f, 173–88
Nietzsche, F. 23 n. 7, 27–33, 49 n. 85
 on metaphor and truth 28–33, 53f
non-being 66f

Oberman, H. O. 220 n. 6
ontology 102 (s.v. actuality; justification)
Ott, H. 174 n. 3

Pannenberg, W. 10
parable 48–50, 120f
Parmenides 42, 97
Paul 107f, 133, 136–43
Pesch, O. H. 190, 193
Pius XII 206f
Plato 4, 39f n. 63, 59, 73, 137
Plessner, H. 129
possibility s.v. actuality
prayer 154–72
Presocratic philosophers 4

Quell, G. 114 n. 55

Rahner, K. 13, 173–88, 190, 192f
resurrection 5f, 112, 142f
revelation 7, 13, 17, 183–5
Ricoeur, P. 9, 22
Robinson, J. M. 113
Rothe, R. 194
Russell, B. 62 n. 107

sacrament 13, 191, 212
 and word 202f
 as liturgical action 201f
 as representation 199–206
Schenker, A. 161 n. 5
Schleiermacher, F. 74, 194, 199, 206
Schmitt, C. 171, 182

Scholder, K. 78 n. 26
Schulz, W. 84
self-evident 182–6
Semmelroth, O. 192
sin 107f, 141f
Snell, B. 22, 49
speech-event s.v. word-event
Spinoza, B. de 4, 59
 on anthropomorphism 74–87
 hermeneutical method 74f
 on historical-critical method 77–80, 87
 on revelation 80f
 on *sola Scriptura* 74f
 on unhistoricality of God 86
statement 45, 145–8

theology 109f
time 120, 217–9
truth 6, 16f, 111
 as *adaequatio intellectus et rei* 16–8, 25f, 171
 as interruption 171f

verification 117f
Via, D. O. 22
Vico, G. 22f n. 7
virgin birth 88f
Vonessen, F. 60 n. 104
von Balthasar, H. U. 210f
von Rad, G. 95 n. 1
Weinert, H. 129

Wittgenstein, L. 51 n. 87, 62 n. 107, 171
Wolff, H. W. 95 n. 1
word-event 4, 9, 14, 118–21, 203f
Word of God 106f, 113f, 126, 166, 208f

Xenophanes 73

Zimmerli, W. 135f
Zwingli, H. 22 n. 7, 50f n. 86, 193f